AF575148

Emil Holzhauer:

The Portrait of an Artist

06/03/02

To Hanna,
my very special
granddaughter.
I love you,
Granmommie
Audrey Edwards

Emil Holzhauer:

The Portrait of an Artist

Audrey Edwards

Pittsburgh, PA

ISBN 1-58501-027-8

Trade Paperback

First Printing—2001
Library of Congress #00-110758

Request for information should be addressed to:

CeShore Publishing Company
The Sterling Building
440 Friday Road
Pittsburgh, PA 15209
www.ceshore.com

Cover design: Jeffrey S. Butler - SterlingHouse Publisher, Inc.
Book Designer: N. J. McBeth
CeShore is an imprint of SterlingHouse Publisher, Inc.

Printed in Canada

Acknowledgements

My deepest gratitude goes to the following people for their contributions to this work: Edward Nowogroski, Marion Holzhauer, Arnie Hart, Paul Koch, Mary Harlow, Lorna Williams, Mildred Baker, Deborah Scofield, Gillis Powell Sr., Marianne Dunn, Teresa Rett, Ann Tutt, Dave and Debbie Pomerenke, Elizabeth Scofield, Eleanor McCain, James R. Richburg, Jean Ruckel, Linda Heflin, Jane Meigs, Julie Nichols, and Zella Tobin.

I depended a great deal on the *American Family Series* paperdoll books authored by Tom Tierney and published by Dover Publications, Inc. of New York for an understanding of fashions worn during the early nineteenth century in America. Almut Flentge-Parker assisted me with descriptions of fashions and lifestyles in Germany during the early twentieth century. My special thanks go to Charles and Eileen Arpke for their unflagging and time-consuming efforts to improve my writing skills.

I am indebted to *Boston Herald, New York Times, Detroit Free Press, New York Daily, New York Evening Post, New York Sun, New York American, Literary Digest, Chicago Art World, Newark Evening News, New York Post, Rochester Democrat, New York World, New York Evening Mail, Macon Telegraph and News, Greenville Piedmont, Asheville Citizen, Atlanta Journal,* and *Palm Beach Post-Times* for their society and art pages that assisted me in understanding Holzhauer's artistic growth. I have not always quoted from these pages, but the knowledge I gained from reading them was invaluable to me.

I am grateful to the National Broadcasting Company, Inc. for permitting me to use excerpts from a 1940 radio program featuring Holzhauer and to Oberlin College's Allen Memorial Art Museum and the Institute of Art, Chicago, for permission to quote from letters these institutions wrote to Holzhauer.

To **LEE ANN**

Her Mother's Plum

Disclaimer

This work is narrative, and creative, non fiction. It is based on the life of Emil Holzhauer, a German-American teacher-artist. The only real people the author has used in telling Holzhauer's story as he related it to her, are Holzhauer and his teachers: Robert Henri and Homer Boss. It is important to recognize that all dialogue, including that attributed to Holzhauer, Henri, and Boss was created by the author and should not be taken as verbatim. All other characters were created by combining several individuals who were associated with or had an influence on Holzhauer, or they were purely figments of the author's imagination. In the interest of brevity, some later events in Holzhauer's life were moved to earlier periods.

One

Emil inched his way slowly out of the tiny bed, careful not to sink into the clumpy horse-hair mattress, or jostle the warped wooden slats. It was nearly an impossible task, this daily effort to emerge from the cover without waking his cousin, Fritz, whose unbridled behavior would bring Emil's father bounding into the room with his walking cane. It was a weapon both boys respected.

He was about to claim triumph when his foot caught in the frazzled coverlet. He grimaced in despair, almost sinking back into the lumpy bed when Fritz suddenly rolled his muscular frame over. Fortunately, he took the cover with him, freeing Emil's foot in the process. Successful at last, Emil tiptoed around the creaky board in the floor and held a sigh of relief until he was safely out of the room and into the warmth of the tiny kitchen. In friendless solitude, his mother punched bravely on a ball of coarse-grain dough. It was an activity that seemed to take more energy than her frail body possessed. The heavy wooden block she stood on lifted her small frame high enough to reach the working surface.

As a small boy, Emil had watched in horror one day when the wobbly stool she once depended on had turned over. The episode sent her head-first into the corner of the table. The fall had cut a deep gash in her forehead, covering her and much of the surroundings with blood. Emil thought she was dying and that he would be left to live with his father. It was a fate too horrible for his young mind to deal with. He fell to his knees and prayed to God that he might be allowed to die with her.

Almut Holzhauer still wore the scar from the accident, and it reminded Emil often of how close he had come to losing her. He wished ever so much to make her life easier, but he seldom saw an opportunity to do that.

Bread-making was only the beginning of the long, arduous day ahead of her, one that would see her trekking across the village to keep house and cook for a factory owner's family. Once her chores were completed there, she would retrace her steps in a weary trudge homeward, where a multitude of household chores awaited her.

She smiled and quickly wiped her hands on an apron that had made several trips around her impoverished waistline before its raveled edges met a final time. The tie string was so frazzled she had resorted to pinning the threadbare garment together to prevent its falling to the floor. The mother and son embraced in a warm but quick gesture. Neither uttered a sound since their voices would echo through the thin walls of the tiny apartment like a yodel from the nearby mountaintop and raise the ire of her husband.

Frau Holzhauer gently pushed her son back the full length of her arms. It was a distance scarcely farther than that of a small child's reach. Still smiling, she reached beneath the work table, pulled out a potato, and swished it playfully in front of his animated face. He broke into a broad grin but not before snitching a bite of raw dough. He loved his mother's *Brotchen*, raw or cooked. When she made bread, it was a delicacy. Everybody said so.

He understood the gesture. Hot potato salad, a dish he savored, would be served for supper. Otherwise, his birthday would come and go in the household without ceremony, for Herr Holzhauer had long since forbade such nonsense.

Unlike most German families, the Holzhauers ate their heartiest meal in the evening since Frau Holzhauer was obliged to cook and serve the noon meal to her employers, leaving her own family to make-do with cold cuts for lunch. It was opposite to the German custom and to their own tastes, but a necessary evil for all concerned.

To avoid disaster, Almut motioned her young son back to his bedroom, where, to Emil's utter delight, Fritz continued to slumber. He smiled to himself for this rare occasion when he could wash up and comb his stubborn hair without the threat of Fritz yanking the makeshift stool from under him. It was a necessary evil, that stool, for he needed the added height to see himself in the mirror.

He tried as always to comb his thick strands straight back, to hold them off his forehead, but the moment he let go, they fell softly into a half-bang and stubbornly remained there. Irritated, he slammed the comb on the chest top, a slight noise really, but one that woke Fritz nonetheless. Startled to see Emil finished with his morning routine, Fritz snarled something unintelligible. Emil answered with a sprightly grin. Getting the better of Fritz was rare and an incident he savored. Among other things, it deprived Fritz of yanking the cover off him, and laughing as his shivering body made a frantic search for warm clothing. As second in line each morning for the wash stand, it meant searching for the stool Fritz always hid from him, then cleaning the filthy basin of fine shavings and dirty water purposely left there to raise his ire.

Fritz's insensitive pranks always reminded Emil of the days when his mother's gentle touch awakened him in the privacy of his own bedroom, but those days were gone forever. Life had been much more bearable back then, except of course for the traumatic visits to his aunt's house, where he was sent to play with his cousin who was four years older. Fritz's coarse behavior during the visits reached beyond what Herr Holzhauer jeeringly called childhood pranks. The trauma of having blackberries and dirt smudged in Emil's face, and briers laced through his hair, and rotten bird meat forced down his throat had become commonplace. In the beginning, he had run screaming to his mother, but Herr Holzhauer had yanked him from her arms, and sent him back for more of the same.

Then came the tragedy, the one that would change Emil's life, and not for the better. Fritz's parents were killed in a train accident, and he was sent to live with the Holzhauers. Among other things, it meant sharing a room scarcely big enough to hold Emil's own belongings, much less Fritz's cumbersome weightlifting paraphernalia. Though only a small boy at the time, Emil knew there would never be any measure of peace in the household again. He did feel sorry that Fritz had lost his parents, but pity for his own predicament always seemed to take precedence over that. Fritz was dedicated to building brawn and muscle, a fact that assured him of physical dominance over Emil and most of the other boys in the little city. The idea of lifting weights bored Emil. His own idea of enjoyment was reading, especially books about art and artists, and he loved drawing and sketching the nearby mountains and the old city factories in Schwabisch-Gmund, Germany, where he was born. The magic of the pencil forming designs at his bidding entranced and delighted him. The problem was, he wanted to go beyond the strictness of the classroom, beyond copying, and into the excitement of creativity. No one had encouraged or assisted him in this endeavor, and nearly everyone laughed at what they considered a waste of time.

Still, he harbored thoughts of opportunities to come. At thirteen, he was only a year away from being apprenticed to one of the local manufacturers. He had reason to believe that Buchhandler and Sons, where he hoped to be trained, would send their apprentices to drawing classes. It was a dream that sustained him.

Herr Holzhauer forbade any hoopla or recognition of family birthdays, deeming them nonsense. He did believe in celebrating, but not with the family. While many Schwabisch-Gmund families had celebrated the recent turning of the twentieth century, Emil's father had abandoned his family for an all night drinking session at the *Bierstube.* Through the apartment's thin walls, Emil had heard his mother's muffled sobs that night as he too lay sleepless. Both were afraid Herr Holzhauer would return in a drunken rage. It had become a way of life Frau Holzhauer and the boys learned to live with, though not without trepidation.

Rather than chance a confrontation with Fritz, Emil gathered his school materials, his coat and his cap and left the room. He loved that woolen cap, not only for the warmth it provided, but for the discipline it imposed on his hair. It was a look that matured him, or so he imagined. He wished often that he might be allowed to wear it in the classroom. Maybe then his classmates would refrain from calling him "the kid".

Physically, he had a great deal going for him. There were the strong jaw, full eyebrows and eager blue eyes that spoke for the suppressed energy shyness had always concealed. When his full mouth could be coaxed into a broad smile, it revealed straight white teeth that sparkled against his lustrous brown skin, tanned from outdoor sketching even during the winter months. His hair, though slightly unruly, was above reproach with its thick brown strands falling softly over one side of a high forehead.

Although ahead of schedule, he hurried, constantly aware that tardiness at the Catholic School would not be tolerated, and fearful as well that Karl, his best friend, might venture off without him.

Grabbing a roll and a sausage in one hand, his satchel in the other, he left quietly after planting a kiss on his mother's sunken cheek. He usually ran all the way to the lamppost where he and Karl met, but with time on his side for once, he munched on the fresh, hot roll as he ambled along the old cobblestone street. He had scarcely begun the daily trek when he heard a familiar whistle, a special signal he and his mother had devised for getting each other's attention. Glancing backward, he caught sight of his mother's tiny arms waving him back. Frau Holzhauer's face was delicate but somber, creased by sorrow and a certain sense of destiny. When the two of them stood facing each other, she opened her shabby shawl, revealing a neatly folded garment tucked inside. "It's for your birthday," she beamed. "Your very own shirt. I've only to sew on the buttons." She smiled, a nervous gesture, but genuine, magnifying the creases in her face.

"Mother," he breathed, "how did you manage this?" He couldn't remember the last time he had received a new garment. Most everything was threadbare by the time Fritz outgrew it. His mother shushed him with her fingers on his lips, then squeezed his hand softly as their eyes met. They were accustomed to talking with their eyes, a glance often serving as a complete message.

"Thirteen is a very special age," she said softly. Her smile faded then, her emotions overcoming the momentary joy. "I'll put it in your drawer. Papa won't notice as long as you have your coat on."

At four feet, eleven inches, Emil was already taller than his tiny mother whose round shoulders spoke for the heavy burdens she had always carried. Her deep-set eyes, once bright blue, had lost their sparkle, her face roughened with anguish. Her compressed lips held off tears that fought for release. Emil knew they were there. They were always there.

The whole episode provoked him. Clothes were of little importance to him as long as they weren't too uncomfortable. He knew there was no money for a new shirt. She must have used the fabric her sister had given her, he decided, fabric intended for Frau Holzhauer's own much needed frock. He wished that she had used it for its intended purpose.

He ambled along after that, forgetting for the moment the chilly air, but fear of missing Karl soon seized him. He grabbed the mass of material in the legs of his *Lederhosen* to prevent the excess fabric from wadding up in his crotch, and he ran to make up lost time. It had become a way of life, the wearing of clothes two sizes too large and well worn by the time they reached him. They never seemed to last long enough for him to grow into them.

First to arrive at the lamppost, he paced back and forth in long strides, his thoughts lingering on the plight of his mother. It was a relief when Karl arrived for it wrested his mind from it all.

"Goddamn this wind," Karl grumbled. The boys loved using profanity, but they were careful to limit it to each other's company. Karl humped his shoulder in an effort to ward off the cold and pulled his wool cap tightly around his face. They ran to keep warm, though Emil was forced to stop periodically to pull his knee-socks up, the stretch having lived its lifetime long before he claimed them.

"Come on, come on," Karl complained. "I'm freezing."

"You're a ninny," Emil teased as he raced to catch up. "You with your long pants."

Karl ignored the comment, buttressing himself further with his hand-sewn satchel in front of his face. He was a year older and a good three inches taller than Emil. Karl's rich brown hair always lay in huge waves with a delightful widow's peak on his high forehead. The mop of hair and full eyebrows called attention to his close-set eyes and tiny mouth, features that made him appear younger than his fourteen years. He was painfully aware of this and he spent considerable time trying to change it. Even at fourteen, he was often preoccupied with his appearance. Before entering the school grounds, he would remove the cap and smooth his hair with meticulous care.

Emil envied Karl his suave demeanor, his outgoing personality, and his charm. All seemed to call attention to his own short-comings in those areas.

As they neared the school, Karl purposely slapped his hand against his bulging coat pocket. "Anybody have a birthday?" he teased. It was like him to offer no hint that he had remembered and then to surprise Emil. It was the highlight of Emil's young life, this friendship with Karl. When Emil had been permitted to begin school at the age of five, he was placed in the company of boys who were six or older, a trying situation for a youngster whose country placed a lot of emphasis on the slightest age difference.

Karl was the only classmate who had reached out to him, and even he seemed embarrassed by the friendship at times. He lived in fear that their friendship would end once Karl graduated and became an apprentice in the factory.

Absolutely no one would be permitted to leave the school before reaching the age of fourteen. That Emil had completed the mandatory work and finished in the top ten percent made no difference; he would have to repeat the last year. It was a fate that monopolized his thoughts as the boys neared completion of their eighth year.

When they reached the school grounds, Karl pulled a small brown package from his pocket, but not before removing his cap and attending to his appearance. "Hurry," he said. "Let's go in the corner." Emil knew the spot, for it had served on many occasions as a secret meeting place for the pair. Though located on the outside of the building, it offered warmth as it was shielded from the wind by a storage building, and its walls were well heated by the cast iron stove inside. The wood and coal burning stove had been fired up long before the boys' arrival.

Emil dutifully followed his friend. "What is it?" he asked repeatedly before they reached the corner.

"You'll see," was Karl's response. After satisfying himself there were no eavesdroppers, he placed the brown package in Emil's hands. "Go ahead. Open it," he urged.

"What is it?" Emil repeated, anxiously unwrapping the package. When a small leather case fell into his hands, he couldn't contain his emotions. "A knife!" he shouted. Karl's own excitement equalled Emil's, but he urged discretion. "Shhh, they'll hear you," he warned in hushed anxiety. "The blade came from my father's knife. Honed it myself and carved the handle too," he boasted. "Better hide it from the Butcher. He'll kill us both." It was a name attributed by all the boys to the most dreaded professor in the school.

Emil fondled the wooden handle, which consisted of two neatly carved pieces of wood glued together. The blade was attached between them. His initials had been meticulously hand carved on one side. The blade was stationary, and might have posed a danger in a boy's pocket except that the leather case, obviously meant for a larger piece of cutlery, was thick with padding.

"Karl," Emil whispered breathlessly. He turned the handle over and over, admiring every detail with close inspection.

"Here, let's try it out," Karl said as he grabbed the knife and pierced his skin. When his blood began to trickle, he thrust the knife at Emil, handle first. "Well?" He grinned condescendingly.

Stirred by the emotions of the moment, Emil scarcely noticed the put-down, a habit of Karl's he had grown accustomed to. He had wished for this moment. He wanted nothing to spoil it. Many Schwabisch-Gmund boys mingled their blood as a symbol of their friendship or as a vow to accomplish something they wanted dearly, but making such a vow with a younger boy led to Karl's being subjected to cruel teasing. Their blood mingled, sealing their vow to pursue their art studies together, no matter the hardships.

Emil fondled the knife periodically throughout the morning classes, then examined it thoroughly during the lunch break, especially during the long walk home and back. The excitement of it all made dreaded Herr Professor Abt's class almost bearable. Once class began, Emil tried to concentrate on the assignment given them, but the events of the morning still absorbed him. While fondling the leather case in his pocket, his arm brushed against the paperwork on his desk and revealed a sketch he had done in his spare time. Quickly, he slapped his arm over the sketch, but not before Abt caught sight of it.

Abt's demeanor was anger with a hint of savagery in his sunken eyes. His large frame might have been a threat to his enemies in the past, but the muscles had long since turned to putty, offering no more protection than his bald head offered covering from the cold. In the classroom of young boys however, he was still very much in charge.

Grabbing Emil by one wrist, he clamped the other with his ever-present walking cane, a move that left the sketch visible for all to see.

"Not enough assignments?" he bellowed. "Wasting paper, wasting time. Is this how you show your appreciation to your professors who try to train you for a job?" His booming voice seemed to shake the walls, as if they feared the man as much as the students did. Emil knew he would not be given a chance to defend himself, to point out that the sketch had been done in his free time and only after he had completed his assignments.

All sixty-four boys cringed in terror as the professor's anger grew and rhetorical questions spouted from his mouth like sparks from a furnace. "Who else is wasting time sketching the mountains, the trees? Speak up! You?" He pointed from one student to another. "Too much leisure? Well, we'll see what can be done about that!" Abt made the rounds, cracking his cane indiscriminately across the desks, and often striking the helpless boys on their arms and shoulders.

By the time he reached Karl's desk, his anger had gained momentum. "You!" he snapped. He looked directly at Karl who dared not twitch a muscle. "Is this a friend of yours? This boy who wastes his time and his parents' money? Well, is it?"

Karl didn't utter a sound, for the boys had learned in the past that it only made matters worse.

"Can't talk? Well, let's see now," he scowled as he pawed through Karl's papers. When some of the boys began to whimper, Abt began delivering blows with all his force. He punctuated every stroke with cries and groans that spoke for the awesome joy he received from it all. With one last crack across Karl's knuckles, he returned to Emil.

Being last on the professor's list was not an enviable position, because Abt seemed to gain strength as he went along. "You see what a fuss you've made?" he growled as he struck Emil a hard blow across the shoulder. The frightened boy writhed in pain before bracing for another blow. When the bell sounded, Abt seemed as relieved as the students themselves that the episode had come to an end. He sank into his chair, exhausted.

The moment they were out of Abt's hearing distance, Emil murmured, "Butcher." It was a title the professor earned daily. The only hope of escaping his wrath was to graduate, and Emil couldn't even look forward to that.

"Why did you bring the goddamn sketches with you?" Karl whispered angrily. "You know it causes trouble." His narrow eyes pierced Emil's own angry glare. But there was no time to argue, as they had entered the next classroom, that of Herr Professor Unruh, their favorite teacher. Unruh detested the sight of the boys' tearstained faces and their bruised skin, but he dared not intervene. Herr Abt was considered an authority on education, as confirmed by their own textbooks, which were written by him and used throughout Germany.

"*Schweinehund*," (swinedog) Emil repeated silently. It was his only recourse except for the tears of hatred that welled in his eyes.

Karl pouted throughout the afternoon and remained taciturn on their way home. It was not until they neared the lamppost that he spoke at all.

"Not too much difference in our hands now," he grumbled.

He had always taken pride in his long, thin fingers and smooth hands. "Hands of an artist," he often bragged, and he would add that Emil's stubby-fingered, unshapely hands were those of the working class.

When they reached the lamppost, Karl turned away without a word. Emil gazed at him longingly. He wished they could begin the day anew, capture the moment with the knife and the mixing of their blood, and remain frozen there until they'd had their fill of it. Maybe then they could make their usual sketching plans for Sunday after Mass.

In frustration, he threw his satchel over his shoulder, but then cried out in pain when it scraped across his bruised back. With the day's events impossible to escape, he trudged homeward. The sight of the massive Gothic church looming up in front of him with its rounded transept arms and double-towered facade grated on him as never before. Since first hearing the story of St. Cecelia, he seldom passed the church without thinking of the popular saint whose delicately carved statue graced the interior.

He had believed the St. Cecelia story at first. It had given him hope on many occasions, hope for a better life for him and his mother, a life that excluded his abusive father as well as Herr Professor Abt. But when fervent prayers to the saint didn't change things at home or at the Catholic school, he grew to resent the adults who repeated the legend of St. Cecelia's golden shoe. Looking back, he realized his mother had reveled in the story, and it had no doubt raised her spirits with the age-old theme of good prevailing over evil.

How realistic she could make it all sound during his earlier years: the story of the poor fiddler who had come through tiny Schwabisch-Gmund, knelt at the feet of the stone image of St. Cecelia, and played a pitiful tune. The saint had thrown the beggar her solid gold shoe.

When the beggar tried to sell the shoe, he was arrested for thievery and condemned to die on the gallows. Before the hanging, he was granted one last request: to play again for St. Cecelia. There, in the presence of the townspeople, the revered saint had thrown him her other gold shoe.

From that day forward, St. Cecelia held a special place in the hearts of Schwabisch-Gmunders, especially the underprivileged. But not for Emil, not any longer. He had made up his mind this very day. Timidly, he approached the massive double door entrance, awesome with its solid construction and bleak countenance. The church was a prison in Emil's eyes, the imposing entry a deathknell to freedom. It was there he was made to attend Mass every Sunday morning, thus dashing any hope of sketching in the distant mountains.

When a timid push on the door yielded nothing, he used the full force of his body, causing the massive structure to burst open and send him sprawling to the floor with all his paraphernalia. The whole thing frightened him, the more so as he had never once entered the church except in the company of his mother, and that was always during Mass.

After satisfying himself that no one had witnessed the scene, he gathered his things and stood gaping at the massive interior as if it were his first time there. In a way, it was. He had attended Mass every Sunday since he could remember, dutifully following the ceremony demanded by the church and his mother, but his heart was never in it. Most perplexing to the boy was that his father, a man who needed to pray, never did, and his mother, a saint to his thinking, prayed constantly for forgiveness. For his part, it was all a farce, the more so as the priest often frequented the same *Bierstube* his father did, and condemned others for doing the same.

Void of the priest and the self-glorifying ceremony of many of the parishioners, the awesome beauty of the interior awed him. The side aisles were of equal height to the nave, itself an impressive three stories high. Tall windows enabled beams of sunlight to puncture the shadows, illuminating the rib-vaulted ceiling and creating a mystical drama of an ever-changing nature. Emil longed to capture the moment with a quick sketch, or even a full-fledged drawing, but remembering his mission, he walked purposely down the long nave to the wall that housed St. Cecelia's statue. By standing tiptoed, he could scarcely reach her bare feet which he touched briefly before jumping back at the sight of her face. A stream of sunlight had illuminated only a small portion of her facial features, but it was sufficient to reveal the contortion there, long since considered by the townsfolk to symbolize her downcast state resulting from the beggar's tragedy.

Struggling with mixed emotions, anxious one moment to capture the drama of the changing scene on paper, and wishing the next he could destroy the whole myth, he burst into tears and ran screaming down the lengthy nave, stopping only when he reached the massive double entrance doors. When his emotions reached a climax, he let out a scream before voicing his concerns in the general direction of the chapel, the nearest thing to the statue he could see. "You never had any gold shoes! Never!" he yelled. His skin rose up from his body, seemingly in protest of what he had done, while burning tears singed his face as he struggled to pull one of the wide doors open.

Once outside, he hurried, for he had to arrive home before Papa, or there would be no opportunity to pour his heart out to his mother.

Again, Frau Holzhauer was bent over her little working area in the kitchen, almost as if she had spent the day there. Before arriving home, Emil had gotten control of his emotions, but the moment he caught sight of his mother, he burst into tears again. "The Butcher," he screamed. "He did it again." He tugged at his clothes, baring the welts on his shoulder, and held his bruised hands and arms out.

"Oh, my poor boy," his mother consoled. "We must hurry before your papa--." Frau Holzhauer stopped there, knowing it was unnecessary to warn Emil. The episode would not be mentioned to her husband. She bathed his hands in a solution made from the medicinal leaves she and Emil had gathered during blackberry season.

"You must be very careful. What if Herr Abt heard you call him names? Or your papa?" Frau Holzhauer accepted things as they were. She tried to instill in her son her own patience and submissiveness. A gentle, sensitive woman, she lived in fear of her husband. A "common housekeeper" he called her. He, a cabinetmaker, had stooped beneath his station by marrying her. Gently, she dabbed the worst spots with her healing potion, and Emil recalled the happy berry-picking days when they had gathered the medicinal leaves. He wished they were there, just the two of them, without Papa and without the Butcher.

"Does that feel better?" she asked as she emptied the potion much sooner than she cared to. "We must hurry. Your papa--."

Emil nodded. The familiar sound of Herr Holzhauer kicking the door open sent Frau Holzhauer scurrying to her chores and Emil to the room he shared with Fritz. Opening his chest drawer, he spied the new shirt, pressed and neatly folded, complete with buttons. His head dropped to his chest. He detested himself for dwelling on his own misfortune instead of thanking his mother for one of her many sacrifices. There would be no opportunity to do so before morning, perhaps not even then.

Two

Emil's dream had come true. He was apprenticed to the Buchhandler factory where Karl was already serving his second year.

In Schwabisch-Gmund, every boy's future depended on his ability to draw. The town fathers saw to it that no industry other than their own, the gold and silversmith industry, was permitted within its walls. Nearly every citizen was employed as a jewelry designer or steel engraver or as assistants in these fields. Boys with drawing talent were lucky, because those who excelled would be the recipients of the best jobs.

All the boys in Schwabisch-Gmund attended eight mandatory years of training prior to being apprenticed to one of the copper concerns for four years of intensive training in the field in which they showed the most promise: steel engraving or jewelry designing. No one was exempt.

Emil and Karl lived for Sundays, the only days they were free to sketch. The boys couldn't go far after attending Mass, but in their old city subject matter was everywhere. Founded some time in the eleventh century, it was situated in the southwest of Germany in an area known as Schwabenland. The city's walls and guard towers, dating from the days of the Hohenstaufen rule, still stood. King's Tower, the highest and most conspicuous of them, was still used as a fire watchtower. By the time Emil came along, the little city had long been at peace, snuggled cozily in the valley and encompassed by gently rising hills.

A map of the city would fail to show a myriad of narrow, winding alleys and lanes or the ancient houses with their high pointed gables and brown tiles interspersed with orange or vermilion. In stark contrast were the city's Gothic churches with their ornate windows, doors, and columns, all stretching heavenward.

There were the Romanesque churches as well with their aisle and nave extensions and their ambulatories and radiating chapels, all of solid masonry walls with covered stone vaults. One church in particular was noted for its bell tower, which assisted the community in keeping time. Few of the inhabitants had watches. During their outings, Emil and Karl depended on the church gong to get them home on time. When the gong sounded twice, signaling the half-hour, they often argued which hour had passed, as their sketching usually removed them from the reality of passing time.

Everything in the direction of the distant mountains where they longed to sketch had to be reached by foot as there were no coaches connecting the city with the surrounding villages and mountains. The idea of sketching in the distant mountains had become an obsession with the boys, and Karl had been given permission to skip Mass for such a venture. Emil knew he would be denied the same pleasure, but at Karl's insistence, he asked.

The result was an outright refusal and a stern warning not to mention it again. Frau Holzhauer held her breath in fear when Emil ignored his father's warning and broached the subject a second time. The timid request came just as his father bent over to lace his boots.

It seemed to Emil that the only emotion Herr Holzhauer ever showed was anger. He wore a constant frown that had caused a deep, permanent wrinkle, vertically situated on his forehead between his cold, blue eyes, which were invariably puffy and bloodshot from too much drink. It took a great deal of courage for the young boy to attempt to penetrate that frightening exterior. "Papa?" His voice was a mere whisper.

Herr Holzhauer grabbed Emil by the shoulders and pierced his eyes with an angry glare. "You see these boots? Have you any notion what I paid to have them made?" he growled.

Emil remained silent, as he knew the story he was about to be subjected to, of how unnecessary walking was a waste of shoe leather, and how hard his father worked in order to put shoes on the family's feet. The more he talked, the angrier he became, finally shaking his clenched fists in the frightened boy's face. When Frau Holzhauer let out a muffled cry, he stopped short of striking Emil, but not before pounding his fist repeatedly into his open palm.

"You'll go to Mass Sunday and every Sunday after that. Do you understand? This Sunday, next Sunday, and the next and the next!" he shouted. Emil couldn't face his father, but he could see in his mind's eye the contorted facial muscles that went hand in hand with the snorting nostrils.

Emil wished he hadn't broached the subject. At least then he had hope. Now even that had dissipated.

Factory life at Buchhandler's was far from the haven Emil and Karl had imagined. Wulz, the foreman, was worse than Herr Professor Abt had been. He assigned menial and degrading tasks to the apprentices, tasks to be performed in full view. Fehrle, Sterner, Holzhauer, and Ott, the four boys who were most often recognized for their outstanding work, were often singled out for mortifying tasks.

Like many of the others, Emil and Karl consoled themselves by threatening to leave the factory. Even though the rules were not in writing, they were expected to work for Buchhandler once their training was completed. It was unheard of for anyone to leave. No one took the threats seriously.

"If he only knew we don't want his goddamn job. That's what he's afraid of, you know," Karl told Emil. "I'm leaving that goddamn factory. I'd leave tomorrow if not for the drawing school," he spouted. The tightness in his lips eased into a dimpled cheek, but fell short of breaking into a smile.

"All hell would break loose if you did," Emil warned. "At least stay until I finish and we can leave together?" The plea went unnoticed, and the questioning glance he tossed Karl's way suffered the same fate.

Emil went on. "If he only knew about our plans to study art, he wouldn't worry about his--"

"Don't dare mention that!" Karl warned. He vigorously shook his finger in Emil's face. "Everybody's laughing at us, you know. The money's in steel engraving and designing. Ask anybody. Artists starve to death."

"Karl!" Emil scolded. "*Verdamnt*! They've always said that. We can make a living in steel engraving and paint in our spare time."

"Don't worry. I'm not quitting. Got the hands for it," he grinned.

They both laughed, but the truth was, Emil's own misshapen hands worried him. He had begun to examine the hands of all the boys who finished higher than he in the annual design competition. None of them had stubby fingers like his.

Karl's shapely hands weren't the only asset he could boast of. He had a certain air of nonchalance that enabled him to enter a classroom without attracting anyone's attention, or he could let everyone know, if he cared to. Talking to girls came easily for him. His jaunty self-confidence made him attractive in spite of his crooked teeth and disappearing chin. He had a way of flaunting his stature, holding his head high and his shoulders thrown back, and his well-proportioned body cut a nice figure on the dance floor.

As for Emil, he had always shunned social gatherings, especially dances. While all his friends had enjoyed the advantage of dancing lessons, he had been denied them. His lack of schooling in this and other social graces had taken its toll on his self-image. He was wretched in the presence of girls.

At home that evening Emil walked past his father, apparently unnoticed and toward the room he shared with Fritz. Greetings or even recognition, were unusual except when he and his mother were the only ones there. He had the strange feeling that the two of them made up the entire family and that his father and cousin were merely unwanted visitors.

In the tiny room he and Fritz shared, his cousin was sprawled across the floor, resting between exercises. His barbells blocked the doorway.

"Will you move that thing?" Emil grumbled. He pushed the heavily-weighted bar as hard as he could, rolling it against Fritz.

Fritz scowled, his broad chest and powerful arms bulging with muscles. His twisted smile revealed a torn lower lip, a lingering scar from one of his many brawls. He had outgrown the need to torment his young cousin, for better opportunities for exhibiting his strength had presented themselves. Townspeople gathered in large numbers to see the weightlifting champion outdo his opponents. Skirmishing with Emil was no longer a challenge, but if provoked, he was not one to play dead.

In the past, Emil would have stepped over Fritz and his weights, but something inside him snapped like a spring that had gradually worked itself lose. He tried moving Fritz's brawny body with his foot, and when that failed, he grabbed him by his massive shoulders and pushed with all his strength.

Fritz found the whole thing amusing. Between raucous peals of laughter, he urged his cousin onward. "Come on. Try Again. Push hard! I won't use my hands," he boasted as he braced his legs against the wall. When Emil lunged toward him, Fritz moved away at the last second, and Emil hit the floor.

The scuffle brought Herr Holzhauer bounding into the room.

His facial expression terrified the boys, but both of them felt some comfort seeing that the walking cane he held was a treasured one with a gold acorn design on the handle. He often raised it over their heads in a threatening motion, but he never used it as a weapon. He delighted, however, in watching the boys flinch.

When Emil stood up, the old man struck him a hard blow to his head, cutting a wide gash, and sending him back to the floor. Frau Holzhauer witnessed the scene in horror.

"You brute!" she screamed. "You'll kill the boy! Emil, Emil," she whimpered. Emil was too dazed to get up, but conscious enough to fear for his mother.

"You keep your mouth shut," Holzhauer warned her as he stomped out the front door. Emil's condition had probably kept his father from striking Fritz and Frau Holzhauer, the three decided.

With trembling hands, his mother prepared a solution and began bathing his wound. "His cane," she sobbed, "he'll never forgive you for breaking the acorn loose." She brushed her tears away with frequent swipes of her old apron, quickly and without ceremony, anxious to get hold of her emotions, to strengthen herself for the consequences she knew would come.

Emil could think of nothing but getting to night school. Tardiness was not permitted, and even if it were, he would still be among the first to arrive. He often arrived before the classrooms opened. He tried leaving home a little later, but fear of being late always seized him and sent him racing to the lamppost and beyond if Karl weren't waiting there.

Coming from the prison atmosphere of the factory and the traumatic experiences at home, Emil thought of the school as a make-believe world. The teachers were, for the most part, masters in their profession, and some were artists. They were chosen on their merits by the young director, a painter and sculptor of no mean ability himself. All instruction, however, was for the sole purpose of training the boys for local concerns, nothing beyond that.

The *Fachschule* brought all the boys in the city together, serving as an auxiliary to the various manufacturers. The integration of all concerns created a great rivalry among the boys for the annual prizes and awards for the best designs. Nearly every citizen in Schwabisch-Gmund bestowed praise and adoration on the winners.

It was not only factory against factory, it was also boy against boy. No one was more aware of that than Karl and Emil, whose keen senses of competition led them to battle each other for the highest awards. Their fiercest rivals were Fehrle and Sterner, both products of their own Buchhandler Brothers' factory. Emil felt it unrealistic to think of outdoing either of these boys, but he harbored thoughts of doing as well or better than his best friend. Not once in all the years they entered the competition had he done so, but he hoped, nonetheless.

At the Holzhauer home, the punishment for the broken acorn was the silent treatment. Fear of the unknown, of what to expect when Holzhauer's bottled-up emotions exploded, kept everyone tense. At no time were they allowed to speak freely in the house, but during these morbid silent periods, they had no voice at all.

If his mother wouldn't cry, Emil could endure it better. She managed to control her sobs until late at night after her husband had gone to sleep, but Emil heard. The thin walls in the little apartment scarcely muffled her cries. He felt responsible for her misery.

To ease his conscience, she confided in him. "It's none of your doing, son. Your papa dwells on something else."

"Something else?"

"He wants more money from your Aunt Rose. And you know, we owe her so much already." Her tiny wrinkled hand clasped his, a sign that he was her only comfort.

For years, her husband had forced her to borrow money from her sister, money they both knew would never be repaid. But there would be no peace in the Holzhauer house until she asked for more.

Emil wanted to take the acorned cane and crack the old man's skull wide open with it. Even while he and his mother agonized over the family's financial crisis, the great cabinetmaker was in town spending money on beer as if he had plenty.

"You could keep a little back from my factory pay," he offered. A paltry sum, seldom affording him the price of a beer, the one extravagance he occasionally allowed himself, it would nevertheless give her the satisfaction of repaying some of the money her husband had borrowed.

With no alternative available to her, she accepted his offer. A slight smile parted her thin, pale lips. "But only until the debt is paid. Then you must keep your money, and save it for your art studies."

But of course there would be no end. Even if the debt were paid, there would be others. They both knew it.

Three

As apprentices, Emil and Karl were not allowed to talk, not even whisper, so they devised the *Kugelpost*, a means of communication via paperballs. They wrapped notes written on scrap paper into very tight balls and sailed them through the air.

Not once had the foreman caught them in this activity. With sunken cheeks, dead eyes, and yellowish complexion, Wulz appeared to suffer from a progressive wasting away of the body, but he had the strength of a bull, and he proved it every time one of the boys broke a rule, however small. He referred to all of them as "*Stifts*" (raw, inexperienced engravers). It was a stinging insult for the young sensitive boys.

The moment Wulz entered the room, things came to order. Though not superior in knowledge or training, he was nevertheless in charge. Given the job years before because of his then superior craftsmanship, his future was no longer secure now that students in the Catholic schools received much more advanced training prior to entering their apprenticeships.

Ambitious students could accomplish almost any goal they set for themselves in arts and crafts because of the schools' superior guidance and training in jewelry designing and modeling. Many excelled in spite of Wulz.

When Herr Buchhandler, the owner of the factory, made his visits to the designing department, he was impressed by Wulz's group. The boys were always working, and since many of them were well-known for their accomplishments in the field of arts and crafts, Buchhandler assumed they had developed much of their skill under the direction of Wulz.

After nearly two years with Buchhandler Brothers, Karl was still polishing, the only task that required no training. Most of the items they were required to polish were inferior. Slovenly journeymen didn't bother to scrape away the ridge of metal, making it impossible to polish their work. If anyone complained, he would be given extra clean-up chores or a harsh blow across the back.

With Wulz out of the room one day, Emil grumbled when a journeyman passed along inferior work to be polished. "*Stift*," he muttered.

Instead of lashing out at Emil, the journeyman smiled contentedly. He had seen Wulz's shadow just outside the door. When the foreman walked inside, no one had to ask if he had heard.

"*Stift*?" he bellowed. The sound came from deep inside his chest. His nostrils dilated like those of an angry bull, and his eyes seemed in a struggle to remain in their sockets. "*Stift*?" He stalked around the room repeating the oath.

"Some problem here, Herr apprentice? I suppose you could do better than the journeyman!" His voice was like thunder, a warning of the awful storm that was to come. Grabbing the first tool he could find, he hurled it across the engraving bench, knocking steel dies, files, and other tools on the floor.

He then picked up the stool Emil was sitting on and flung it in the direction of the filthy cuspidor, emptying its slimy contents. Unhurt, Emil knelt quickly and began picking up the tools. It was a common practice, this jerking of the apprentices' stools from under them. They tried to stay poised for it, especially if the foreman was angry.

With slavish quickness, Emil retrieved the objects, grabbed his stool, and continued his work without a word or glance in either direction.

Wulz's rage had brought on a coughing spell. He gloried in exaggerating his condition. He never covered his mouth or turned his head. The sound of the phlegm breaking loose nauseated his defenseless audience as they were forced to watch him heave back and forth to emphasize his torture. The apprentices and journeymen alike sat glued to their seats throughout the performance. They were lucky if they escaped the spray of the flying saliva, which Wulz aimed in the general direction of the cuspidor.

Regaining his strength somewhat, he returned to Emil. "Holzhauer!" he yelled. The intensity with which he bellowed almost sent him into another coughing spell. Rather than chance that, he lowered his voice to an ugly whisper. "If you know so much about steel engraving, you know working areas must be kept clean. Show us how to clean a cuspidor."

Nothing was more humiliating, especially since Wulz had overturned the cuspidor and most of its contents had emptied on the floor. On hands and knees he had to clean the fresh, slimy phlegm and other vile spittings from the cuspidor and surrounding areas while all the boys watched.

While Emil carried out his punishment, Karl cleared his throat, signaling that a *Kugelpost* was imminent. Emil was afraid to look up, but afraid not to. Wulz was still eyeing the clean-up activity. Emil had often voiced concern over the *Kugelpost* signal. His own throat-clearing had always sounded suspect to him.

"You're just imagining things," Karl had always assured him. "There's no rule against clearing your throat. Just be accurate, and remember the rule. If caught, swallow the evidence."

The message arrived safely, and amazingly free of slime, but it was a full twenty minutes before Emil had a chance to read it. "All the way to Lauterberg Sunday," he read.

Good old Karl. Nothing could have eased the pain better than the thought of the two of them sketching on Lauterberg, the most inspiring mountain of all, and the one farthest from Schwabisch-Gmund. They had never undertaken such a trip, but they had often dreamed of the day they could. It would mean leaving at two in the morning to see the sunrise from the mountaintop. The possibility would sustain him.

The remainder of the week, he used every tactic he could muster in an all-out effort to obtain permission from his father to skip Mass the following Sunday. Even his mother intervened. He could hear her soft voice late in the night pleading his cause. Emil cringed. Her efforts usually made his father more determined not to bend.

When permission came, it was delivered in anger. "All right! Let him go!" her husband yelled. "Then you can pay the cobbler for a new pair of shoes when he wears them out."

No matter the bickering. It was the nearest thing to consent Emil would ever get.

The days dragged on relentlessly, and when Saturday night finally came, Emil lay sleepless most of the night, listening to the clock slowly ticking away. Fear of his oversleeping or Karl's oversleeping, or worse, that his father would suddenly spring from his bed and refuse to let him go, and a dozen other worries gripped him like a vice. At fifteen minutes before the designated hour, he grabbed his belongings, slipped out of the house in the clothes he had slept in, and ran as fast as he could toward the lamppost. He didn't pause for a good deep breath until he caught sight of a lone figure casting a small shadow under the flickering gaslight. It had to be Karl.

It was rare and delightful for everything to go well. Lauterberg was to be theirs for a few hours. All the mountains in the area had their respective characters, but Lauterberg was considered by nearly all citizens of Schwabisch-Gmund the most exciting, and it wasn't unusual to see hikers from the little city making their way to the famous mountain on Sundays and holidays.

Moving hastily along, the boys wound their way through the narrow alleys, up the hills, and onto the dusty country road that led to the mountains. They looked back occasionally at the city nestled in the peaceful valley below, its gas lanterns clearly marking the streets and various public buildings. As always, King's Tower stood out from all the rest, a constant reminder of less peaceful days.

Once over the hills, they missed the light afforded them by the city's lanterns, and the white sand road was their guide. The only sound in the villages along the way was that of dogs barking. The boys chuckled as they watched the farmers' lights come on to see what danger lurked.

Sharing the dusty country road with no one, they paced themselves so as not to miss the sunrise. By the time they reached the second village, many of the farmers were already milking cows and tending to other chores. When they reached the Rosenstein, the first mountain of the chain, they wanted to climb its steep front and enjoy the view of the valley below with its red-roofed villages and tilled fields. But the sky was already turning gray; they had to hurry on.

Once they put the other peaks behind them, they nearly ran to the foot of Lauterberg. The path led them alongside the mountain and gradually to the top. The sun could slip up somewhere on the horizon without their seeing it, because the dense wood along the ridge only lent a vista of the sky above. A clearing in the woods led them to the edge of a steep cliff, and there they saw the red edge of the sun peering over the ridge on the opposite side. They burst into song, proclaiming "*Die Sonne erwacht mit ihrer Pracht*" (the sun awakens in her glory).

From Lauterberg, with its jagged and broken walls rising from a ravine, they viewed the sun-warmed red roofs and pinnacles appearing in the valley below. Church bells rang in the glory of a Sunday in July. They were calling the peasants to worship while Emil and Karl saw proof that God existed.

Subject matter was everywhere. They wasted no time getting started. In a little while, they heard a church organ and a simple melody, sung by an angel it seemed to them. Even the noise of the charcoal moving across their papers interfered with their listening.

"Look!" Karl shouted.

"What?"

"Between the broken walls. She must be the one who was singing." They stared.

"She's an angel," Emil declared. "Look how she moves." The only women they had seen were earthy peasants, heavy and awkward in comparison. They held their stares.

The girl began to walk in their direction.

"What will we do?" Emil whispered, while suppressing the pounding of his heart with a charcoaled hand."Karl, she's coming," he whispered, raising his hand to his mouth to quiet himself and smudging his shirt in the process. Every effort to brush himself made it worse.

"Keep quiet," Karl begged. His attempt to sound confident failed.

Emil bowed his head in the direction of his sketch but saw nothing. Sensing her nearness, his head bobbed up without his permission, and he smiled self-consciously.

"Good morning," she said. "I thought you might be artists. Do you mind if I see your work?" Her speech was as angelic as her singing, as pleasant as her chiseled features, as warm as her friendly blue eyes. Ringlets of blond hair hung softly over her high forehead while soft curls framed her oval face. Her lengthy tresses were tucked into a soft bun at the back of her long slender neck. She wore a high-necked linen blouse whose soft bodice enhanced her full breasts. Her ankle length skirt fitted cozily around her tiny waist.

She didn't sound like anyone they had ever heard. She used exquisite High German, with no trace of the local Schwabían dialect.

Emil opened his mouth to speak, but as no sound came out, he closed it again.

"I'm afraid you'll be disappointed in our sketches," Karl managed.

He used such good German, foreign to anything he had ever used before, Emil couldn't resist glancing at him. The girl brushed the remark aside and peered over their shoulders.

"Oh, you've done the corner of the courtyard. Those are both nice. I envy you your talent. Are you from Stuttgart?"

To be taken for Stuttgarters instead of boys from the province was a great compliment. To Karl's dismay, Emil found his tongue long enough to admit they were only Schwabisch-Gmunders. She didn't seem to care. Her interest in their work finally put them at ease enough that they introduced themselves and asked questions of their own.

The girl's name was Anna. Her mother was the widow of the former school teacher, and she lived in the little house near the entrance to the yard. It was one of the few houses still intact on Lauterberg. The Countess of Lauterburg, who had lived in a castle close by, had always taken an interest in the family and had offered to educate Anna, the younger daughter. She had received an excellent education and became governess to the countess' only child. Their home was in Frankfurt Anmain, but they came to Lauterburg for lengthy vacations.

The dumbfounded boys were captivated by her fairy tale. It seemed to Emil that he was imagining the whole thing. But there she was, proof that the working class could rise above their station in life and get along with the other classes. Without the Countess, Anna would have grown up into the same peasant girl as the others in the village. Now she was a *Weltdame*, a society lady.

After she left, the boys had private thoughts of her, each living an imaginary life of association with her. When lunchtime came, they ate their sausages and rolls, washing down their meager lunches with water from the fountain in the courtyard. Karl daydreamed himself to sleep, but Emil was far too excited for that. Eagerly, he sketched.

Suddenly, Anna appeared again, this time with a book in her hand. As she walked toward an arbor, Emil could see her quite well through the overhanging vines. Quickly, he began a charcoal sketch. His eyes wandered over her features. The excited young artist reached beyond himself, inspired as never before.

Just when things were going well, his subject stood up, put her book aside, and began walking in his direction. Quickly, he tried to bring it all together, but his clumsy fingers wouldn't cooperate. He contemplated tearing it up or moving it to the bottom of the stack, but before he could settle on one, Anna was in speaking distance.

"You were drawing me, weren't you?"

He managed a nervous smile and then instinctively raised his hand to his quivering mouth. Again, he had to clean his charcoal-streaked face with his shirt, and in full view of Anna.

"May I see?" she asked.

He stammered something unintelligible, then prayed silently that Karl would wake up and come to his aid.

"So that's the way I look?"

"No, no, it's much too-- I should-- you're much more beautiful." He blushed.

Anna leaned over for a closer view. Her breasts touched his head and her breath mingled with his. He swooned with delight, convinced that he was in love. Suddenly, Karl jumped to attention, self-consciously tugging at his clothes and needlessly smoothing his hair.

"Look," she said excitedly. "Your friend has done a sketch of me. A very nice one too, though he doesn't admit it."

When she left, Karl lashed out at Emil. "Goddamn rotten trick!" He glanced repeatedly at Emil's sketch of Anna, and once he reached out as if he might tear it in pieces.

"There wasn't time to wake you. I hardly--"

"Sure. Time to sketch her, but not to wake me." Karl's tiny mouth was so tight, it took on the uneven character of his teeth.

Silently, they sketched until the shadows lengthened. Without a word to each other, they packed their things and began the long trip home. They took turns leading the way through the difficult mountain path until they reached the white dust of the Schwabian Alb country road, which once again became their guide.

Mile after mile, Karl nursed his anger in silence. Emil's efforts to make plans for the following Sunday failed. They were nearing the lamppost before Karl spoke at all.

"I'm going to Munich," he declared. "I need to watch a real artist at work. I mean a master. There should be plenty of them in Munich.

Maybe even Berlin." It wasn't the first time Karl had suggested the idea, preposterous as it was.

"A mere peasant meet a master artist? I never expect to see one, much less know one," Emil moaned.

"No real artist is going to waste his time teaching. Would you, if you were a master? No, you would be painting."

It was difficult to ignore Karl, but this was much too idealistic for Emil. The truth was that tomorrow morning he would be back at the steel engraving bench, polishing the inferior work of untrained journeymen.

"There's a lot of excitement in the cities," Karl continued. "We can't learn anything from these peasant women." He broke into a knowing grin as he raised his eyebrows up and down. "Remember what we read about von Stuck and the other artists? They had plenty of women."

Emil agreed with some of his ideas, but his own experiences with girls, or lack of them, caused him great concern. He was seldom in their company, and when he was, he didn't know what to do or say.

At the lamppost, Karl turned toward home without a word. "You're in love with her too?" Emil called.

Emil heard the suppressed giggle. He took advantage of it. "Lauterberg next Sunday?" he asked.

"Wouldn't have it any other way," Karl retorted.

Emil waited, hoping Karl would turn around, or say goodbye, or wave, but he didn't.

At home, the idea of returning to the distant mountain met opposition. "You'll do nothing of the sort," his father assured him.

"Papa, I could wear my old shoes, you know." It was a desperate attempt to gain his father's sympathy. Not only had Emil outgrown the shoes, the cobbler had deemed them beyond repair.

His plea was ignored.

Karl had completed his two year apprenticeship and was now a journeyman. As such, he had been freed from the task of polishing, and he was allowed minimal conversation with the other journeymen as long as he didn't upstage Herr Wulz in any way. He also had the distinct pleasure of assigning tasks to the apprentices.

It was a sad day for Emil, for it meant the burial of the *Kugelpost*, his only diversion from the daily drudgery. Outside the factory walls, he begged Karl to continue using it, but he only laughed at the idea. "Why should I? I can talk to you anytime I want."

"Yes, but I can't talk to you. We can never discuss our sketching plans or anything personal."

The relationship itself seemed buried along with the *Kugelpost*. Karl soon became moody and uncommunicative, often taking advantage of his superiority in the factory.

By the time Emil became a journeyman, their relationship had deteriorated. Karl's attendance at the arts and crafts school had gradually tapered off as well, and it was a rare occasion for him to attend the new Sunday class. Emil sorely missed him, but his own enthusiasm for the classes never wavered, especially the exciting Sunday classes where they were allowed freedom of expression for the first time.

Teaching in the *Fachschule* was supposed to be held within the narrow horizons of the industry requirements, but there was one teacher, Herr Kreisel, who encouraged any student's attempts beyond that. His specialties were jewelry design and color theory.

It was his idea to offer voluntary Sunday classes for the more ambitious students. It was a marvelous substitute for the Sunday sketching trips, which were not possible in the winter. Although usually too sensitive to let go without Karl's approval, Emil cast his doubts aside one Sunday and began a life-size watercolor of a crane. He was unaware of the instructor even during the most trying moments when the crane looked like anything but a bird. When it finally took on the shape he struggled for, Herr Kreisel wrinkled his round face in a warm smile, and his eager brown eyes attested to the joy he felt. "Now he's in his element," he announced proudly for the class to hear. Emil would never forget the words or the familiar chuckle that accompanied them.

His first thought was to share the moment with Karl, but as they no longer walked to the factory together and there was no *Kugelpost*, he would have to wait for the arts and crafts class. Even as a journeyman himself, Emil wished for the revival of the *Kugelpost*, almost putting a message in Karl's open tool drawer on special occasions such as this.

While contemplating the notion, Herr Buchhandler made a rare appearance in their department. The director walked purposely to Karl's workbench. "How long before you leave us?"

"Saturday, sir," Karl answered. His voice was barely audible. To avoid Wulz's cold gaze, Karl's eyes darted from object to object, finally fixing nervously on the director.

Mumbling, though not usually permitted, was overlooked by Wulz, who was himself in a state of shock. He would doubtless be happy to be rid of one more threat to his job, but Karl's leaving the moment his contract was up, without mentioning it to the foreman, was a slap in the face. It could mean trouble for Wulz.

The minute Buchhandler left the studio, there was an uproar, but Wulz's booming voice soon brought them to their senses. "What gratitude!" he raved. "And after all I've taught you." He shifted his attention to Emil. "And did you keep this little secret too?"

Emil blushed deeply. His body had stiffened from outrage in the beginning, but when Wulz singled him out, he slumped over the bench, speechless. Everyone in the room knew he and Karl had been friends since early childhood.

At closing time, other journeymen and apprentices showered Karl with questions. "Why didn't you tell us? How long have you known? Where will you go?" Karl's answer was a smug and satisfied grin.

On Saturday, he packed his tools and left, never to return to the factory. He and Emil parted like strangers.

Four

Spring, though it seemed a lifetime in coming, had finally arrived in the little German city. It was a season that traditionally renewed the artist within Emil. Still, things were not the same. Factory life without Karl had been more painful and depressing than repeating the eighth year at the Catholic school. At least then he had the apprenticeship and Karl to look forward to.

As a fourth-year journeyman, he had become something of a tyrant toward all the apprentices as well as to third-year journeymen. He did assist them in the learning process, which was more than Wulz could lay claim to, but if they didn't grasp new concepts immediately, he was quick to rant and rave.

He continued to sketch daily, racing out the door the minute the factory whistle blew, but there was a conscious void in his life, a yearning to change things as never before. He made up his mind to give notice when his contract ended, but as the time drew nearer, his courage began to dissipate.

One day, Josef, one of the apprentices, aroused the ire of Wulz to such an extent that the foreman beat him unmercifully about the face and neck. In backing away from the blows, Josef lost his balance and fell against a bench, cutting a gash in his side. Enraged, Josef grabbed a stool and flung it at his tormentor, jabbing him in the stomach. Wulz managed to subdue the boy and beat him unconscious.

During the beating, one boy sneaked away and summoned Herr Buchhandler. Josef, having regained consciousness, cried out to the director. "Look what he did to me. He's a monster!" the boy screamed, his bloody face and neck offering ample proof of his testimony. "Why do you think Karl left? I want my contract cancelled now!"

It was not until Josef's father threatened suit against the factory that the contract was cancelled, and Josef left triumphantly.

The episode gave Emil the courage he needed. He was further encouraged by a card he received from Karl. Postmarked in Ulm, it read, "Lenbach is dead." The boys had pored over textbook prints of Lenbach's paintings and both of them admired the artist. It was Karl's entire message. No matter. They were friends again.

In a few days, another card arrived, this one from Nuremberg. "On to Munich," was the brief message. Finally, he received a card from Munich. No message, just an address. Karl was taking the first steps, and, just as they had planned, he would lead the way. Emil fondled the knife Karl had given him, and smiled contentedly. He wrote Karl to ask if he might visit him in Munich as soon as he could leave Buchhandler's. There was no answer. He decided to go anyway.

News of his plan to leave Buchhandler was met with extreme hostility at home. "No, you can't do that!" his father raved. When Emil didn't give in to the demands, the old man revealed a serious problem at his own employ. "There are changes being made at my factory. I may be without a job any day now. You'll have to contribute to the household expenses."

If it were true, Emil's life would be ended. He couldn't accept that without a fight. "But Papa," he protested, "you have a life job." In reality no such thing existed, but most Germans liked to think they had one. Emil uttered the words out of frustration.

"You stay with Buchhandler," his father demanded with a familiar scowl.

It was with trembling voice Emil responded. "Papa, I'll stay in Schwabisch-Gmund, but I'm leaving Buchhandler."

Realizing he had no means of holding the boy, as he was of age and ready for compulsory service, the proud cabinetmaster mellowed a bit. "Then don't leave so soon after your contract is over. You'll create a scandal and nobody will hire you. Stay for a while before you quit."

"No, Papa. I'll have no trouble finding a job."

In one day, he was hired by one of the best designers in the city. It was there the steel dies for the trade were made. The manager hired him on the strength of his achievements at the arts and crafts school.

Just one day prior to the end of his contract, Emil spoke with Herr Buchhandler, expressing his displeasure with the indenture.

Then he walked out.

Five

Nearly two years had passed since Emil's encounter with Anna at Lauterburg. He had spent many lonely and sleepless nights fantasizing of their joyous reunion, of her posing for him, and of his completing the sketch he had only begun that day. Frankfurt had seemed far away then, but now that Karl had broken the bonds that held him to Schwabisch-Gmund, anything seemed possible.

It was a rainy day in June when he relaxed on the train to Munich and allowed his thoughts to wander. Everything was working out the way they had planned. Karl was leading the way. No more Abts and no more Wulzs. As to the insecurity of his father's job, he believed the situation had been exaggerated. Once he realized it, Emil would be free to leave Schwabisch-Gmund and study art. It was a grand feeling.

With that in mind, he tried to visualize what art school would be like, and he began to worry about entrance exams and other requirements. Karl had scoffed at these and other concerns. "An entrance fee will get you in," he had always promised. Emil remembered vividly the boldness in Karl's manner and a tone of certainty in his voice. How he envied him that self-confidence.

When the train pulled into Munich, he immediately spotted Karl in the waiting crowd. He appeared to be drenched though he tried to shield himself from the driving rain. *The weather's perfect for reminiscing*, Emil thought happily. *It would hamper sightseeing and most other activity.* His heartbeat quickened just thinking about it.

"Karl," he mouthed. Emotions colored his voice. They sought shelter from the rain, then embraced warmly. An awkward moment followed as they talked generalities: the cool breezes from the Alps, the unusual amount of rain, and the weather in general. Karl finally broke the spell.

"Let's make a run for the *Hofbrauhaus*."

"Wonderful."

The *Hofbrauhaus* with its huge, low-vaulted hall was furnished with long wooden tables and benches, which were always crowded with beer drinkers. It was just the spot for the boys to reminisce. Like most young German boys, Emil loved beer, but he seldom had the price of one. With his new job, he intended to indulge a bit more often, though mostly he would save his money for the day he could leave Schwabisch-Gmund and study art.

At the *Hofbrauhaus*, waitresses flitted back and forth delivering beer on their heavy-bosoms. Emil blushed at the sight of it, particularly when his own order was delivered. He was much too shy to remove the beer from its tray.

Karl laughed at him, deepening the crimson in Emil's face. "I'll take it," he told the waitress, then shoved the beer stein in front of Emil. Strangers at their table laughed with Karl.

For the first time in months Karl was talkative. He was full of stories about Munich and its art galleries. "Wait until you see the classical paintings. Durer, Allderfer, Grunewald, and Lenbach, Bocklin, Kaulbach," he crowed. "We'll make the tour tomorrow and the next day and the next. You can never see it all or tire of it."

Caught up in the excitement, Emil finished his beer quickly instead of savoring it as usual. To his consternation, the waitress delivered another on the same platter.

Again, Karl yanked the beer off the girl's bosom and shoved it in front of Emil, calling attention to his timidity. This time Emil was determined to savor each swallow, never allowing himself to take a drink until the taste of the last one faded.

Karl was well into his fifth beer when he asked what brought Emil to Munich. The coldness with which he spoke seemed to minimize their relationship, to wipe out any memory of their promise to each other to study art together. It was painful for Emil, who remembered their vow as if it were yesterday. Even then, he fondled the knife in his pocket.

"Isn't it obvious? To find out about art studies. It's what we always dreamed of, isn't it? Studying art in one of the cities? Getting away from

Schwabisch-Gmund? But you wouldn't answer my questions, so when I got the chance, I came to see for myself what the opportunities are. I'm anxious to hear about your job. What do they pay? Are jobs plentiful?"

Karl's only response was a twist of his head, a movement that precluded eye contact with Emil but fell short of a blank stare at the wall. It might have been meaningless to others, but it was a familiar gesture to Emil.

"Heaven's sakes, Karl. You have no job?" The news was startling, so much so that he stood up as if to leave, then perched lightly on the edge of the long bench they shared with other drinkers.

Karl fondled the beer stein. His head remained cocked, more in defiance now than embarrassment.

"But how do you exist?" Rather than take a chance on damaging their relationship again, Emil changed the subject. "All right then. Tell me about the galleries."

"No, I'll tell you what you really want to know. I came to Munich to get into an artist's studio as an assistant, helper, handyman, anything. Just to be near an artist, you know. I stayed away from most of the big names except for a few I found by accident. Everybody I talked to advised me to take a regular course at the art academy, but I didn't want that."

"Didn't want it?" He stared at Karl in disbelief. "You turned down a chance to take an art course? You're not serious?"

"Art classes might be all right for you, but not for me. I need to watch an artist work. Do you think anybody would waste his time teaching if he could paint?" He faced Emil now, looking squarely in his stunned eyes.

"Maybe, but still—" he pondered. "They have to make a living. What if they can't sell their work?"

"You have to take an entrance exam to get in the stupid school." Karl's tiny mouth protruded in a childish pucker.

"So that's it." How painful it must have been to admit that Emil had been right all along. "You mustn't let that stop you. You can pass it. Maybe you can get in with an artist later. You can't spend your time walking the streets."

"I went to see Franz von Stuck," Karl said with an air of importance.

Emil gasped at the idea of calling on the well-known artist. "But how did you know, I mean, where does he live? You mean at his studio?"

"Didn't say I saw him. Only that I went to see him. Got as far as the iron gate. The porter gave me a terse `No' when I begged for a moment with Herr von Stuck. He slammed the iron gate in my face when I refused to leave."

"Refused?" Again, he stared at Karl, half expecting him to laugh, exposing the whole thing as a joke.

"I finally went to see a priest."

"A priest? What for?"

"Advice, of course. Wanted me to enroll at the academy."

"Well, you see. Everyone agrees," Emil railed.

"Not everyone," he spouted. "I don't! It's a waste. I won't take an examination and—" he stopped in the middle of his sentence and returned to the story of the priest. "He suggested I do some religious art in some studio he could help me get in. Promised to look into it the next day."

Emil remained on the edge of the bench; anxiety and distress his unwanted companions. "Well? What happened? Did he—"

"I didn't go back."

Emil gulped his last swallow of beer, denying himself its full flavor and bringing a big-bosomed waitress to his side. He jumped to his feet, urging Karl to leave with him.

Reluctantly, Karl agreed. "Don't worry. That idea didn't appeal to me, but I'll get in with an artist yet."

Somehow, Emil believed he would. He certainly had the courage for it. How wisely Karl had spent his time as far as canvassing the city's art galleries was concerned. He was an excellent guide. Prints in a book, mostly black and white, were as near to an original as either of them had previously been. Now they were studying originals, old and new, in a variety of styles and techniques.

The perfect renderings of the old masters with their dark, low-keyed tone qualities, and the pointillist technique of the French, Italian, and Swiss impressionists intrigued them. But the most striking thing was the Munich school headed by Emil's idol, Franz von Stuck. His bravura technique in broad, heavy strokes and strong contrasting colors came closer to Emil's conception of artistic expression.

Hans von Zugel, also one of his favorite artists, was well represented. Both boys had read a great deal about him and had heard personal stories from their beloved Herr Kreisel, a classmate of von Zugel.

Day after day they trod from gallery to gallery, sometimes spending a whole day in one of them. The Alte Pinaketheke, Neue Pinaketheke and Schack were their favorites. Emil loved the old masters' work in the Alte Pinaketheke, but he felt more at home in the Neue among the moderns. Again and again he returned to admire Bocklin's *Spiel der Wellen.* Throughout Germany, Bocklin was considered the king of painters, and Spiel der Wellen, a large canvas depicting a sea god and nymphs cavorting in a dance of the waves, was one of his masterpieces.

The boys made their pilgrimage through the art galleries from opening to closing each day until the time came for Emil's departure. The thought of returning to Schwabisch-Gmund dampened his spirits. For the first time in his life, he contemplated disobeying his father and giving up the new job at Jansen's. He longed to bid farewell to Schwabisch-Gmund and meet whatever challenges the world might bring. They had arrived at the train station before he could bring himself to mention it. "Should I stay, Karl?"

"What do you mean?"

"You know. Look for a job? Should be easy finding something in engraving or designing. I've heard the manufacturers are always happy to have a product of the Schwabisch-Gmund factories." His voice reeked with uncertainty.

"Stay if you like," was the curt answer. "But don't expect me to get that kind of job."

"Not work in the factory? But how will you exist?"

It was not until the conductor called passengers aboard that Karl said anything at all, and when he did, he requested a loan.

Astonished, Emil nevertheless handed him twenty marks. "God's sakes, Karl. Come back with me. I'm sure I can get you a job at Jansen's."

"Never!" Karl yelled as the train pulled away. "You can go back, but I never can."

The disappointment of the farewell lingered with him throughout the journey home. Parting was an emotional moment filled with memories and uncertainties, but it was a moment he wished to savor, not deplore. He would have given part of his life just to be in Karl's shoes, with no responsibility except for himself. For Karl, it apparently meant nothing.

The farewell found Emil caught up in the emotions of the moment, but he knew in his heart he could never leave Schwabisch-Gmund without his father's permission. It wasn't easy breaking the bonds of discipline he had been subjected to all his life. He returned home but more determined than ever to study art.

The newness of the job at Jansen's shoved the picture of Munich into a remote corner of Emil's mind. He was intent on doing good work. His first pay envelope contained twenty-one marks, six marks more than the customary pay for a first-time journeyman. He had the distinction of being the highest-paid man his age in the entire city.

By contributing substantially to the household capital, he hoped to prove his worth to his father. Confident of the boy's sense of responsibility to his parents, he hoped his father would allow him to leave Schwabisch-Gmund. And since his father's fear of losing his job was apparently ill-founded, Emil again broached the subject.

"Other cities pay more, Papa. And I could still help with the expenses at home."

"No! Fritz never sent a penny home and was always writing for loans."

Fritz had taken a job in Berlin at first and had made good wages, but he was always broke. Even now, while serving in the army, he continued to write home for loans.

Emil had to live with the decision, but he harbored hopes of changing the old man's mind.

No word from Karl. Still, Emil was confident he had been successful in his quest to study with an artist. Before falling asleep each night, he visualized Karl knocking on the masters' doors, imploring them to let him enter. The mere thought of doing such a thing made Emil quiver, but that was part of Karl's charm. It was like him to keep it all a secret and then glory in surprising Emil. Knowing that made waiting a bit easier.

When Emil made his nightly entrance to the arts and crafts library a few weeks later, Karl awaited him, with a roguish grin on his face.

"Karl!" he shouted.

"Shhh," Karl warned. "This is a library."

"What are you doing here?"

"I've come for the job you promised me. Is it still open?"

"Yes. What changed your mind?"

"Oh, I don't know," he shrugged. His feigned indifference didn't fool Emil, but he let it pass. Nothing mattered now that he and Karl would be working together again, sketching side by side, and studying and planning. He was ecstatic.

His joy soon dissipated. Karl joined the *Burschenshaft*, a fraternity consisting of students and white collar workers who spent most of their time in the beer halls and put a lot of emphasis on the latest designs in apparel.

Emil hardly recognized his friend in stylishly-cuffed wool slacks and matching jackets, white high-necked shirts and ties, and buttoned vests. It was only recently Emil had succumbed to purchasing gabardine for a pair of slacks his mother made. For rare special occasions, he wore his only suit, a dark brown pin-stripe he had worn throughout factory days. He wore work clothes to the factory and for sketching. There was little else on his agenda.

For him, it was life as usual: work, library studies, and sketching, all without Karl. One evening after work, he grabbed his stool and pad and hurried toward the outskirts of the city. A glance in the direction of the Rosenstein Mountain sent him scurrying across the newly-plowed fields. The fast-setting sun sent its last rays through a narrow strip of clear sky and onto the mountains of the Alb, painting Rosenstein gold. Emil stopped momentarily to gaze at its beauty, then quickly reprimanded himself for wasting time. Long shadows reminded him the scene before him was temporary. Hastily, he set up his materials so as not to miss a moment of the spectacle before him.

From the beginning he had been vaguely aware of someone approaching in the distance. He was almost certain it was Karl. When the footsteps became audible, he turned around, hopefully. It was his father.

"Papa!" he shouted. Something terrible must have happened. His father had never sought him that far away from home. His expression was different somehow, not like anything Emil had ever seen.

"Papa, what's wrong?"

"The worst has happened," he said, focusing his eyes on the ground.

"Dear God. Mother's dead?" It was the worst thing Emil could think of.

"No, I've lost my job." The proud cabinetmaster raised his eyes, but looked in the distance, apparently unable to face his son.

Hatred for the old man seized Emil. He felt like screaming that it was none of his concern and that he would go away and study art anyway. But to his surprise, he pitied the old man.

"What should I do?" his father asked.

Emil was stunned by the question, an indication his father had quickly switched roles, transferring all responsibility in the family to Emil.

"Do? Well, what about a lesser job in your factory? Pride isn't everything."

Herr Holzhauer shook his head vigorously. "The factory is to be closed. No one has a job. The owner's son could have kept it going, but he isn't interested. Has his own factory in another city."

"But couldn't someone else run it?" Silently he cursed his father.

On the way home, he talked of looking for work as a common jeweler. With all the young men available in the trade, both of them knew he would be laughed at.

"Don't worry," Emil heard himself say. "I won't leave you." The words echoed like the sound of a prison door slamming shut.

He longed for the dreadful night to end, to give him a chance to talk with Karl. Arriving early at the factory the next morning, he waited, certain Karl would quell his emotions.

Karl agreed it was rotten luck, then sheepishly revealed his plans for leaving Schwabisch-Gmund. "I'm giving notice today. Going to Berlin."

Emil stared at Karl in disbelief. Again, he had intended to leave without saying goodbye. If not for Emil's poignant story, he would have done just that.

"Don't worry," Karl told him. "I'm going to stop wasting my time. But first I have to get away from them." He nodded in the direction of some of his *Burschenshaft* companions. "You know how it is. Nobody here is interested in fine art. Things will be different from now on. You'll see." He patted Emil's shoulder reassuringly. He seemed contrite and genuinely sorry that things were going bad for his old sketching partner.

"Yes, I believe you've learned your lesson," Emil said. "Getting away from your drinking friends is a start."

The friendship was renewed, and Karl promised to keep in touch.

That he might yet lead the way to art studies was Emil's only hope.

Karl wrote regularly and excitedly about art galleries, plays, concerts and recitals. Emil lived for the day when he could join him, but he wondered when that might be. His father's efforts to secure a job were mostly unsuccessful. Nothing but part time and little pay. In order to survive, his parents decided to rent a larger apartment where they could take in boarders.

Emil was skeptical. Since Fritz left home, he had enjoyed the privacy of his own room and had become somewhat obsessed with the idea. His mother tried to comfort him. "It'll be better for both of us, Emil, and you'll still have your own room." Nothing was more comforting than his mother's soft, reassuring voice. He was ashamed for focusing on his own selfish desires when she would have the brunt of the disadvantages. Faced with cooking and cleaning for obnoxious and demanding boarders, the frail woman accepted her fate without a moan.

Emil had scarcely unpacked at the new apartment when his father announced he would have a roommate, a cobbler.

"No, Papa," Emil pleaded. "I need my privacy. I pay for it."

The old man's eyes fixed on the boy in a cold stare. Even as Emil spoke, his new roommate, a filthy man, stood in the doorway. His belongings were fastened to his waist with a dirty bootlace.

Emil ached to catch his mother alone, to scream at her for agreeing to the arrangement. The opportunity finally came one evening when he returned from the factory. He stood in the doorway, his anger rising within him. In a faded but frayless apron, Frau Holzhauer persevered in the kitchen. Her thinning cotton dress hung loosely over her frail body except where the apron string held it close to her tiny waist, giving her a hint of substance. She worked a batch of dough, almost too massive for her frail arms to knead, stopping only when the cauldron of soup needed stirring or called for another vegetable. Rolled up in the corner of the kitchen was a thin mattress she and her husband were obliged to sleep on now that the other beds were occupied by paying customers.

Emil was ashamed for directing his anger at her. He knew in his heart that she, a woman of deep moral convictions, must have been appalled that the cobbler's women visited him in their rooming house. How painful it must have been to know her only son was always obliged to take a walk until the cobbler's woman-of-the-evening left.

With no hope of leaving Schwabisch-Gmund, and reduced to rooming with a filthy cobbler, Emil treasured moments of privacy. He rushed to the apartment after work each day to tend to his affairs before his roommate arrived. Saturday was especially traumatic, as it was the cobbler's big at-home entertainment night.

After work one Saturday, he fled to his room, but the shoe repairman was already there with the whore of the evening. Emil stood frozen in the doorway. The only sexual acts he had witnessed were those in his mind, and they were always beautiful, nothing like he witnessed there. When the cobbler caught sight of Emil, he winked in triumph. Emil responded with an incriminating blush before rushing out of the house and down the cold, impersonal street.

He thought of the good home-cooked food his mother had prepared, and his stomach ached for it. But he couldn't go back and face the cobbler across the kitchen table. It wouldn't be the first time he satisfied his hunger pangs with a beer and a roll.

At the *Bierstube*, Felix rushed to Emil's side and insisted he join him and the other Jansen boys. Felix was their self-appointed leader. His fleshy lips dominated his small face, and his oversized, protruding ears added to his facial dilemma. A thick mop of black hair, slitty eyes and massive eyebrows completed the picture of a man who refused to allow his facial flaws to intimidate him. His outgoing personality, unflagging ego, and stylish attire enhanced his appearance considerably.

When the other Jansen boys spotted Emil, they broke into song: "Bring beer, bring beer, or he shall collapse," they sang.

One beer, perhaps two, had always been Emil's limit. But not on this occasion. He drank until his mind was a blur and his usual timidity was obliterated. Before leaving the *Bierstube*, he was as bold as any of the boys, sometimes singing a full verse all by himself. The later the hour, the louder he sang:

If a girl falls in love,
The devil breaks loose.
Useless the bolts, useless the lock
If you close the door and lock the house
Love will sneak through the key hole.

It was a popular song with German adolescents. They often sang it to tease the waitress, especially when she played favorite with any of the customers. The minute a beer stein was empty, Emil and the others changed their tune to the beer song.

From then on, every Saturday was the same, the cobbler entertaining himself in their room, Emil at the *Bierstube*. And every Sunday, he faced depression. This new way of life continued until the Christmas season, the most depressing time of the year for him. The Holzhauer house would probably be the only one in Schwabisch-Gmund without a tree. They used to decorate a tree, or so his mother told him, but he couldn't remember. He did recall begging for one and crying bitterly when his mother told him "maybe next year."

When he was old enough to understand, she told him the story. "We waited until midnight for your father one Christmas Eve so that we could light the candles on the tree. He promised he would be home for supper, but we waited and waited. Finally, I put you and Fritz to bed. But you both cried so, I lit the candles on the tree, quickly snuffing them out so he wouldn't know. But that very minute, he walked in the door. He said there'd never be another Christmas tree in our house, and of course, there never has been."

Without ceremony, Christmas came and went at the Holzhauer apartment. As the New Year approached, all the young people were talking about the annual skating party at the pond just outside the city. In the factories, on the streets, in the homes, and at the *Bierstube*, the party took precedence in their conversations. It was a rare opportunity for Emil to join mixed groups.

But he couldn't get in the mood. What would he celebrate, he wondered. Certainly not 1905, because he hadn't achieved anything. By 1906 he should have a year of advanced studies behind him, but of course, he wouldn't. He and the cobbler's women would still be competing for half the bed.

Skipping the skating party, he walked through the open country, past the snow-covered fields and villages with their steepled churches and peasant houses, remembering the days when the scenes before him had dominated his artistic efforts.

At the foot of the Hohenstaufen, far from the confines of the city, he sought cover from the howling wind and allowed his thoughts to wander. Climbing the mountain was out of the question, but he could easily visualize the breathtaking view from the top, a view that had stirred his restless soul on many occasions.

There has to be a way out of this, he thought in near mourning.

Jansen's factory vibrated with reminiscences of the skating party and intermittent stories of the *Bierstube* celebration. Though he had taken part in neither of them, Emil's spirits were higher than usual. He could still see no future for himself, but he was encouraged that he had survived the holiday without succumbing to the will of the crowd.

Felix was the first to reprimand him for his absence. "Missed a great party last night," he chortled with a sensual thrust of his hips. "But that's okay, boy. We took care of the women without your help." The hearty laughter that followed was painful, but he had learned to live with it.

Felix was a drinking companion of Karl's when he was in town, and the two subjected Emil to endless teasing. They tried goading Emil into joining them for their sexual exploits, but he always shied away from any encounter with young women. The more he cringed, the more pleasure the two found in teasing him, and they finally accused him of being stiff in the wrong places.

Emil walked away. To his dismay, Felix followed.

"Did you hear about Hans?" asked Felix.

Emil pretended not to hear. He dreaded the exaggerated stories Felix entertained himself with.

"Owns his own horse and buggy," another employee said. "And owns his house too. Just imagine."

Emil cackled. "Hans? Owns all that?" Hans was only an employee at Jansens. "He must have another job," he retorted as he proceeded to his desk.

"No," Felix demanded, shushing everyone. "He hasn't heard!"

Everyone talked at once, jumping at the chance to be first with the story. But Felix sent the others to their respective work areas. "It's Hans' brother, Alfred, who has all these things. He came from America with all expenses paid. Fifty dollars a week he earns!"

"Fifty dollars a week? For jewelry designing? Impossible. Fifty dollars a week is more than the factory owners make." Emil brushed past Felix and began working.

"See for yourself," Felix challenged. "Alfred's coming to the *Bierstube* tonight." His fleshy lips stretched into a broad smirk.

Word of Alfred and his story reached all the factories, arousing the curiosity of every young designer in the city. The *Bierstube* was so crowded, Emil had to strain to hear what Alfred was saying. His heart pounded furiously when Alfred said chances were good for fellows in the steel engraving and jewelry designing trade to find jobs in New York.

"Americans don't have the training we have here," he explained. "Mostly, they go to trade school for six months or so and learn what they can after getting into the business. The companies are always glad to hire a man trained in Germany."

Emil exulted. *What could a new man expect to make*, he wondered. *Would it be sufficient to support his parents, pay for night school and other expenses*? He tried to elbow his way through the unruly group, but it was hopeless. Everyone fired questions at Alfred, seldom waiting for a reply. It was a fun night for those who had no intention of leaving Schwabisch-Gmund. For Emil, it was his future.

"Ask him about a new man's salary," Emil begged of those in front of him.

Finally he heard the answer. "I would guess about eighteen dollars a week. Ten dollars would easily cover your expenses and allow you small luxuries."

He needed no further encouragement. Without a taste of beer, he hurried home to tell his father.

"Where's Papa?" he demanded. "Papa!" he called boldly.

"What is it? What's wrong?" his mother asked.

When the old man appeared in the doorway, Emil grabbed him by the arm: an unprecedented gesture. "Papa, wait till you hear," he squealed.

"What's the matter with you?" his father grumbled.

For once, Emil wasn't intimidated. With hardly a good breath, he told the story of Alfred, and concluded with his own intentions to follow in his footsteps. "I can get a good job, send money home, and study at night," he finished.

Pausing for the first time, he held his breath in anticipation of his father's reaction. But there was only silence.

"Papa?" he pleaded.

"Surely you don't believe this story?" he mocked.

Emil rubbed his sweaty palms together: a nervous motion, but one that quelled his anxiety a bit. "Why should he lie to me, Papa?"

"Why? To impress you, of course, and he has obviously been successful," he laughed.

Emil realized for the first time the depth of his hatred for his father, but he managed to remain calm in spite of an urge to strike him. "Papa, Alfred is a designer just as I am. He trained right here in Schwabisch-Gmund. He's not a braggart. If you would only talk to him, you would see. Please, Papa."

Herr Holzhauer was unrelenting, but Emil wouldn't give up. "Papa, he says I can save more in a week in America than I can earn here."

"No!" his father snapped. "I won't let you go. What gratitude!" he raved. "I have supported you all your life and now you want to run away. We'd never hear from you. Just like Fritz. You'll stay here in Schwabisch-Gmund."

"Please," a soft voice intervened. "We mustn't stand in the boy's way. He won't forsake us. I know," his wife promised.

Emil was shocked by her courage in speaking out and further shocked that his father allowed it. Tight-lipped, they both watched anxiously as he stalked out the door in angry denunciation.

When she was certain he had left the apartment, Frau Holzhauer spoke with trembling voice: "Perhaps you should go anyway."

Without his father's consent Emil knew he couldn't go. Respect for authority had been instilled in him since early childhood. No matter what the injustices he felt at the hands of his father, he had to abide by the rules.

Efforts to discuss the matter ended in violent outbursts by the head of the household. As always, Emil and his mother remained quiet with an alert look of respect painted on their faces.

Finally, one night he relented. "All right!" he raved, pointing an accusing finger at his wife. "Let him go. You'll see I was right. We'll never hear from him again unless he wants money."

As insulting as the accusation was, it was the nearest thing to consent that Emil would get. He wrote to Karl and begged him to come along. It was the chance they had been waiting for.

Two days before he was scheduled to sail, Karl's reply arrived:

> No, I shall never follow you across the ocean.
> I shall never leave the Fatherland. Fate has decided
> we each go our separate ways. Let us abide by it.

Emil was certain Karl would change his mind. He was just as certain his friend would some day be as well known and respected as Bocklin, von Stuck, or von Zugel. But as things stood, he must go alone to a new country and a new language with no money and no guarantee of a job. It was quite a challenge for a boy who had never been past Stuttgart.

As much as the idea frightened him, he wished to be on his way. His father acted so strangely that Emil feared a last-minute refusal. He had been given the passage money, a loan from the savings made up mostly of his own contributions. Still, his father was not like Emil or his mother had ever seen him.

When the time came for Emil to leave for the train station, the atmosphere bore the weight of a funeral procession. He fully expected a fight at the station, after which he would not be permitted to go.

For the last few days he had silently repeated an address: "George Keller, 2600 East 14th Street, New York, New York." It was the address of a jeweler who had advertised in the *Jeweler's Gazette* for a designer. He had written the name and address everywhere: his trunk, jewelry designs, an envelope inside his wallet; and he had committed it to memory in case everything else was lost. Repeating it was more of a therapeutic thing, as it helped him cope with the deadly silence he and his mother had been subjected to at home.

By the time they reached the station, the building number and the street number ran together in his mind. He tried hard to discount its importance and concentrate instead on the most pressing problem: that of getting to America in the first place.

Frau Holzhauer talked as much as she dared under the circumstances, mostly cautioning Emil to care for himself properly and to write often. "You know, son, Fritz would never write to us. And it means so much to hear." Emil squeezed her hand hard. The worst thing she could do was mention Fritz at that point. If anything would enrage his father, that would.

Just then, he felt the powerful grasp of his father's hand on his shoulder. In agonized terror, he turned to face it, but he was totally unprepared for what he saw. As far as Emil knew, it was the first time the old man had ever cried.

Awkwardly, he threw his arms around the boy, holding him for a long moment before letting go. "Goodbye, my boy. I know I'll never see you again."

Frau Holzhauer cried openly just as Emil had expected. But to his surprise she didn't seem to be in need of comfort as much as his father did.

"I'll be back," he promised. "Really, I'll be coming home for a visit. You'll see," he added, surprising himself, for thoughts of a return trip to the little city and the iron rule of his father had not occurred to him.

As soon as Emil boarded the train, Herr Holzhauer walked briskly away. In abject wretchedness, his wife followed.

Six

It was almost morning before Emil slept at all on the train, and then he only dozed, awakening to the conductor's every call. He was conscious always of the sound of the wheels that carried him farther and farther away from his Schwabenland. *If only Karl were here*, he thought in near terror.

At daybreak he watched eagerly as the landscape and villages hurried by. He felt the discomfort of a foreigner as he listened to the sharp, harsh sounding speech so different from his own soft Schwabian dialect.

In Hamburg, he had difficulty locating the hotel he had been assigned to. *My God*, he thought. *This in my own country. What will I do in a foreign land?*

He ventured outside the hot, dingy hotel room where his fears subsided. He was captivated by the bustle of activities along the waterfront. Boats and tenders plowed through the river while scores of workers loaded and unloaded the mass of cargo at the docks. He wished for time to take it all in, perhaps even sketch the whole thing.

The next morning, he boarded a tender that carried him to the massive *Augusta Victoria*. Once he found his cabin, he ran back on deck for one more look. He felt a tinge of discomfort upon taking one last look at the shore. He knew it would be his last glimpse of German soil. The thought of never seeing his mother again engulfed him, but there would be no tears shed for his father.

The trip itself was a nightmare because he suffered from seasickness. It was only during the calmest weather he was able to take in the wonder of the ocean, to watch the receding water from the stern of the ship. The virgin green of the churned up water with its everchanging design reminded him of Arnold Bocklin's *Spiel der Wellen*. And that brought back memories of Munich, and of Karl. It was a calming and hopeful thought.

Emil was confused when Bruno, a passenger who had befriended him during his bouts with seasickness, told him they were nearing their destination.

"But how do you know?" Emil asked.

"The sea gulls," Bruno explained.

"But we saw them before," Emil reminded him.

"But only in the beginning when we were not far from land. Now it means we're near land again."

Then one golden Saturday morning, the electrifying cry of `land' jolted Emil from his bunk. He ran on deck and caught his first glimpse of America.

He was seized with fright. *What if I can't find employment*? he worried. He watched in disgust as New York's skyscrapers came into view, reminding him of ugly upended shoe boxes. He wondered if this was his adopted country's idea of architectural beauty. Then cries of "Look, the Statue of Liberty!" captured his attention and softened his demeanor a bit. He knew of its sculptor, Bartholdi. Once, he had copied one of Bartholdi's bas relief lions.

While the first and second-class passengers were landed at Hoboken, Emil and the others had to remain on board overnight. Early the next morning, a boat carried them to Ellis Island where they were taken in hand by an official of the emigrants' home. He was assigned to another hot, drab hotel room.

Gladly, he accepted an invitation to join Bruno on a trip to Long Island. As they walked along Broadway to the Brooklyn Bridge to catch a trolley, Emil quickly developed an aversion for New York's lack of sanitation. In Munich and Stuttgart, the only cities in Germany he knew, the streets were kept immaculate, the horse droppings swept away immediately into holes in the street.

The wonder of the Brooklyn Bridge soothed him, however. The river's dock-lined shores, the warehouses, and the heavy traffic reminded him of Hamburg, a scene that had delighted and entranced him. The bridge and the river were the only highlight of the New York City trip. In addition to making him nauseous, the trolley ride was endless and boring as they changed from one trolley to another only to view row after row of ugly one and two-story buildings.

Soon after breakfast he followed Bruno's directions to the George Keller jewelry concern. "George Keller and Company, Jewelers, 5th Floor," the plaque on the building read. Once inside the office, he spoke slowly and deliberately just as Bruno had instructed him: "Mr. Keller, please." He had practiced the three words all morning, but he could tell by the employee's expression that his English had been anything but articulate. He was nevertheless shortly presented to Mr. Keller.

Bruno had written a note of introduction, stating Emil's purpose in coming. Mr. Keller read the note and smiled. Emil was certain it meant rejection.

"I'm familiar with Schwabisch-Gmund," said Mr. Keller, in German. "I'm from Stuttgart."

The German language had never sounded so good. Emil almost relaxed, then thought better of it. Keller questioned him about his training and experience and asked for samples of his work. Timidly, Emil handed him a folder containing some of his jewelry designs. While Keller studied them, Emil noted with interest the documents and diplomas gracing the office walls and signifying awards the company had received in major competitions. Even though printed in English, he knew the significance of the awards, and the thought occurred to him at the time that he should leave, perhaps saving himself a great deal of embarrassment.

"This is certainly new. I doubt whether the trade here is ready for it. We're way behind Europe in matters of taste. It's always been that way." Keller spoke highly of the steel engraving samples as well. "The job is yours," he said.

Emil broke into a rare grin. On his return to the immigrant house, he caught himself skipping now and then, something he hadn't done since early school days. He was duly congratulated by the others to whom the security of a job meant everything. "What does the job pay?" he was asked, but his flushed face told them he hadn't bothered to ask. He prayed it would be at least the eighteen dollars Alfred had told him well-trained newcomers could expect. Anything less might prove to be grossly inadequate for what he wished to accomplish.

With the assistance of a man at the immigration office, he found a room on East 18th Street and reported to work as soon as his trunk arrived. His first assignment was to design ladies' lockets.

"The American ladies want them more than anything else," Keller told him. "I want them in your own modern style." To Emil's astonishment, Keller seemed quite excited over the idea.

As soon as the designs were completed, Keller offered them to his customers. All were delighted, but only one lady was bold enough to order a locket with the revolutionary design.

"Much too radical for the moment," Keller had to admit. "The damn fools," he said. "Here they had a chance to be among the first to wear them, but they didn't have the courage. Women! Bah! Well, from now on, try a combination of the old with the new and maybe we can sell them."

Emil was astonished. In Schwabisch-Gmund, intricate designs like the ones he rendered for Keller were considered old fashioned. Combining would require research in his spare time. There had been precious little of that. After nine hours of working at the crowded and badly lit working area, he was unwilling to work at night, too. He needed time to explore the new country, time to study English, and time to look into the possibilities of art schools.

Unwilling, but afraid to refuse, he produced the combined designs. Again, the American ladies balked, afraid to venture forth with something other than the norm. He was told to adapt himself to the old styles, particularly to Keller's way of rendering, because his was not understood by the trade and could not easily be executed by the jewelers and engravers.

More research. And still no salary. Keller was apparently waiting to determine Emil's worth to the company before deciding on a sum.

Emil began to wonder about the possibility of another job. A steel engraver didn't have to worry about new designs and styles. A great deal depended on what his salary was to be, so he waited. When Keller finally handed him a pay envelope, Emil couldn't bring himself to open it inside the factory walls. It was not until he was on the bottom floor of the building that he allowed himself a peek at the contents. "Forty-five dollars!" he yelled in protest. "Only fifteen dollars a week? After all the extra work and the self-training?" He was bitterly disappointed.

However, it was more than he had ever received before in a dozen pay envelopes, so he soon adjusted to the idea. In the safety of his pocket, he fondled the crisp bills all the way to the post office where he sent a money order to his father for thirty-four dollars, a partial payment on the passage loan.

Eleven dollars left to be used as he wished. Already he found he could live on six dollars a week and afford some luxuries. Anxious to become acquainted with the new country, he began crisscrossing the area from the East River to the North River. On Sunday he would take a trolley to the end of the line, wherever that might be: Dykman Street, 180th Street, or Van Cortland Park. From there he walked, covering as much of the sparsely settled sections as he had time for.

The trolley was a necessary evil for a young man who suffered motion sickness. He spent a great deal of time exiting one trolley long enough to vomit before riding another one until the turmoil inside him reached its climax. The subway might have been less grueling for his delicate equilibrium, but his ignorance of the language made using it impossible.

One Sunday while making his tours, he accidentally discovered the Metropolitan Museum. From then on, he became a regular visitor. He quickly fell in love with the barefooted, dreamy-eyed, flaxen-haired peasant girl in Bastien Le Page's *Vision of the Maiden of Orleans*. He was disappointed, however, that there were so few modern paintings. The same was true in arts and crafts, and even in design. Ancient styles were the thing. There was nothing to indicate an art nouveau or youth style which even Schwabisch-Gmund flourished in. The visits inspired him nonetheless, and finally prompted him to ask Keller about an art school.

"What kind of art school? Design or fine arts?"

"Fine arts, I guess," he answered timidly. "I'm particularly interested in the figure." Herr Kreisel had always stressed the importance of knowing the figure.

"The figure!" yelled Keller. "Why that would take ten years to learn anything about," he laughed. Emil was put down by his condescending manner, but he knew nowhere else to turn for answers as similar questions put to his fellow employees produced no information at all. None of them had any ambition to train or learn anything beyond what they had already done.

"As long as that? Well, even so, I need to start sometime. Do you know a place?"

"I would advise you to start in a course for design. You're very weak in your knowledge of the old styles. You need to know more about them than about life drawing." Keller made quick, agitated gestures as if the whole idea annoyed him.

Emil resented the time spent in old style research already. To prevent suspicion, he asked where he should go to apply for the training.

"The Mechanics Institute is best, but they're closed for the summer. Meanwhile, I suggest you make copies of all the ornaments you find on public and private buildings in the city and anything you find in the museums that might be of use to us here in the shop."

At the Keller concern, he had disciplined himself to the strain of drawing under conditions heretofore unknown to him. Schwabisch-Gmunders would be appalled at the poor lighting and lack of working space furnished the designers. In order to draw the intricate designs, he had to cram his legs into the narrow kneehole of a tiny desk in a poorly-lit working area. His legs ached from lack of circulation, and rest periods were not allowed during working hours except for a short lunch break.

Hoping to find better conditions elsewhere, he approached other companies with samples of his work. Just as he had hoped, the samples substituted nicely for his lack of communicative abilities. He accepted an offer from a silver manufacturing company.

Keller was furious. "Leaving in two weeks? No way. If you leave, you do it now. Out! Out!" he yelled, pointing to the exit. Emil tried to explain that two weeks' notice was customary in Schwabisch-Gmund and that he had not meant to anger him.

"You're not in Schwabisch-Gmund, Holzhauer," Keller smirked.

No wages for two weeks would mean drawing from his meager savings. Fortunately the passage loan had been paid in full, but he had continued to send his parents five dollars a week. Rather than alarm them so soon after his arrival in the United States, he tightened his belt a bit and sent their allowance as if nothing had changed.

The new job was easier and free of demands on his spare time. But, just as in Keller's concern, none of the men had any interest in art. Nobody could tell him anything about an art school, and his English was too poor to read the newspaper ads with any degree of success.

Faithfully, he had written to Karl, always pleading with him to come to America. Karl's response was always the same - "Never." Emil decided to forget about art classes for the moment and devote himself to the study of English.

He had hardly begun his new studies when a letter from home brought disturbing news. Fritz was on his way to America. He could tell from his mother's letter that she and his father had bragged about their son having sent over two hundred marks home in the four months he had been in the United States. Their bragging had also brought scores of requests from Schwabisch-Gmund for loans. He had singled out a few worthy requests, specifically those engravers and designers who excelled in their work and work habits. Felix, though a tiresome braggart, had been one of them.

Fritz was quite another story. Given the chance, Emil would have told him about the inferior working conditions, the language barrier, and the frugal existence he was subjected to in order to support his parents and still save a few pennies. It must have appeared otherwise on the other side of the ocean, and it was too late to rectify that.

Reluctantly, he met the boat and brought Fritz to share his room until he could secure a job and find his own. It was a nightmare he never dreamed he would be subjected to again. Fortunately, it wasn't long before they found a job for him, but Fritz griped about the pay and accused Emil of misleading him with the large sums of money he had sent home. As fast as he made money, he spent it, mostly on beer and women, then begged Emil for loans, loans he never intended to repay. He drifted from one job to another, usually as a result of having been fired. One day Emil returned to find him in a drunken rage.

"You tightwad," he accused, shoving Emil into a corner of the tiny room. "You live on a sausage a day just so you can look good to everybody at home." Having abandoned his weight-lifting program for a life of leisure, heavy drinking, and late hours, Fritz's muscles had long since turned to flab, but he still liked settling arguments with force. "You're a goddamn skeleton."

Emil was enraged. "You're complaining, and you don't even share the rent? No more loans and no more free board for you," he warned. "What brought this on? You lost your job again, didn't you?"

A faint snarl escaped from Fritz's lips. "Just as I thought," Emil said. In a rage, he began throwing Karl's belongings in the floor. "Go find yourself another room."

Fritz let out a low moan as he slumped in a chair, his head drooped to his chest. He quickly gave in to a deep and drunken sleep.

Before settling down to his nightly study of English, Emil read Karl's last letter, for the third time. In it, he mentioned that a colleague was attending sculpting classes in one of the master's studios. Suddenly, Emil rallied. "Of course!" he yelled. For once, he had seen through Karl's tricks. The "colleague" he mentioned had to be Karl himself. He was to lead the way after all. Emil was exultant.

Seven

There were no jobs for Fritz. The only openings, aside from the factories that had dismissed him, were in Niagara Falls or Philadelphia, and he refused to leave New York City. Emil knew it was the companionship of the Schwabisch-Gmund boys, all of whom enjoyed the night life, that kept him there. The boys met nightly at the rathskeller, an American equivalent to the German beer hall. Emil relished the companionship of his countrymen and the comfort of his native tongue, but fear of making it a habit kept him from joining them on a regular basis. Too, German acquaintances to the exclusion of others meant slow progress in English. He knew command of the language was a must if he was to study art.

Felix was an exception to the others. With little outside assistance, he had made real progress with the language. A superior engraver and designer with many honors to his credit, he was working his way up in the Newark factory. He and Emil could have helped each other a great deal, but Felix scorned the idea of studying together. Emil concluded it was just as well. The self-praise Felix would have subjected him to would have been boring in any language.

Unlike Felix, Fritz could claim neither style nor intellect. An insensitive bore, he continued to ride roughshod over his focused cousin. Rather than furnish him room and board and live with him, Emil applied for a job in Niagara Falls and was accepted.

The change was just what he needed. The engraving department in the Niagara Falls factory offered marked improvement over the city factories. The working area was well-lit and spacious. Actually, he needed little space for cutting the intricate patterns in steel, where, except for delicate manipulations of the hands and fingers, he was immobile by necessity. Having mastered the ability to sit rigid hour after hour in producing the subtle lines, gradations, and tones, he accepted the cramped position and hovered over his work hour after hour, peering through a magnifying glass. But it was a comfort to know he was not crowded against the other engravers, breathing the same air in a poorly ventilated room as he had done in the big city factories.

Again, none of the engravers had cultural aspirations or knowledge of art classes anywhere. Their work called for artistic skills obtainable only through knowledge and practice in drawing and modeling, but they had no interest in pursuing them. They were as confused by Emil's interest as he was with their lack of it.

What he missed in cultural stimulus and native German contact in Niagara Falls, he made up for in forced practice of the English language. Surrounded almost entirely by Americans now, he had to speak and understand the language in order to survive. Advantageous, but frustrating. Also lonely. After more than a year in the United States, he barely managed to understand the language and make himself understood. He sorely missed the German element in his life. More than ever, he treasured the letters from home, as correspondence was now his only contact with German speaking people.

In the little restaurant where he took his evening meal, the waitress asked him if he was from Germany. The question brought a rare smile to his face. "How could you tell? Surely I have no accent," he teased. She laughed, though not derisively. The whole thing relaxed him, and for the first time since arriving in Niagara Falls, he felt comfortable talking with someone. "If you only knew what a struggle it is," he whined.

"But I do know," she insisted. "My cousin went through the same thing, but after two years in the States, she's doing great."

"Your cousin is German?" His spirits brightened.

"Yes. Would you like to meet her?"

The meeting was arranged, happily for both of them. Katy was nineteen, lived with her widowed mother, and waited tables to help with the household expenses. Katy's flushed cheeks were as round as her large breasts that stretched her soft cotton dresses to the limit. Her gentle brown eyes exuded warmth. Their relationship grew as they exchanged stories of hope and dreams and disappointments in the old country. For the first time in his life, Emil took someone other than Karl into his confidence and shared his dream of becoming an artist. He even told her of Anna and of Karl's jealousy at his sketching her on Lauterburg.

Katy assisted him with the language and the culture but she did more than that. Her warmth and passion strengthened his deteriorating emotions. He liked her immensely.

As the relationship grew, his long pent-up fear that he would never know a woman sexually became a thing of the past. Katy's warm and yielding body offered sexual gratification beyond anything he had imagined, and it relegated to the background the ugly memory of the cobbler's dirty sexual pursuits.

As satisfying as the relationship with Katy was, he was disgusted with himself for becoming hopelessly involved without so much as enrolling in an art class. In an effort to regain that sustaining confidence of old, he tried reading or going for a walk alone, but nothing worked. If he wasn't with Katy, he was clamoring to be.

In hopes of wresting his mind from her, he questioned the factory manager about possible art classes in the area and was told to try Buffalo. He was given a day off for that purpose. The Albright Art Gallery did offer art classes but the train service and the distance from Niagara Falls to Buffalo made it impossible to attend.

The day was not wasted, however. It had been some time since he lolled around in an art gallery. One painting in particular captured his attention: Hans von Bartels' famous torpedo boats. What memories it brought to mind. His introduction to the work had been through a *Kugelpost* from Karl about a new biography he had found in the library. All day at the factory Karl had carried the book in his knapsack, waiting to share it with Emil. In it, they had seen a reproduction of that painting. It had provided food for thought on many sketching trips.

Impressed as he had been with the reproduction, he was shocked to see the injustice of it. There was such force and power in the massive original. Planted in front of the painting for some time, he could almost see the crashing of the waves against the torpedo boats as they plunged through the turbulent sea. "*Mit Volldampf Voraus*" (Full Steam Ahead), the plaque beneath the painting read. Silently, Emil admonished everyone who wasn't there to view this wonder of the art world.

The director at the gallery told him his best hope for classes was in New York City. But if he went back, it would mean leaving Katy. And if he stayed in Niagara Falls, it would mean the end of his art studies before they had begun. He knew what he had to do, and Katy would have to understand. He had told her from the beginning it was his reason for coming to America.

But Katy didn't understand. "Why not paint here?" she asked innocently. "I'll pose for you." Reading the rejection on his face, she added, "Why not? You painted Anna. It's Karl, isn't it? You're afraid to try it without him."

"Heaven's sakes!" he retorted angrily. "You don't understand how meager our efforts were then. I have no doubt misled you."

"You told me yourself you were instructed by well trained professors even in the first grades of school," she reminded him. "My dear girl," he admonished. It was an expression he used when angered. "You know nothing of these things. The training we had was highly stylized in preparation for our trade, engraving and designing, but not painting. I'll have to return to New York City for art classes where I'm certain Karl will join me. I told you about our vow to each other." His haughty tone revealed a side of him she wasn't familiar with.

She looked away. "From all you've told me of Karl, I doubt he took that vow as seriously as you did."

"That shows how much you know." He laughed condescendingly. "Karl is my best friend. He took it very seriously."

His determination instilled in her a certain reality, one that frightened her immensely. She couldn't hold back the tears any longer. Emil's cold demeanor softened. He cupped her round face in his hands, and kissed her wet cheeks.

His tenderness gave her hope. As the sun highlighted her short brown hair with golden-red glints, her moist eyes sparkled, giving her whole countenance an exciting glow. She saw in his face, the same desires she harbored. She pulled him close and ran her fingers through his thick hair. "You're just the most gorgeous thing in the world you know," she teased, gently closing his eyelid with her finger. "That luscious full mouth, so sensuous, so desirable." Passionately, she fingered his lips. "You can't leave me, Emil. We love each other," she whispered. Pushing him an arm's length away, she gazed at him longingly. Her lips parted sensuously, making his job more difficult. He resisted the urge to hold her close and make promises he didn't want to keep.

Dear sweet Katy, he thought, as he watched her glowing expression of joy. Her life was centered around him. She was always praising his lovemaking, his intellect, and his good looks. What warmth she had added to his lonely life, what meaning. Constantly, he had to call on all his strength to help him overcome the power she had over his emotions. Daily, he chastised himself for considering marriage, then quickly rationalized that he could have Katy and study art too.

When a letter came from Karl, his thinking took a new course. "I'm ready to come to America," he wrote. Emil threw his head back, cast his eyes on the ceiling, and blessed himself with the sign of the cross. "Good old Karl!" he shouted. "He has saved me from ruining everything." In his excitement, he almost forgot to read the rest of the letter. A paragraph or two describing the poor weather and other inconsequential things was followed by Karl's now famous one-liner: "Need passage money."

What a disappointment. *Same old Karl*, he thought mournfully. Grudgingly, he sent the money, then made arrangements for a reunion at Felix's apartment in Newark.

The worst part was yet to come: saying goodbye to Katy. She begged to go with him or to join him later. He lacked the courage to tell her the truth, that neither was an option. At the train station, he promised to write and return for a visit once he had become established in an art school. "Please, Katy, you must be strong. Try to understand, darling. I must have this chance."

Nothing soothed her. "Emil, how can you do this?" she cried. The strong arms that had once coddled him, flailed hopelessly in the air, stopping only to dab the swollen eyelids on an emotionally scarred face. Even as the train was boarding passengers, she posed another question. "Emil, when will we see each other again?" It was a question she had posed a thousand times, and it was a question Emil had no answer to.

The train was moving out, the boarding step already taken away. At the last second, he forced her clasped arms from around his neck, ran along the platform and pulled himself up. He couldn't bear to look back, but he could have painted the scene from memory, for it was one he would never forget.

Katy's memory haunted him, but he was soon comforted by her long letters proclaiming her love. She didn't seem to understand that he missed her as much as she missed him. It was a miserable life without her. He longed to hear her soft voice and he ached to feel her warm and yielding body. Except for his mother, she was the only one who had ever loved him, perhaps the only one who ever would.

He consoled himself with the knowledge that Karl would soon be arriving. They would be inundated with their study of the language and art studies and library work. There would be no time for reminiscing or longing. As he waited for Karl's arrival, he felt the happy spirit of the Christmas season as never before.

He joined Felix on a rare Sunday walk through the decorated streets, crowd-gazing and window shopping. Felix's stylish double-breasted wool topcoat with matching spats and hat drew attention to Emil's year-round gabardine slacks and shabby coat he had brought from Germany. Felix was not one to pretend.

"Why the hell don't you buy some new clothes?"

It was an oft-repeated question and one Emil didn't care to discuss. He stopped to view the paintings in the window of a small art gallery.

Felix shook his head. "You still have some silly idea about being an artist? You're a damn fool. Work your way up in the factory, why don't you?"

Reluctant to discuss his plans, Emil only shrugged in reply.

"I suppose you paid Karl's way? Hell, you got all of us here. You should spend some of that money on yourself. Live a little."

Emil had financed Felix's trip to America, along with a few others he felt deserving. All of them had repaid the loan. Certainly he couldn't refuse his best friend something he had offered mere acquaintances.

Emil could scarcely take in Felix's banter, as he could think of nothing but Karl's impending arrival. He worried constantly that some turn of fate might prevent his coming, especially as there had been no word of late. He returned to the rooming house, his spirits dampened by the thought. As both men fumbled for the apartment keys, the door suddenly flew open and a man stuck his head out. It was Karl!

"You devil!" screamed Felix. "Smooth talked the landlady into letting you in, didn't you?" Karl grinned proudly.

Emil remained in shock. The secret arrival was like Karl, depriving Emil the pleasure of meeting the boat, but no matter. They were together again. It made all the waiting, the anxiety, the heartache worthwhile.

Emil and Karl tried to say everything in a warm and endless handshake and anxious glances. Karl's shapely hands and long slender fingers brought to mind a dozen memories as Emil pressed them warmly with his own stubby hands. Both boys looked down at their hands and broke out in laughter.

All three talked at once as if in competition to see who could talk the most and listen least. Felix insisted the arrival of their friend called for a beer at the rathskeller. For once, it met with Emil's approval.

With Felix answering a nature call down the hall, Emil and Karl embraced. "At last, Karl. I thought you would never come. Now we can really begin. Are you all right? You don't look well. Have you been sick?" His usually tanned skin was pale, the areas around his eyes puffy, and his features were drawn.

"No, just the trip. I'll be okay in a day or so," he insisted.

The explanation didn't satisfy Emil, who knew his friend had the stamina of a bull, and that an ocean voyage, while taxing, should have no noticeable effect on a strong, healthy boy. Factory work, without outdoor sketching, probably explained Karl's lack of color. Realizing that, Emil dropped the subject, as it was obviously not a popular one.

"Does Felix know about our plans?" Karl asked.

"No, of course not. None of the boys do," Emil assured him. "1You know how they laugh. It's still our secret. We'll move away from Felix as soon as possible." Karl seemed comforted.

At the rathskeller, the skeletal Schwabisch-Gmund group welcomed him with a round of beer, then followed that with another and another. While Emil nursed his stein, Karl indulged in several. He talked excitedly of the open sea, the marvel of which he had never seen.

Emil had an occasional chance to carry on a private conversation with his friend. "Just wait!" he gasped. "Didn't you think of Hans von Bartels' *Spiel der Wellen* when you saw the waves from the back of the ship? Just wait until you see the original in Buffalo. The print we saw is pitifully inadequate, capturing none of the force, the life, or the power displayed by the artist." He scarcely noticed Karl's lack of interest. His own mind was filled with thoughts and dreams and ambitions that he had harbored so long, they ached for release. "When do we start?" he asked in suppressed hysteria. "I've already looked into the possibility of art classes. There are some available in New York City, only thirty minutes away."

"Hey, be reasonable. I don't know the language."

Emil felt like a fool. Felix entertained the group with stories of women, and Karl responded with descriptions of an exciting life in Berlin where women figured prominently. By contrast, not once in his letters to Emil had he mentioned a woman.

Karl took a room in the same boarding house where the three could share an adjoining sitting room. Night after night they celebrated just as they had the night he arrived. Emil was glad when they found him a job as it would force him to get more rest. Or so he thought. At the rathskeller where they ate their evening meal, Felix and Karl drank until well past midnight every evening. At the end of the first week, Emil excused himself after dinner, hoping Karl would take the hint.

He didn't. Time and again, he lost his job and had to borrow money from Emil until he could find another. Such occasions afforded Emil his only private moments with Karl. He took advantage of one.

"You can't continue these nightly sessions," he warned. "Pretty soon no manager will hire you. You should be studying English every minute you can spare. You're a lucky devil because I can help you. Let's move away from Felix. I've located another place." He spoke harshly.

Karl said nothing, his eyes cast to the floor.

"Very well then. I'll go alone. I can't bear to watch you drink yourself to death."

"No, don't go yet," Karl begged, catching Emil by the arm. "I didn't want to tell you this, but this sickness I have, well its not from the late hours I keep. Got this infection from a goddamn whore in Berlin. Syphilis." He looked away, the confession having required great effort on his part.

"Oh my god," Emil gasped.

"Don't worry. I'll be okay. I'll come home after dinner from now on. You'll see."

Emil agreed to remain as they were, to give him another chance. With his twenty-first birthday coming up in a few days, he knew the event would bring them together again. Karl had always remembered.

The day came and went without a word from Karl. Emil locked himself in his room and threw himself across the bed. Tears stole from his eyes and bobbled down his nose. He wiped his face repeatedly with the knotty old spread and silently reprimanded himself. He finally admitted to himself the nightly sessions were Karl's way of life, and the sooner he accepted it, the better. Katy's last letter lay on the nightstand. Darling Katy, he reminisced. She had not forgotten his birthday. Her love had grown stronger with his absence, as had his. He read her letter again, even though he knew it by heart. He especially liked the closing lines:

> Darling, think of me on your birthday and know
> I am thinking of you. I love you more than
> anything I have ever known or wish to know.
> I live for the day we will be together.

His thoughts were jumbled, but quick. It was impossible to get off work without losing his job, but he could find another one easily enough. Before he could act on the notion, Karl approached him with a passionate apology.

"Please forgive me. I forgot your birthday. I know I've been acting disgustingly, but I am determined to stop it."

"Forget it," Emil said. "All that matters is that you're finally ready."

"I'm afraid you don't understand. I lost my job again. I've been looking all day without success."

Karl looked pitiful. No matter the torment he had caused in the past, he could still muster compassion from Emil.

"I'm truly sorry, Emil. I should have gone with you when you asked me to leave Felix. Then this wouldn't have happened. I would like to get started with our art studies now, but first I have to find a job."

It proved to be much more difficult that either of them had imagined. The only openings were in the Newark factories from which he had recently been fired. He was finally obliged to take a job in Philadelphia. They consoled themselves with hopes of an opening in Newark soon. They both agreed that Emil should find another rooming house in preparation for that day.

From Philadelphia, Karl wrote long letters proclaiming to be happy and healthy. Not once had he mentioned the hundred-dollar loan for passage to America or the numerous loans after he arrived. For over six months he had earned from twenty-five to thirty dollars a week with no obligation to anyone except himself. Pondering the situation, Emil decided it was time Karl learned to discipline himself, his time, and his money. That evening, he penned a letter to Karl, telling him so.

Before posting the letter, he received a request for more money. Karl was jobless and broke. Tearing his original letter to bits, Emil enclosed twenty dollars in an envelope along with a warning:

> I had just been on the verge of reminding you of the money you owe me when your letter arrived asking for more. This is all I shall send you. Buy yourself a train ticket to Newark. You can live with me while you look for a job. I won't furnish money for beer and other luxuries, but you won't go without the necessities.

While waiting at the train station, Emil was reminded of the Munich meeting a lifetime ago. Karl should have begun his studies then. He wondered what the answer was. Suddenly a solution presented itself. He had always waited for Karl to lead the way. The answer lay not with Karl, but with him. He had enough discipline for both of them.

Karl arrived remorseful, ashamed, and filled with self-pity. Emil greeted him warmly, initiating their embrace. As they walked together, both were uneasy, not knowing what to say. Generality after generality presented itself in their conversation, all of which came to nothing, and they were uneasy again.

Again, Emil was reminded of the Munich meeting. "Too bad it didn't rain all day," he laughed.

"Why?"

"Well, in Munich at least we had the damp weather as a topic of discussion. By the time we exhausted the subject and jumped all the puddles, we had loosened up."

Karl grinned broadly, and all was well. For the first time since his arrival in the United States, he talked to his old Schwabisch-Gmund friend. They covered all the subjects: Munich, Lauterberg, Wulz, Professor Abt, and other memories. It was the happiest Emil had been since saying farewell to Katy.

"But there'll be no coddling this time," he warned Karl. "No drinking, and no late hours," he added. He looked directly into Karl's eyes, noting the torture that confirmed his self-disgust, but Emil showed no mercy. "As soon as we find you a job, you're going to pay your debt. And save your money. Why should you borrow at all? You've made far more money than I when I first came here and what have you to show for it? You who have no one but yourself. You should be ashamed." The more he said, the angrier he became, but he couldn't stop. Karl had to be taught a lesson. "And don't ask me for another mark," he warned.

Karl sat throughout the rage with his head bowed. To save them both further embarrassment, Emil revealed his plans. "I'm going to enroll in the Fawcett Drawing School here in Newark. I strongly urge you to do the same. Why let your talent go to waste? It comes so easy for you, much easier than for me. I have to work at it. You have no idea how hard. Maybe it would be better if things didn't come so easy for you. Maybe you would have been more conservative if you had the responsibility of your parents." Recognizing self-pity in his own words, it infuriated him. "Goddamn it Karl, why not apply yourself like you did in the Lauterberg days?"

"All right!" Karl shouted. "I'll go with you to the drawing school." Significantly, he used English, something he rarely did unless forced to.

Emil had never been happier. He had waited an eternity for this day. Even though it was in the middle of the term, they were accepted in the class where twenty to twenty-five others sketched from a costumed model. More than anything, Emil and Karl needed training in drawing the figure, but they would have to wait for that opportunity as nude models were banned in Newark.

The instructor emphasized strict rendering rather than presentation of an idea. It amounted to copying, the one thing they needed the least.

Engraving and designing demanded the reproduction of precise lines nine hours a day, six days a week at the factory.

They were bitterly disappointed, but Emil still saw it as a beginning. "It'll lead to more and better schools and training. At least we can meet other men with the same interests," he pointed out.

The second class was a repetition of the first one. They understood why their joining in the middle of the term didn't matter as it was always the same thing. One night Karl slammed his sketchbook shut and walked noisily out of the room. When class was dismissed, Emil found him downstairs, pacing back and forth.

"What's wrong? Are you sick?"

"Yes, sick of that class. They call that creative? Well, it's not for me."

"Karl, be reasonable," he begged. "At least it disciplines us, and who needs that more than you? If we can just stick with this, think how easy it'll be when we do get into something inspiring. There have to be better schools somewhere, and we'll find them. But for now—"

"No! I won't let you talk me into it." He turned away, indicating the subject was closed.

Emil attended the classes alone, but he was heartened by Karl's diligent study of the language. Soon they were going to the library together, devouring information on artists just as they had done at the arts and crafts library in Schwabisch-Gmund. Once he learned to read English, Karl became a devoted student. Fascinated as always by the impressionists, they read everything they could find in the local library on the subject. Discussions were further enhanced by their visits to the art galleries on Sunday. Karl, though not enrolled in a class, had quit drinking and was paying his debt to Emil at ten dollars a week. It was a hopeful time.

Disillusioned with the art school almost to the point of quitting himself, Emil nevertheless stuck with it. Through association with the others, he learned of several schools in New York City, most of which had life classes. He wrote to all of them, requesting either night classes or Saturday classes. With Karl's interest aroused, and with his own knowledge of the language, he felt certain they would soon be attending one of them.

Within a week he received news of a night school. "Nudes," he cackled. Finally, the chance had come. He glanced through the papers hurriedly while waiting for Karl to return from work. When he didn't arrive at the usual time, Emil began to pace the floor. Too jittery to wait in the small room any longer, he opted to go downstairs where he could keep watch from the sitting room window. As he started toward the door, he noticed a note on the chest-of-drawers.

"What in the world?" he said aloud. There was a ten dollar bill attached to it. Anxiously, he read the one-line note: "This ends my debt to you."

In all the excitement, he hadn't noticed that all of Karl's belongings were gone.

Downstairs, the landlady told him, "Why, Mr. Holzhauer, your friend gave notice a week ago."

Eight

The trauma of dealing with Keller, his first employer, had been a hard lesson for Emil. Still, it had its merit. Calling on all the diplomacy he could muster, he asked the factory manager for a five-day work week. "I feel I need to improve my knowledge of design," he explained timidly. Reluctantly, the manager agreed, but only with a substantial cut in salary. It was "a first for the factory," Emil was reminded often, "and temporary depending on what you contribute as a result."

Emil knew that his superior German training set him apart from the other engravers, and that was the only reason the manager allowed the break in an otherwise stiff tradition. He was afraid of losing him to another factory.

He enrolled in Saturday art classes at the New York School of Fine and Applied Arts, but continued his search for night classes. There were a number of classes available, but all were taught weekdays or they were highly stylized drawing classes such as the one he and Karl had enrolled in. Meanwhile, his interest in studying art had become a laughing matter among other engravers, and he soon found himself alienated from all of them.

In his haste to catch the train for that first Saturday class, he skipped breakfast altogether, but not without raising Frau Kessler's ire. She had sensed the emotional strain he suffered at the hands of Karl, and had begun to play a protective role toward him. The only food she served the lodgers was coffee and biscuits in the morning, but after Karl disappeared, she often invited Emil to have dinner with her and her husband.

Having thus adopted Emil, Frau Kessler fussed about his poor eating habits, insisting each work day that he take an extra sausage biscuit to the factory. Every morning, she wrapped the biscuit and placed it beside his coffee cup. What ranting he would have been subjected to if she ever learned he kept it until noon and made it his entire lunch, thus saving his lunch money.

Once he boarded the train, the ride seemed as endless as a day at the steel engraving desk. He was tormented by thoughts of interrupting the class with his tardy entrance, a spectacle that would be most humiliating. He ran the last two blocks to the school, pausing to catch his breath only when he reached Broadway and 80th Street where the school was located. Once inside the building, he covered the stairs two steps at a time, pausing briefly when he reached the studio door. He tiptoed through the doorway so as not to call attention to himself or disturb the class.

The welcome odor of turpentine, paint, and varnish greeted him inside the large room, where lockers, stools, screens, and a model stand were the only furnishings. Everything was paint-splotched: ceiling, floor, walls, and furniture. All was a welcome sight to him, warm and inviting in spite of its bareness.

There was a problem, however. Class was due to begin in fifteen minutes, and he was the only person there. He didn't know whether to take a seat or remain standing or wait outside. He was still tussling with these decisions when a young woman came in and disappeared behind the screen at the other end of the room. *Portrait model?* he wondered. With no one to ask, he floundered in distress. Finally, he settled on a stool and readied his materials, just in case.

Just then a voice from the direction of the model stand broke the awful silence. "Would you like the same pose the others had all week?" she asked.

With eyes planted on his paper, he shuffled uncomfortably on the stool before deciding "of course" would be an appropriate response. When he raised his head to look at her, the words stayed somewhere in his throat. The woman was naked! She had assumed a sensuous pose and she wanted to know if it was to his liking. Even if he had known what to say, he wasn't at all certain he could say it.

He knew there was to be a nude model, but it never occurred to him it would be a woman. He wished that for once in his life, he hadn't arrived well in advance of everyone else. He busied himself as long as he dared arranging his sketching paper even though he had already done that several times. The model, obviously bored with it all, held her pose in silence.

Once he took his eyes off her, he couldn't bring himself to look again, and as he had to appear busy, he attempted a sketch from memory. The alabaster skin remained most prominently in his mind and the rich black hair that framed her face in soft ringlets. The sparkle in her eyes, the breasts, large and firm, the nipples touched with just the right amount of red, he recalled, but then he realized it was Katy's body nudging its way into his memory.

He had not allowed his gaze to go below the breasts, but that was not to say he didn't benefit from peripheral sight. When he had exhausted his memory, the excitement of drawing the nude overcame his shyness and he plunged into the sketch. By the time other students arrived, he had already done several charcoal sketches from different angles. The men crowded around him, apparently quite taken by his enthusiasm if not his talent, but none of them showed any interest in sketching the model themselves. They sauntered back and forth, smoking, rummaging in their lockers, chatting, perhaps waiting, Emil assumed, for the instructor.

It was nearly noon when the instructor came and began criticizing his sketches. Emil was bitterly disappointed as he was unfamiliar with the terms.

"I was hoping for a lecture and perhaps a demonstration," he said timidly.

Instead of responding, the instructor riffled through some of Emil's sketches. "Well, now, I see you have a natural bent for the human figure. You should go into illustration, or perhaps fashion designing. Marvelous opportunities there."

Emil quaked with disgust and he made no attempt to hide his disappointment. "I'm not interested in the commercial aspect of art."

"Why paint? There's no money in painting. With your knack, you could make money as an illustrator or fashion designer. I market a lot of the students' work. I could do the same for you." He noted Emil's displeasure. "You'll change your mind," he added knowingly.

It was a bitter disappointment. As the tuition had been paid and he was furnished a model, he opted to complete the month's studies, and continue his search.

The next Saturday he was the only student in the room. He voiced his disappointment to the model, Maurice, a young Jewish boy.

"I'm sorry you had to work today. It's obvious you wouldn't have to pose if not for me."

"Oh, but then I wouldn't get paid," Maurice answered warmly. He surprised Emil with his refined use of the German language.

Following suit, Emil continued the conversation in German. "Oh, I see. Are all art schools like this? There's no competitive spirit here. No spirit at all, it seems."

"I can understand your disappointment. I'm an art student myself. I pose in the daytime to make tuition for night classes. Too bad you can't attend at night."

Emil abandoned his sketch immediately. "Night classes? Where?"

"The Henri School."

"Henri? Where is that?"

"The Henri School? Right here on Broadway. Henri's the most exciting name in the art world." Maurice was shocked that any art student would be unfamiliar with the name. "If Henri doesn't inspire you, no one will. Electrifies the whole room with his lectures and demonstrations." He paused, but the passion he felt for the teacher lived on in his facial expression.

Emil squirmed with delight. He felt as if his life was about to begin. At his insistence, Maurice continued.

"Henri's lectures are spontaneous. Quite phenomenal the way he can put you in control of your own emotions. Never know what he'll ask of the model next or of the student. Sometimes he has us attend the ballet just to observe the dancers' movements."

Maurice's passion alone painted the picture Emil had coveted most of his life. He could scarcely control his emotions.

"Say, why not visit the class Monday evening and see for yourself?" Emil didn't bother with formal enrollment procedures for fear the process would take a week or so. He didn't want to miss a single class. When he arrived at the school the following Monday evening, Maurice ushered him into the room where a life class was in session. Fifteen or twenty students formed a half circle before the nude model who had taken her pose only moments earlier. His heart fairly leaped with excitement as he gloried in what he considered the atmosphere an art class should have. One thing in particular caught his attention. Floating in the sink was a large board with rainbow-colored paint mixtures spread over its surface. There appeared to be a hundred different colors.

"I'll tell you about that later. Belongs to George Bellows," Maurice told him.

"Who?"

"You're going to have to read the paper. Bellows makes the art pages. Been a Henri student for some time. Lives in this very building."

"If you only knew the trauma of reading an American newspaper," he explained. "You have a woman in the class," he noted, almost as if he expected Maurice to be surprised. In Schwabisch-Gmund, the sexes had always been separated, so working or studying beside a woman would be a first for him.

Maurice snickered. "We call her 'Vamp,'" he whispered.

Some of the students were obviously drawing her instead of the paid model, and it was no wonder. Her huge, marbled eyes sat deep in her forehead as if pushed there by some misfortune and they appeared to have no relation to the rest of her face. Her sallow complexion pointed to a life devoid of sunshine. She reminded Emil of his childhood notion of a witch.

Eager to begin, he gladly accepted Maurice's offer of a stool and a big board palette, and rooted his way into the group. He was especially grateful that no one seemed to notice him.

The group, though focused on their work, occasionally engaged in light-hearted banter. A fat boy they called "Tiny" was noticeably older than the others, and for a second, Emil had mistaken him for the instructor. But that conclusion was based solely on a quick glance that failed to reveal distinguishing characteristics. He appeared to have slept in his clothes for months, and his pants were coming apart at the seams, baring a delicate area of his body. He apparently wore no underwear. Emil was astonished that nobody called the dilemma to the poor man's attention.

It was a congenial bunch of men and boys, and one lone woman, all with the same interest and many with the same problems. They attended school by night and made their tuition by day. In many ways, Emil was luckier than some because he had a trade, and a well-paying one at that. The class abounded in clerks and salesmen, jobs totally unrelated to art, and jobs that offered no advancement in position or salary. All of the students dreamed of going abroad to study the work of the masters, but none had hopes of accumulating the funds for such a trip. As for Emil, he harbored the notion of saving money to invest in securities that would bring him a monthly income, leaving him free to paint.

There were at least two students in the class, Tiny and Lamberty, who wielded a brush by day, but only for billboard painting. Aside from earning a paltry sum, it was degrading work for a student of fine arts.

When Emil enrolled in the class the following night, he was introduced to Henri's assistant, Homer Boss. Unfortunately, Henri was in Europe, but Emil soon learned that Boss had a great deal to offer. The main problem was his voice, a squeaky, irritating quiver that verified his uncertainty. His hands shook during his demonstrations, almost cancelling out the value of his excellent work, and solidifying his lack of confidence in himself.

"He's intimidated by Henri," one of the students explained. "But once you get past his delivery, you'll find he has a great deal to offer."

"Yes," Maurice agreed. "If only he would speak forcefully, it would be grand."

Emil agreed that Boss' poor delivery was regretful, but it didn't nullify the content of his lectures. The instructor stressed the importance of learning the fundamentals time and again, advocating the outline as a starting point for their drawings. "After drawing your foundation, add to it without hindrance or restriction. You'll find the outline does not restrict you. On the contrary, it will afford you freedom. Once you master the idea of good drawing, you'll find the possibilities limitless as you bring the painting to life." He had no difficulty convincing Emil, as Herr Kreisel had already done that. The problem was the three-hour class period disappeared too quickly. Once there, Emil didn't want to go home. Given an opportunity, he would gladly have slept on the hard floor in the corner of the room instead of fighting the train and ferry schedule home.

The twenty-minute trolley ride from the factory to his rooming house for a quick change of clothes proved to take too much of his precious time. He took a room a few blocks from the factory where he could catch the five-fifteen train immediately after work, grab the ferry, then make his way to Broadway and up to 66th Street where the school was located on the top floor of the building. On the way, he dropped in at a small restaurant near the school, for a nightly ham omelette, rice pudding, and coffee. The waiter, knowing of Emil's constant battle with time, placed his order the minute he spotted Emil coming through the door.

At school, nobody knew when Henri would make an appearance. "What does he look like?" Emil asked Lamberty one evening.

"Don't worry, my friend. When Robert Henri enters the room, nobody will have to tell you who he is."

"Tall and handsome," offered Vamp. "Wears a moustache. Has thick arched eyebrows and warm, inviting eyes," she breathed as her own bulb-like eyes bounced in their sockets.

"Look for a sloppy dresser," countered Tiny. "Maybe his new wife will iron his shirts."

Emil laughed, but he wished he hadn't, for he laughed alone.

"Well, he always covers his ass," chided Lamberty. Unabashed at capturing the class' attention, he eyed Tiny's backside. Tiny made a quick search of his vital parts and a feeble attempt to pull his clothes together. As soon as the laughter died, his pants gaped open again, leaving his fat buttocks in full view of all who cared to look, as well as those who didn't.

Lamberty continued the conversation. "When the so-called Frenchman does come back, we'll have no warning," he said with a touch of sarcasm. At twenty-five, Lamberty was a mere thread of a man whose thin body appeared taller than its five foot eight inch frame. His thin upper lip drooped on either side of his mouth giving him a constant angry demeanor. His baggy threadbare clothes scarcely made contact with his thin frame as they had been stretched over a much larger physique before belonging to Lamberty.

He was preoccupied with anything French as he had an uncanny attachment to his French-born mother. "He lives on a boiled potato a day in an effort to save enough money to travel to his mother's birth place. He can think of nothing else," Maurice had told Emil. "His paranoia has built up an antagonism toward Henri because of his ability to come and go to Paris."

Emil paid little attention to gossip as he was much too engrossed in his meager efforts to draw. He was soon to learn that there was some truth in Lamberty's description of Henri. One night with no hint to anyone, in the middle of the class period, a stranger appeared in the doorway. There was no question in Emil's mind of the tall, thin man's identity. Not since Herr Professor Abt's grand entrances had he witnessed such devoted attention from students. But this time, the captive audience was sincere. The students' effervescence pervaded the room like the warmth of the fired up pot-bellied stove. The atmosphere was electrifying, just as Maurice had promised it would be, even though the man hadn't said a word.

Maurice ran to Emil's side. "Don't tell me. It's Henri," Emil gasped.

"He's going to lecture," Maurice bubbled.

Henri spoke slowly, deliberately, and confidently. Emil cursed himself for not studying English more.

"How many of you noticed the puff in the model's sleeve?" he began. In a dramatic gesture, he moved toward the model, eyeing her purposely. "Note the soft pleat here," he said, touching the fabric gently. "Don't think of it as a sleeve, but as a part of the woman herself. Use it as a part of the whole idea, to bring out her femininity, if you see her in that light. Then carry that idea forward. And this wisp of a curl?" he said of the model's hair. "Again, use it to create that vision you wish to convey of her, the one that made itself clear to you in the beginning when you organized your thoughts and settled on an opinion. Choose from your model the things that make this vision manifest. Use them to construct your idea, and express the emotion of it."

He used no notes, but spoke without faltering. "You must give your work life. Show the relation of things. Life is not piecemeal. Everything you choose to include in this composition must have a purpose, and that purpose must be to enhance your original opinion, to give it form, living form. Every element in the sketch must be constructive of an idea, your idea, the one you wish to convey. You see why you must work toward expressing an opinion? You must make a statement. Say something. You're not here to reproduce a likeness, but an emotion, an idea—"

The lecture continued, well past the designated class time, Henri's exuberance never waning. Neither did that of the students. Once, Emil had a nature call, but he refused to answer it for fear of missing something. By the end of the lecture, he noticed the pain had subsided, the intensity of the evening producing enough perspiration to solve the problem without his leaving the room. Following the lecture, Henri went from chair to chair, observing. Emil was near panic when he heard the criticism of some of the long-term students' work. He watched as Henri grabbed the brush from Tiny's hand and slashed fervently across the drawing paper. "Don't be afraid to let go. Make your own language. Your ideas are better than anyone else's because they're yours."

Exactly the words Emil wanted to hear, and precisely the goals he wished to attain, but he wondered if he ever would. Suddenly he was grateful he didn't work with the myriad of colors Bellows used in the daytime. He had trouble enough with a pencil, the lines of which could be erased.

Henri gave no indication he knew of a new student in the class. When he came to Emil's stool, he riffled through his sketches. "You have discipline," he said.

Was it a compliment? Emil didn't know. He was afraid to ask. He was keenly aware that the training he had received in Schwabisch-Gmund had its merit. His craftwork in design and jewelry and silverware helped him in observing and rendering things, a background the others didn't have. Without it, he would have been floundering in the open sea.

The anxious two hours in the presence of the exalted instructor, straining to understand his meaning and trying to meet his expectations, exhausted him. He fell asleep on the train and missed his stop.

"Rahway! Rahway!" the conductor called, jolting Emil's consciousness with his deep raspy voice.

"Rahway?" he asked. He looked around to discover he was the only one on the train. "I'm going to Newark."

"Not tonight. We've already been to Newark."

He spent the remaining hours slumped against a vacant building, catching a nap now and then. It was early the next morning before he could get the milk train back. Somehow, he survived the nine hours at the steel engraving desk without falling asleep, then eagerly returned to school that night.

Henri made another appearance at the school the following Friday. It was "sketch night," a fellow student told him. There were quick, thirty minute sketches of one pose only, followed by twenty-five minute sketches, then ten, and eventually five. The students made quick responses after each pose, and the drawings were placed against the model stand for Henri's critique. With an uncanny understanding of their weaknesses, he criticized their work, tantalizing them with his unusual philosophy on how to improve it.

Henri had studied and trained in Europe, but he never identified with the European masters. His own work was chosen for permanent collections in European galleries, but in the United States, where he was considered a revolutionary, he was not so highly regarded. He appalled the academicians with his freedom of technique and choice of subject matter: dirty waterfront, slums, and laborers. They were unheralded, if not restricted, subjects for an artist.

While making his rounds one Friday evening, Henri pulled up a stool beside Emil, observing him quietly at first. "You're accustomed to copying from a textbook print, aren't you?" He didn't wait for an answer. "Free yourself from that. It requires no real thought and affords no freedom. It'll stifle you." Again, he watched in silence. "Forget about the detail. You can get that with a camera. Reach for an innate characteristic in this model, not a likeness," Henri told him.

Everyone in the room was keenly aware of the instructor's words. When he walked away from Emil, he spoke with the continuity of a lecture.

"Art is an individual effort without rules or methods for success," he said as he approached Lamberty. "Art is a search for truth." He paused before adding that European masters were still searching for it. "The works that grace the walls of the museums are valuable only as a means to an end. The search for truth remains open to you. All you have to do is probe."

"Have you found truth?" Lamberty asked.

His impertinence irritated Emil.

"I'm still searching," Henri confessed, undaunted by the remark. "This man never allows detail to get in his way," he said of Lamberty. "But be careful, even so. You mustn't disassociate your lines from life itself, from feeling. Remember, lines are beautiful only when they correlate with human feelings. Even when you paint still life or landscape." The remark produced a murmur throughout the room, heads bobbing up to look at him. "Yes, you should always use feeling as described by human forms interwoven within the painting or sketch. What's more important than life?" he asked rhetorically, addressing the entire class. "You see, you have no answer. Give your lines life."

Emil vacillated between visions of grandeur and despair; Henri's inspiration sent him reaching for the highest goals, the very ones he had set for himself as a lad. He quickly found his strict training prevented his attaining anything close to that ideal. Night after night he tried to ease the lines that produced his sketch, to free himself of that unyielding stiffness. And every night, he failed.

In total frustration one night, he threw his hands up in despair, calling attention to himself, the very last thing he wanted. Above all else, he didn't want sympathy or unwarranted praise. He needn't have worried. "This drawing distinguishes itself by its utter weakness," Henri told him.

Exhausted again, he fell asleep on the train, missing his stop. By catching the early milk train back, he arrived at the rooming house in the wee hours of morning. He set the alarm for two hours later, and climbed in bed in his work clothes.

The next morning, Frau Kessler knocked on his door. "I worry about you," she told him. "I don't mean to pry, but I heard you coming in early this morning. I'm afraid you'll be sick if you don't get more rest."

"I sleep some on the train you know, and I feel rested. Honest," he assured her.

"You haven't even picked your mail up lately. I couldn't help noticing the pretty handwriting on this one," she teased.

It was from Katy. She had continued to write often even though Emil hadn't. He had begun to dread her letters as he had once dreaded those from home for she was always pleading for him to visit, something he couldn't do. This one was different:

> I have waited long enough. I'm tired of your
> promises. Since you won't come to me, I'm coming
> to you. Arriving two weeks from Friday. Please
> meet the 10:40 night train...

Instinctively, he grabbed pad and pencil. *What to say? There might not be a warning next time. What if she has the same control over my emotions as before?*

A few minutes' delay would mean a late arrival at the factory, an unforgivable violation. There was no time for phrasing a lot of niceties and goodbyes, so he borrowed a farewell from Karl:

Fate has decided we each go our
separate ways so let's abide by it.
Good luck to you.

Nine

Classes at the Henri School gradually filled the void Emil felt from the loss of Katy. After four months at the school, he had finally learned to relax during the long trip from the Newark factory to the school. There had been times when he skipped dinner altogether even though it was the only nourishment of any degree he allowed himself. His weekly salary had increased to thirty-six dollars, so he could afford one good meal a day and still save eighteen dollars a week even after increasing his parents' allowance. With his newfound security, and with assurance he could make the class on time, he began to savor the omelette and rice pudding in the evening rather than gulp it down.

His enthusiasm for the night classes had not waned. Indeed, the excitement of it all sustained him through the tedious factory hours. He lived for the moment when he could enter the barn-like studio with its palette scrapings, pot-bellied stove, model stands, easels and uneven-footed stools.

No one ever knew if Henri would show or not, but no one was willing to skip a class, just in case. "All part of his act," Lamberty explained to Emil. "Likes to keep us guessing." His smirk lifted his drooping upper lip and brightened his demeanor.

"It's part of his charm," declared Vamp as she rolled her witchy eyes.

"I don't know about charm," laughed Maurice. "I doubt it's a conscious thing with him."

Lamberty bristled. "He likes to keep us guessing," he repeated.

Emil had come to realize Lamberty actually idolized Henri, but he was childlike in his jealousy of the teacher who often traveled to France, an opportunity Lamberty wanted desperately for himself.

In spite of the obsession, Lamberty was one of Emil's favorites in the class. Dedicated to his ideals, he saved every cent he could toward a trip to France, where he had visions of studying the French Movement. It was heartwarming to Emil to know someone else was willing to give up the material things in life in order to pursue a goal.

It was quite another story with Tiny, whose obsession was limited to food and his idea of the good life. He often directed his songs to Vamp even though her only response was a cold glare. The seven dollars a week he earned as a billboard painter, he spent on food. While Lamberty made do with boiled potatoes, Tiny dined at the Greenwich Village Inn, at least until he ran out of money. He had established a reputation at the Inn as a singer, and he was always prevailed upon by the manager to sing for the customers who responded by tossing a few coins his way now and then. It was enough to keep him eating, but fell short of providing funds for new pants or repair money for the old ones.

At the school, his musical aspirations were reduced to humming, always *Barcarolle*. Emil wanted to join him but never had the courage until one night when all the boys chimed in. When the others tired of it, Tiny and Emil continued, their jovial voices permeating the large, sparsely furnished room, lending it an atmosphere of warmth and frivolity. Their only accompaniment was the sound of charcoal moving across the students' drawing boards.

They hushed when Boss entered the room, and hurriedly cleared their space in full anticipation of his lecture. The whole class respected Boss for his ideas and depth of emotion, but his painful delivery seemed even meeker in light of the forceful and passionate lectures Henri delivered.

Neither Boss nor Henri told the boys to work with the skeleton, but Boss often used the bony creature to point out some part of the human structure. "Know the bone structure and the muscles," Boss began. "If you can't draw them from memory, you don't know them well enough." He was deliberate and methodical in his efforts and his teaching. With Plasticine, he built up muscles in the body and placed them on the skeleton in a brilliant explanation of how they worked. As Emil watched, he was amazed at the man's understanding of how the muscles looked in action and at rest.

Lamberty had benefited the most from Boss' expertise. The would-be Frenchman was highly respected among the group for his ability to express movement of the body, and he could do so with one line when others needed a dozen. His talent had not come easily. Emil watched that evening as Lamberty drew and revised and drew and revised until the sketch met with his approval. His laborious task complete, he threw the charcoal aside and fell into a slump.

"Fantastic," Emil remarked, genuinely astonished by the drawing's subtle beauty.

"I nearly ruined my paper erasing it," Lamberty complained.

"If I could do as well, I wouldn't worry about the paper." He forgot that to Lamberty, the price of drawing paper was no small matter. "No one can accuse you of copying," Emil moaned. "I wonder if Henri will find me freer? Look at that," he fussed, jerking his paper off the drawing board. "Mechanical, just like he said."

"Bah! He copies too," accused Lamberty. "You're surprised? Doesn't he use the Maratta system? What's that but mechanics? He has no feel for dipping his brush, mixing his own colors. No sensitive hand. Has to have them mixed for him." The excitement of revealing a flaw in Henri's work brought color to Lamberty's dull face and lightened the dark circles under his gargantuan eyes. He thrust his bony jaw forward in a show of contempt.

Tiny voiced his objection, his fleshy cheeks wobbling up and down as if they were made of jelly.

Lamberty ignored him, and directed his conversation to Emil. "You won't like Henri any more when you see the new French art."

Tiny hummed Barcarolle, getting louder and louder.

"We have a constant concert right here in the studio. I wonder why Henri thinks we need attend others?" Lamberty grumbled, then purposely moved to the other side of the room.

In a moment, Tiny began putting his things away. "I'm getting hungry. Say, why not join me at the Village Inn?" he asked Emil. "I'll sing for you."

The idea was preposterous. Nothing would induce Emil to leave before they closed the studio doors. "Maybe another time. Say, do you ever attend the concerts?"

"Only now and then. You?"

"No, but Henri's always pushing it. Wish I could."

"Tickets are free for art students you know. You should join the German Society for Culture. They sponsor all kinds of concerts, lectures, and exhibitions."

Lamberty's feigned disinterest in their conversation quickly dissipated. "I'll take you there," he said with obvious satisfaction.

Fortunately, the society met on Sundays, the only day Emil could attend. The group's purpose was to promote interest in cultural affairs and make them available to anyone interested. Although it had been initiated by Germans, and its original membership was made up of Germans, it had expanded to include many nationalities. There were doctors, artists, authors, diplomats, and other intellectuals in the group.

Meetings, which were held once a month, were short and to the point, leaving plenty of time for the members to enjoy speakers, musicians or other performers. Since Emil could remember, he had longed for the companionship of people who appreciated the artistic things in life. At the society, he found himself surrounded by intellectuals whose broad experiences enabled them to talk on any subject. The problem was, he couldn't join in their conversations as he had nothing to offer. He was, however, an excellent listener.

One Sunday, they were to be entertained by a concert pianist, a new member of the group. Lamberty, who had missed the business meeting, made his entrance to the performance in the same threadbare clothes he wore every night in class. His long, shaggy hair spilled over his forehead, hiding his equally shaggy eyebrows.

Emil had invested in a new suit, a light brown year-round gabardine with a tan vest. His muted brown tie picked up the darker color of the suit's subtle stripe. His white shirt featured a detachable celluloid neckband collar. He fought the high, stiff choker the entire evening, marvelling at others in similar attire who didn't seem to mind it.

At twenty-five, his poor eating habits kept him thin just as he had been as a young lad, a fact that would preclude his purchasing another suit prior to wearing this one threadbare, and the collars could be replaced separately.

Lamberty rushed to Emil's side. "Come, I want you to meet the Isaacs."

"No, please. Isn't the concert beginning?"

"Don't worry," he scolded. "We've plenty of time."

Emil was overruled. They joined a distinguished-looking couple dressed in the latest fashions, the man in a double-breasted sack-suit, the woman in a woolen suitdress featuring a high neck and narrow skirt that came within inches of her ankles. Lamberty introduced them as Helen and Charles Isaacs.

"Emil Holzhauer, a fellow art student," Lamberty said, seemingly with pride, Emil noted.

Soon, everyone was talking, except Emil. The Isaacs, a couple in their late thirties, seemed endowed with worldly wisdom and resourcefulness, enabling them to talk about any topic that might come up. On several occasions, they tried bringing Emil out of his shell, but he refused to do more than nod in agreement with whatever they said.

"Are you familiar with tonight's performer?" Mr. Isaacs asked, gazing hopefully into Emil's eyes.

"No."

"Ah, you're in for a treat," declared Isaacs. "I caught his practice session once. Has tremendous volume and variety of tone. I"m afraid he lacks sensitivity, though. That feeling of restraint is either there or it isn't. Don't you agree? So important now with the new approach to music."

Just then a Mr. Schliemann, a friend of the Isaacs, joined them. Emil was taken aback by the man's attire, a loosely-fitted black wool suit and matching vest with a neckband shirt and blue silk tie. His cuffed pants touched the top of shiny black pointed-toe shoes. He was tall, thin and wiry.

Emil hated the intrusion just when he was getting used to the Isaacs. Schliemann was introduced as a Wall Street broker. "I wish this was Marcy's concert," he said. There was a distinct yearning in his voice.

Emil could think of nothing but Schliemann's profession. For years now he had harbored thoughts of investing his savings, but he had never had the courage to approach a broker with the meager sum he had to offer.

"Well, Marcy's young yet," Charles offered.

"Yes," Schliemann agreed, "but with her talent, she should be at the top already." His firm jaw tightened.

"I must apologize for both of them," Helen said. "They're talking about Marisa Didrikson. Mr. Schliemann is one of her benefactors. Friends call her Marcy."

Schliemann continued his praise. "Nobody can interpret the new music like she can. She can make you feel the ocean wave. A genius at mixing the overtones."

Lamberty seemed to understand. "Impressionism," he said knowingly. "Naturally it's a French idea."

Deep color rose in Emil's face. He felt like a fool. Perhaps nobody had studied impressionism more than he, and yet he never associated it with music.

"Presently, Marcy's on a European tour," Helen explained to Emil and Lamberty.

Schliemann turned his attention to the art students. "Have you exhibited your work? At the school I mean?"

Both were quick to admit they hadn't. The Henri School held annual exhibitions, and often had others in between, featuring all the students in both the day and night classes. Each student could make his own invitation list, but Emil had no one to invite. The thought of actually exhibiting his work was preposterous to him; the idea of inviting someone to ogle it, even more. Emil quickly explained that he was only beginning his studies, but Isaacs and Schliemann scoffed at his humility and urged him to show some of his work at the next exhibition the society sponsored.

"I wouldn't dare," admitted Lamberty. Emil agreed.

"You're much too modest, I'm sure," offered Helen. "I envy you the training you must be getting from Henri." Her enthusiasm was shared by all of them. Emil had wondered why the Isaacs and Schliemann wasted their time with the likes of him and Lamberty. Apparently, it was to Henri's credit, not theirs.

"We admire his enthusiasm for change in the art world, and his courage to fight the academy."

"I hope you have a chance to meet Marcy, Emil," said Helen. "She loves the German people, and she loves a chance to speak German." Her voice was warm, as if she were talking to an old friend.

"She's German?" Emil's interest peaked.

"No, but she speaks the language fluently. She was born in Poland, but her family lived in Germany when she was a small girl."

"Does she belong to the society?" Lamberty asked.

"Oh, no. There's no time. She teaches at the New York Institute of Music when in town. Then on Sundays, she performs for private audiences. Busy, busy girl," she added.

Emil knew at that point he would never have the opportunity to meet her, and he was glad. *What would I say to her, even in German*? he asked himself. His curiosity, however, was not quelled. As soon as he and Lamberty were alone, he questioned his friend.

"What do you know about Miss—ah, you know, the pianist?"

"Nothing," admitted Lamberty.

"I assumed since your friends talked about her so much?"

"Not really friends. Just society acquaintances. They never mentioned her prior to this. They were obviously interested in you, my friend. Or at least in your German background."

"Me?" Emil was astonished.

"Didn't you notice how Mrs. Isaacs kept probing into your background?"

It was true, but Emil had dismissed it as kindness. Lamberty hadn't enjoyed the conversation, especially during the high praise for Henri. He had departed the society a bit moody. Emil wanted to lift his spirits. "You should exhibit. I mean it. You've done some excellent studies."

"And where would I get the funds for framing?" he asked in a huff.

Yes, that was a problem, but one that Emil could manage, if only he had something he would be willing to exhibit. Only recently had he attempted a painting, having insisted all along on improving his drawing first. Mostly, the night students resigned themselves to drawing because the artificial lighting was not conducive to painting. Even in the best of times, and at Henri's urging, they limited their colors to red, yellow, green and blue, with black and white for enhancement.

But on Sundays Emil had begun to test his skill in oil. There were no Sunday classes, but the Henri studio was available to any student who wanted it, and it offered a golden opportunity to meet with the day students, many of whom had exhibited and had been recognized for their talent. Besides Bellows, there were Kuniyoshi, Marsden Hartley, Rockwell Kent, Sarah and Mac McPherson, Edward Hopper, and many others whose names Emil hadn't yet put to memory. When the weather was nice, they took their materials into the Orange Mountains or other outlying areas for important outdoor experiences.

Eventually, Emil had quite a collection of his own work, most of which lay in stacks on the floor of his room. Exhibiting it was out of the question. He wouldn't even let the landlady see it.

On the walk home from the train station, he noticed a familiar figure approaching from the opposite direction. It was Felix. They rarely saw each other even though they lived only a few blocks apart. He often thought of calling on Felix to see if he had heard anything of Karl, but he never seemed to have the time or the courage. Contact with Felix was better left to chance, or at least in a mixed group of Schwabisch-Gmund boys during Sunday hikes. As the two approached, they broke into wide grins.

"Felix! How are you?"

"Handsome as ever and rich as hell. I'm gonna be the factory manager soon." When he laughed, his big lips seemed to cover half his face, giving him a clown-like appearance.

As soon as Emil could break into the personal encomium, he asked about Karl.

"Karl? Why, he lives with me. You didn't know?"

"How should I know? Karl living within blocks of me and not getting in touch?"

"Well, it's your own damn fault. I hear you drove him out."

"I?" he asked, startled by the accusation. "Felix, he's my best friend."

"Oh?" Felix guffawed. "He said you were a tyrant."

Emil was grateful for the darkness as it would conceal the flush that had temporarily immobilized him. "Because I asked him to pay his debt? You repaid your loan, didn't you? Why shouldn't Karl?" His voice quivered in the beginning, but gained strength as embarrassment turned to anger.

For once, Felix was at a loss. Emil continued. "I only tried to teach him a lesson in economics."

The news dulled Emil's spirit, pushing aside the happy memory of the concert, the Isaacs, and the pianist.

All the next day at the factory, thoughts of Karl wove in and out of his mind. It took the night class to relieve the stress. To his dismay, the thoughts surfaced again as he began the train ride home.

At the apartment, he was happy to see a letter from his mother, as it had been longer than usual since he had heard from her. He had begun to look forward to news from home now that his parents had accepted the fact that he couldn't leave his studies for a visit to Germany.

"Papa is dead," the letter began.

Ten

The letters from home grew more and more depressing. The closing lines of his mother's letters were always the same: "Please don't let me die like your poor papa did without seeing you again."

The words tugged at his emotions, bringing a mix of tears and anger. He wanted to help his mother, but he resented her references to "poor papa."

His death had added a new wrinkle to Emil's tortuous life: what to do about his mother. Apparently, she too had been quite ill from an asthmatic condition. Unable to keep up the rooming house, she was at the financial, as well as physical, mercy of her son. To appease her temporarily, he invited her to come for a visit or to make her home with him in America, whichever she wished. The moment he posted the letter, he was ashamed for tantalizing the poor woman. She who had never been outside Schwabisch-Gmund, would never attempt to cross the ocean. Instead of easing his conscience, he found it merely intensified the pain.

In less than a month, he received a letter from his mother that showed spunk he never dreamed she had. The idea of coming to America appealed to her, and with the assistance of her sister, Rose, she had begun preparations.

Meanwhile, summer was approaching. The Henri School would be closed from June through August. Some of the affluent students in the day classes joined their instructor on a trip abroad. Even the not-so-affluent students planned trips to Monhegan Island, an artist's paradise Emil had only heard about. Lamberty had finally saved enough money to assure himself of a prolonged sojourn in France. He was set to leave the day after classes ended.

While others celebrated the closing of the school, Emil was in a downcast state. Three months without instruction was not appealing to him. Henri tried to prepare students, like him, who had to remain in the city.

"This is not a vacation from school," he reminded them.

"Quite the contrary. Think of it as a sabbatical, a time for practicing what you have learned. You know by now subject matter is everywhere in the city. Paint the riverfront, the street vendor, the beggar, and the Brooklyn Bridge from every conceivable angle, every conceivable time of the day. They're all studies of nature. Your goal is to see the unusual. Don't sacrifice the initial impression the subject made on you and caused you to paint it. Bad weather? Take out your drawings you did here and rework them. Draw the models from memory."

With only one day a week for painting, it was more than ample assignment for Emil. And if his mother came to America, there might be no time at all for painting. He knew the worst was not over. With her deteriorating health, and no one to assist her in obtaining a passport, or storing her belongings, the prospect seemed hopeless. As conservative as he had always been, he felt a need to tighten his belt another notch for what might come.

Meanwhile, he dived into the ocean of ideas awaiting him in the city. He began with the riverfront, a place called the Neck, a filthy, smelly place, but one that enchanted him, and called him to return six afternoons a week and all day Sundays. Neither hunger nor thirst could entice him to leave the scene before darkness fell, no matter his firm intention each Sunday to take a break. Even when he remembered to bring Frau Kessler's biscuit, it remained untouched in his pocket, often serving as part of his evening meal. Total involvement in his work erased from his consciousness the idea of time, and he was quite astonished to see nightfall close in on him long before he thought it should.

Once darkness settled in, he proceeded to the library and read until the attendants pushed him out the door. French impressionism and impressionists remained his favorite subjects. He and Karl had already done a great deal of reading in the field, but once he graduated beyond sketching and into painting, he had a little better understanding of what they meant by visual truths.

He followed Henri's suggestion, painting the fascinating Brooklyn Bridge in all its splendor, Sunday after Sunday. 'Search for simplicity,' he could hear Henri say as he faced the complicated man-made marvel. From nearby rooftops, from the bridge's promenade, and from the East River beneath the bridge, he painted the towering wire-suspensioned wonder. Such an undertaking was often time consuming, requiring permission from the managers or owners of nearby buildings to climb to the rooftop, and promises to the bridge attendants to disperse any crowd that gathered around him while he painted on the walkway. As July approached, he returned to the Neck, where he began to practice the choppy brush strokes the French artists were finding effective in their quest for visual truth. The strokes were not strokes at all, but mere dots. It was a painstaking job trying to depict a scene, to make a statement with nothing but small round dots. He was engrossed in his efforts when he became aware of familiar voices nearby.

"Lamberty! What in the world? I can't believe it."

"I didn't go," he said. His thin face was furrowed by long-term brooding.

"Not go? But why?"

His answer was a disheartened wave of his hand as he plodded past his friends and into a directionless path somewhere.

"His mother," said Maurice. "She was very ill."

"I'm sorry," Emil offered.

Lamberty stopped, but didn't turn around to face them. "She's dead," he said mournfully.

Emil was stunned. He knew how Lamberty doted on his French-born mother and how he hated his father. But if she was dead, why postpone the trip, he wondered. What could be better to ease the pain of losing his mother than the long-awaited trip to his beloved France? "Maybe after another year of study you'll benefit more from the trip. Believe me, I can understand your enthusiasm for the French artists. I've been working on Monet's dot system. God, what discipline it took to develop such a method."

"That's old stuff," Lamberty said, mockingly, then headed up the river's bank.

"Sorry," Emil offered, but Lamberty was well out of earshot. "I didn't know what to say," he explained to Maurice.

Maurice filled in the blanks. Lamberty's mother had been gravely ill, and there was no money for her medical expenses, so Lamberty used his life's savings to pay the bills. When she died, he became depressed, isolating himself from everything and everybody. It was only by accident Maurice had learned of his fate when he ran into Tiny on the streets. "It took some coaxing just to get him out of his room," Maurice said.

"Will he be able to continue the classes? What about the fee?" Emil asked. "Where will he get eight dollars a month? Perhaps we can all chip in?"

"Henri will see to it. If he thinks they have promise, but can't pay, he charges it, so to speak." The revelation only served to prove to Emil that he was always the last one to be apprised of anything. How many others attended free, he wondered. No matter. Even if he had qualified for free lessons, he couldn't accept charity. He studied his unfinished painting. "What would Henri think of this?"

"Hard to say. Have you made a statement?" Maurice teased. They both burst out in knowing laughter. The comment was straight from Henri's lectures, a constant reminder to the class that painting is like speaking. "Don't talk if you have nothing to say," he often told his students.

"Say, did you hear about Rockwell Kent?" Maurice bubbled. "The Met bought one of his paintings." Kent was one of Henri's day students.

"No! The Metropolitan Museum?" It was almost too much for Emil's imagination.

Success for others in the school encouraged him to continue with the dot system until he came up with something he felt might be good enough for exhibition at the German Society.

He had become quite friendly with Helen and Charles Isaacs since their initial meeting. They had pressed him to enter the next show. He had occasionally been invited to dinner at their home where Schliemann was often a guest as well.

Reluctant at first, Emil soon learned to enjoy the get-togethers as conversation was never a problem. Schliemann was an enchanting man, easy to listen to, knowledgeable, but not in the least condescending. Like the Isaacs, he could talk with ease and assurance about anything, it seemed. Modern in thought, he spoke favorably of Henri's battle for artistic freedom. He was intrigued by the new American artists, and he blasted Americans for looking overseas for their purchases.

When the subject of music came up, and it always did, it inevitably led to a discussion of Marcy.

"You really must meet this lady," Schliemann told Emil. "The two of you should have a lot in common. Helen and Charles could arrange it."

Emil was astonished by the suggestion, coming from a man like Schliemann, obviously a man of means and background. His response to meeting their Marcy was always the same, a quick glance toward the floor. *If indeed the meeting were arranged, what would I say to her or she to a dullard like me*? he thought.

Emil was glad when summer ended and classes began again. He was equally glad that he had improved as much as most of the students even though some of them had studied abroad under the guiding hand of their instructor. When Boss spoke of marked improvement in Emil's action sketches, he began to entertain the notion of having his work singled out as the best of the evening. The selection, made by Boss or Henri, was displayed on the wall for everyone's perusal. Emil's work had never been chosen.

When the honor finally came, it was not an action pose as he had expected, but a sketch of the nude model. It was his first real classroom thrill since Herr Kreisel had singled out his watercolor of the crane. That memory had sustained him through many a trauma, and like this one, would last forever.

Before selecting the painting, Henri discussed it at length with Emil. Using his slow but forceful voice, he made certain the entire class could hear. "You're a master," he began. "You have solidified here. That's great. All parts of the model are joined in one single theme, each playing its part in bringing out the whole. I suggest you do the same with the background, even making the curtains harmonize with the model's face. Everything in your painting should be a part of the portrait."

Emil's confidence was renewed. From then on, his work was chosen as often as anyone's, boosting his ego to the point that he agreed to enter the German Society's upcoming exhibition. He chose two dot paintings, wood interiors, and framed them for entry. Before the exhibit was opened to the public, he previewed the display and was delighted with his own entries.

His pleasure was short-lived, however. On opening day, the paintings took on a new appearance, a public display of his ignorance. He felt certain everyone was laughing to themselves that he could hang such atrocities. Rather than face anyone, he headed for the exit, but paused when he heard Lamberty's voice.

"Where to, my friend?"

"Lamberty! Oh, I wish I hadn't allowed it," he cried, glancing anxiously in the direction of his exhibit.

"Don't be silly. Nobody looks at it with the same penetration you do. Half the people here are your fellow artists. They'll see the merit of your work."

Emil tried to listen, but it was impossible to focus on anything but the two small Holzhauer paintings that spoke for his blatant ignorance.

How easy for Lamberty to dismiss his concerns when he hadn't the courage himself to exhibit, Emil thought. Indeed, he hardly painted anymore. Emil couldn't ignore the wrinkled, threadbare shirt, the ill-fitting pants, two sizes too large, doubled around his waist and held precariously by a cracked, paper-like belt. True, it was the same garb he wore in the classroom, but somehow it hadn't the same significance there where linseed oil and turpentine odors prevailed, where nobody wore his Sunday best, and where poor lighting painted a false picture of things anyway. "Lamberty, you should be exhibiting instead of me. I mean it. You shouldn't let your talent go to waste. You need a job."

"I have a job," was his haughty answer.

"You know what I mean. Billboard painting doesn't pay enough." He declined to say it was frowned on by others in their pursuit. "Even if you have to seek training in something, it would be worth it." Lamberty's response was a vigorous shake of his head. "Heaven's sakes, man, you're going to need an occupation in order to paint. Look at Henri. Even he has to teach for a living. In Germany—"

Lamberty interrupted. "If you're satisfied with working in a factory, do it. It's not for me."

It was a common opinion among the students though most didn't voice it. They envied Emil his salary but not enough to trade places with him at the engraving desk. Bums on the street, not always having the price of a meal, yet factory work was beneath them.

The conversation with Lamberty, though not always pleasant, at least eased the pain wrought by his exhibit. Suddenly, Charles Isaacs was beside them. "Congratulations," said Charles as he reached for Emil's hand and shook it vigorously.

"Believe me, I wish I had never allowed them to be hung," he moaned.

Helen approached him with her arms outstretched. "Ah, just imagine," she exclaimed joyfully, "you've sold your very first exhibits." She gave him a warm hug.

"Sold?"

He followed the excited Isaacs through the crowded room as a flood of emotions raced through his mind. Sold signs hung on both exhibits. "Fifteen dollars," the price tag read, and someone had apparently paid it. Emil gloried for a moment, then eyed the Isaacs suspiciously.

Lamberty rallied, his mood suddenly lighter than Emil had seen it since the tragedy. It must have been a moment of vicarious pleasure, imagining a sale of his own work.

He couldn't be certain about the Isaacs, but he wouldn't embarrass himself by asking either of them or the society's treasurer the purchaser's name. He left the exhibition not knowing whether to celebrate or cry.

At the Neck later that afternoon, he painted until darkness set in. On the way to his rooming house, he noticed a familiar figure coming from the opposite direction. Even in the darkness, he knew it was Karl.

More than two years had passed since Karl left the note and final payment in Emil's room. No matter. The sight of his old Schwabisch-Gmund sketching partner was a welcome one. He gladly responded to Karl's outstretched hand. When he felt the warmth of the tapered fingers in his own thick-set hand, all was forgiven.

"Karl, its been a long time, my friend," he said warmly.

Karl returned the warmth. "Where do you live now?" he asked.

"Didn't Felix tell you? The same place. Why not come home with me for a visit?"

At the rooming house, Karl was visibly impressed. "Jesus, look at all that!" he shouted, obviously shocked by the mass of sketches and paintings on the floor and chest. He jumped at the chance to view them one by one.

"What about you? Been painting?" Emil asked eagerly. "No," he admitted. Emil decided to take advantage of the situation, hoping it would be just the push he needed. He spoke freely, purposely, of his exciting experiences in the Henri School and the exhibition at the German Society, even mentioning the sale of his two paintings. There was so much to talk about, he hardly knew where to start; in his haste he began in the middle. "Oh, I forgot. You don't know about the organization. You really must join it, Karl. It's a necessity for any serious artist."

"Just Germans?"

"Oh, no. Nationality doesn't matter." With Karl's interest at a peak, Emil jumped at the chance to tell him everything. He went on and on with stories of the Henri School and the society, and Karl seemed enthralled by it all.

"Why not start your studies now, Karl? I can help you so you won't have to stumble your way around as I did." His eager eyes searched Karl's face for the excitement of old.

Finally, he was persuaded to visit the class. Emil arranged the visit on a Friday night when he could be relatively certain of Henri's presence.

Karl seemed entranced by the warm, inviting atmosphere with its aproned students, the simple stools and easels and hard-board palettes, and particularly the nude model whose naked skin took on the warm glow of the pot-bellied stove. He studied the walls, taking in one at a time as each projected quite a different story, one filled with prints of Hals, Goya and Manet's work, one displaying the students' work, and another decorated with globs of splattered paint. "I didn't realize you use paint that much," he noted.

"The day class is mostly responsible for the wall decoration," Emil explained, laughing. "We do use paint, but it's always a waste of time under these conditions." He stole a grudging glance at the dim gas lighting. "Both classes meet here on Sundays and we throw our palette cleanings at the wall," he admitted. Karl was childlike in his fascination.

Talk of an upcoming student exhibition circled the room as the edgy group sought to relieve the anxiety they always felt prior to Henri's arrival. Suddenly, there was a shuffling of feet, followed by anxious mutterings of the group as a whole, an indication that Henri had made his presence known. Karl declined Emil's offer of a palette and easel, but eventually took charcoal and paper in hand.

Henri eyed the model, seemingly piercing the outside in an effort to probe within. Except for the sounds of classical music coming from the old Victrola, there was silence. Slowly, deliberately, he began, his lecture bouncing with spirit, yet held in check to accommodate the students' understanding.

"Don't begin until you have something to say," he warned. Again, he studied the model. "Ah, yes, you must be aware that you have more than a body here. You have refinement, you have beauty. What do you want to say about it? Paint the look, not the body. Paint an idea, not the woman. Sing the picture, hum it, let it flow out of you."

On and on he spewed, his spirit never wavering, his ideas never dulling, his articulation flawless. Karl sat spellbound, his charcoal and paper clutched by his side, unused.

With his lecture ended, at least for the moment, Henri began his rounds, singling Maurice out. "Don't get carried away with painting as if it were something separate from drawing. One and the same. When you paint, you draw."

They were well into the class when Henri charged the atmosphere further with instructions to the model. "Get dressed, would you? Right here in front of us," he directed. "Everyone watch closely now, then paint what you saw. Not what you see later, but what you saw during this process."

Emil rustled uncomfortably on his stool. "Karl, you should try this. You could always sketch from memory. I never could." Karl only grinned in recognition of the compliment, evidently too excited to divert his attention from the goings-on.

"Show the sensation of motion, remembering what Boss has taught you about the nature of each muscle. Fifteen minutes should be quite enough," he warned.

Following critiques of their efforts, he asked the model to undress, again in view of everyone. "Feel the energy now. Capture the spirit. Look for these things as she undresses. Then capture what you saw. Ten minutes."

As always, the class ran past the ten p.m. curfew, but no one was aware of the time, not even Karl. Emil could scarcely wait for Karl's reaction.

It was to be a lengthy wait. They were nearing their train stop when Emil finally exploded. "What did you think, for Christ's sake?" He waited a moment, but Karl said nothing. Rather than alienate Karl again, he lowered his voice. "It's just what we always dreamed of, isn't it?" Even as he spoke, he imagined the two of them commuting each night to the Henri School. No more trips to Rahway and no more early milk trains back. Surely one of them would be able to remain awake, he reasoned. Karl's response was submerged by Emil's private thoughts.

"Maybe later."

"What?"

"Maybe later," Karl repeated.

"Later," Emil mocked. "Always later, isn't it? Well, I haven't the leisure you have. Later may be too late for me." Mournfully, he shared the plight of his mother. "Frankly, I don't know what's going to happen. Her sister, Rose, was helping her, but she was taken ill of late. If only there were someone to help her with all the arrangements." The thought of it deepened his gloom.

Karl showed genuine compassion for the dilemma. "I wish I could help you. If your mother does come here, let me know. I would really like to see her again."

With their friendship renewed, Karl began to join Emil on his Sunday sketching trips, and nightly, they studied together in the library. Emil felt certain it was only a matter of time before they would be studying together at the Henri School.

Only one thing marred their get-togethers. Though Karl didn't admit it, his health had deteriorated. With little or no warning of nature calls, he was often obliged to urinate in his pants. Even so, he appeared determined to overcome the problem and pursue his studies. Then when he didn't appear one Sunday, Emil began to worry.

Week after week went by, and still Karl didn't show. When he could bear it no longer, he gathered his courage and went to Karl's rooming house. For days he had prepared himself for what he might learn there, but he was totally unprepared for what he did.

"Mr. Ott?" the landlady asked. "Why he went to Germany over a month ago."

The news shattered Emil's composure as Karl's shenanigans had never done before. "That *Schlampig*!" he shouted.

Anger rose within him with every step homeward. *He knew about my mother's plight. Could at least have offered to help her with the necessary arrangements. Even accompany her to the States.*

A final thought struck him. *What if he's gone to stay*? To his own surprise, he hoped so.

Eleven

Karl's last trick had made an impact on Emil as never before. He finally realized that his childhood sketching partner lacked the discipline needed to study art. The reality of it depressed him.

To make matters worse, he remained imprisoned in the engraving factory while other students studied in Europe or painted on Monhegan Island or other artists' paradises. With his mother to support, perhaps even coming to America, or in need of full-time care in Germany, he might have felt hemmed in by it all except that life had gotten better for him at the Henri School. No longer did he feel like an outsider. His improved English enabled him to read the art pages of the New York papers and to become aware of how revolutionary his teacher's ideas really were. He could listen intelligently to German Society members, and even enter the conversation occasionally, and order a meal in a restaurant without cringing with embarrassment. His new understanding of things had sparked an interest in recent American art history, which he gleaned from students, old newspapers, and from Henri himself.

Henri's constant encouragement to break with tradition brought to Emil's mind the battle the instructor had fought on behalf of his students, and American art in general. "Submit your work to the academy, but don't be disappointed when they reject it. Such rejection doesn't mean it isn't good, only that it's innovative." As he began to see the big picture, he developed a passionate zeal for educating himself about his adopted country's art. The Macbeth Gallery, it seemed, had been one of the few willing to show the work of a living American painter. In a city with only a few private galleries, and most of them interested in showing only European work, especially the old masters, Macbeth was a godsend for innovative American painters like Henri and his followers.

Emil began to realize that he had left the heart of the art world when he left Germany. He had left the world of the masters and innovators, as well as patrons, to study in a country where art nouveau was not only frowned on, it was rejected.

Ignoring the name-calling by the critics, or perhaps reveling in them, Henri had continued as he had begun, preaching individuality, the artistic message over the subject itself, and, above all, he fought for every artist's right to exhibit, free of the jury system. "Ignore the critics' reference to your subjects as ugly. Keep on painting the ditch digger, the street vendors, the slum dwellers, for in these faces you'll see more character than in the faces of queens," he had assured his students with conviction. "Reach for the character within the subject, not the physical features," he implored them.

As always, Henri's stimulating lecture created a constant challenge for Emil. At Henri's urging, he began to join the day students on their Sunday outings. Boredom was never a factor.

But rumblings of discontent among the day students brought an unwanted change in Emil's life. Just when things were going well, Henri resigned! Day students had complained about Henri's preoccupation with the Maratta system. With night students not so involved with paint, and certainly not with all the hues of the spectrum as in the Maratta, the subject never came up.

"But how can he resign from his own school?" Emil asked one evening, earnestly hoping it was indeed impossible.

"It's just a name, you know. Change the shingle on the entrance and you have another school," Lamberty scoffed. Determined to belittle Henri publicly, in reality Lamberty was in mourning.

Maurice offered enlightenment. "I understand Henri sold all the furnishings to Homer Boss some months back. The school will be headed by Boss and will be known as the Independent School."

In an effort to minimize the loss of Henri, Lamberty soon informed his classmates of an international art show that would make their former teacher look like a conservative. As a frequent visitor to the Steiglitz Gallery, he had become friendly with Arthur Davies, a man bent on introducing modern European art in the United States. "You'll see Cezanne, Matisse, Toulouse-Lautrec, and more," Lamberty promised knowingly. The big event was to be held in the enormous 69th Regiment Armory on Lexington Avenue.

Lamberty had alienated most of his classmates with his notion of anything French being better. Emil remained friendly with him, but often ignored his ravings. He swallowed his pride, however, when the doors of the Armory opened in February, 1913.

With thousands of others, Emil stood in line to enter the huge arena, now disguised as an art gallery. The show had been cleverly arranged so as to offer the viewers an historical lesson in art, beginning with the nineteenth century and ending with the post-impressionists.

For once, Emil dropped his public conservative guard and stood speechless in front of Duchamp's *Nude Descending A Staircase*. While most of the viewers laughed, he didn't. He was astounded by the liberties the artist had taken with his brushes, but secretly admired him for his courage as well as his insight.

The reviews were mostly derisive and biting, the Europeans receiving the brunt of it. The American work was ignored for the most part. The original idea for the show, that of showing American art, was nullified. Just as Lamberty had predicted, Henri was no longer considered a revolutionary.

Like most of his classmates, Emil's spirit was renewed by the exhibits. Anxious to try some of these new ideas, he and Lamberty began to frequent the Orange Mountains and Saddle River. While Lamberty tried to emulate Cezanne, Emil worked with the palette knife in an effort to copy the unusual action in van Gogh's canvasses.

At the school, Emil missed the enthusiasm of Henri's lectures, but he actually preferred Boss' painting because it had more solidity. And unlike Henri, Boss encouraged the students to copy. He saw it as a genuine effort to find one's niche. Like most of the students, his whole point of view had changed with the advent of the Armory Show. He was working with a new style and mode of expression himself. Classes were as exciting as ever.

Emil had a new worry, however. His mother was on her way to America. Would he be able to continue his studies?

In preparation for her arrival, Emil took a small apartment on the first floor of the Kesslers' rooming house, as his mother would not be able to climb the stairs. There was a kitchenette available where she could cook when she felt like it.

He met the ship in Hoboken, and was directed to the sick bay where his mother had been detained by the ship's doctor. Entering the compound, he took a quick glance around the room but saw no sign of his mother. Turning to go, he heard a faint voice calling, "Emil, Emil." From a corner bunk, he caught sight of thin, frail arms on the fragile body of an old woman struggling for the strength to rise up from her prone position.

He stared in disbelief, his forehead muscles forming a mass of uncharacteristic wrinkles. He was quite unprepared for the toll eight years had taken on her. Bravely, Frau Holzhauer managed to stand, and with the assistance of the doctor, she took a few feeble steps in Emil's direction.

Emil remained rooted in the doorway, too stunned to move. "Mother?" he whispered. "Mother, I'm afraid the trip was too much for you," he said as he reached out to her. He embraced her carefully and with genuine concern that the passionate hug he had envisioned might be her undoing. Even as he held her, she began a prolonged, agonizing coughing spell. In broken sentences, she promised she would be all right.

"Emil, Emil," she called weakly. "You've been working too hard. You're so thin."

Emil laughed nervously. Seating her back on the cot from which she had so bravely risen, he joined the doctor for a conference. "Your mother is a very sick woman. She has heart trouble and a severe case of asthma. She mustn't exert herself in any way," the doctor warned him.

But being with Emil again was like a curative for Frau Holzhauer. She delighted in cooking his meals, keeping the apartment in order, and caring for his clothes. Emil hadn't the heart to leave her every night, so he attended art classes only three nights a week. As difficult as it was to give up a moment of his studies, he rather enjoyed the warm atmosphere his mother had created in the apartment, cooking his favorite foods and fussing over him.

From the beginning, she wanted to get in touch with Fritz, but Emil refused. "No, Mother. He's a drunken bum. Never can hold a job and never saved a single mark," he told her.

"Please, Emil. He's like a son to me. You should have seen him the last time he was in Schwabisch-Gmund. He brought me flowers. And once, he gave me a box of candy. Think how your poor papa would feel."

Already irritated by her constant reference to "poor papa," the notion nevertheless took a back seat to her praise of Fritz. "He did what! Where did he get the money?"

"Oh, I gave it to him," she admitted.

It had to be money Emil had sent home, for there was no other source. He knew the rooming house only met expenses, leaving no money for flowers and candy. But the pride with which she told the story discouraged him from prolonging the argument.

It took some doing but he finally located Fritz in New Hampshire and invited him for a visit. Fritz responded by visiting them just long enough to partake of the good German homecooking.

Within a few months, Frau Holzhauer's health had worsened. Almost from the start, she had difficulty breathing in the smoke-filled factory area in Newark. Within six months, her condition had declined so much that the doctor warned Emil she would die if he didn't move her to the outskirts of the city.

Before he could arrange such a move, Frau Holzhauer's condition had worsened to the point that she required hospitalization. In a matter of days, her features were hardly distinguishable because of severe swelling around her neck and face.

As soon as she realized she was dying, she began to beg Emil to take her back to the apartment. "You know what a disgrace it is to die in the hospital," she told him through convulsive sobs. It became a constant plea that turned his nightly visits into mortifying experiences. At his request, Mrs. Kessler agreed to care for her in the rooming house during the day, but the doctor strongly advised against moving her.

Night after night, Emil faced the same problem and heard the same pleas. He begged her to understand. "Mother, I don't want you to suffer. They can ease your pain here. And it's not a disgrace. Quite the contrary. The wealthiest people die in the hospital. Poor people can't afford the care."

His pleas were ignored. "It's my last request," she sobbed. Tears flowed down her bloated features, the whole process taking its toll on her already fragile body.

It was the same scene nightly as he faced her seemingly lifeless body. She seemed to be hanging on for the sole purpose of persuading Emil to take her to the apartment to die.

Finally, her pleas became too much for him. He broke down and cried convulsively. For days, this heavy-heartedness had been building up within him, but he had refused to give in to it. But now, broken and dejected, he seemed suddenly to have returned to his childhood, having abandoned a grown-up world he found quite intolerable.

She tried to soothe him. "I look worse than I feel, Emil. Really, it isn't so painful. You mustn't cry," she begged. "See, I can still give you our signal," she wheezed, but efforts to pucker her swollen lips ended in failure.

Emil broke again as he pictured her in Schwabisch-Gmund, a gentle, submissive woman going about her daily chores in their simple home, and bathing his wounds with her homemade solution. She had been abused all her life and made to feel inferior. The thought of her having to suffer one more humiliation threw his emotions out of control again. Rather than put her through the trauma of watching him, he kissed her swollen cheeks and said good night.

When the factory manager called him to the phone the next day, he needn't have told him the reason. He was granted permission to leave in order to make funeral arrangements.

As she requested, he had his mother's remains cremated so that he could return her ashes to Germany to be interred with her husband. Then out of respect for her, he contacted Fritz. The moment the service was over, he paid the expenses, and escorted the Kesslers out the door, all without a word to his cousin.

Twelve

The memory of his mother's agonizing death lingered with him through the summer months, depriving him of his usual enthusiasm for outdoor painting. He felt her loss keenly, having become closer than ever to her during the eight months she lived with him in the United States.

Emil had always imagined freedom of responsibility for anyone other than himself would bring with it a feeling of euphoria.

It didn't. With his mother's death, the whole atmosphere around him had changed, not only because those closest to him had died or disappeared, but because of the impending war.

He was grateful his mother had been spared the news of German aggression. As for Karl, he had apparently been caught in the middle of the senseless war with no hope of escape. War talk dominated everyone's thoughts and conversations, but Emil soon learned that he was excluded from the conversation at the Independent School. That he had recently become an American citizen made no difference to the others. He was still a "stinkin' damn German," and they were quick to remind him. Even Lamberty was cool towards him, often giving vent to his own anti-German sentiment.

The prejudice was not limited to the school. It abounded in the factory, on the streets, at organizations, in the news, and at the boarding house. Hourly, he listened to his native country and its people being castigated, cursed, and belittled, with no regard for people like him, who hated war.

According to the newspapers, all Germans greeted the outbreak of the war with fervor. They were war-lovers who thrived on killing. Every

German in America became a whipping boy. Efforts to explain his position were met with failure. Lamberty's animosity toward him was especially painful.

It was a relief to talk with other Germans at the German Society for Culture. The association continued to exist after the outbreak of the war, but only after changing its name to Society for Culture, thus discouraging protests and demonstrations by anti-German elements. The new name did not soften Lamberty's heart. He resigned.

Emil was happy to learn that neither the Isaacs nor Schliemann held him personally responsible for the war. They had remained friendly, and the Isaacs invited him to a special dinner party to welcome Miss Didrikson, the concert pianist, back home. Her tour in Europe had been cut short because of the war. Emil was finally going to meet her.

On the Saturday preceding the event, Mrs. Isaacs became ill and had to cancel the dinner plans. However, they had made arrangements with Marcy for Emil to call at her apartment that evening.

"Riverside Drive," he repeated after Charles. His heartbeat quickened at the thought of calling on someone in the fashionable part of New York City. The idea ran hot and cold in his thoughts. One minute he was glorying in the opportunity, and the next he was castigating himself for considering it. As disturbing as it all was, he went.

Almost immediately, Marcy broke into German speech and Emil felt at ease at once. She was vivacious, talented, and desirable. Her dark brown hair lay in soft waves framing her oval face. Her deep brown eyes glowed with warmth and passion. Her slender body gave the impression of height beyond her five-foot-nine-inch frame which was an inch taller than Emil. Her firm handshake called Emil's attention to her strong forearms, an obvious result of years at the keyboard. He could readily see how her open personality and contented laughter must have endeared her to everyone who knew her.

"Your German is flawless," he told her. "How did you happen to study the language?"

"You're very kind, but I can't take much credit for that. I was born in Poland to Jewish parents but my early years were spent in Berlin."

"But you have no accent," he said, almost in protest. His own thick accent continued to make conversation difficult and always seemed to bring about ridicule, especially in the factory. "I shall always sound like a

German trying to speak English, and not doing a very good job of it." He laughed a little, but it didn't conceal the frustration and anger.

"Oh, but I love your accent. You don't want to lose that. It's absolutely charming." Her compassion and her sensitivity brought his mother to mind.

A rush of contentment flooded his body, insulating him from earlier misgivings. To his amazement he was at ease in the company of this gracious and sensitive woman.

"But how did you happen to—"

"How did I get to New York?" she interrupted. "My parents eventually settled here with me and my two sisters and brother."

All evening, it was the same, Marcy anticipating his questions as if she had always known him, Emil alight with excitement and totally immersed in her every word.

She had prepared a simple dinner for the two of them, and, after they dined, she played for him. At the piano she was radiant, living her music as if she had composed it, never showing signs of tiring.

Emil was entranced by the graceful movements of her slender body. Not since Katy had he felt a burning desire for a particular woman. It was a grand and exciting feeling, albeit a frightening one.

"Listen to this one, Emil. It's my favorite little piece. I hope you like it as much as I do."

He was certain of it, for he was smitten to embarrassment by everything she did and said. It was not possible to dislike something of her choice.

"It's *Capricio*. Brahms, you know," she said, smiling.

He knew nothing of the kind, but nodded his head unashamedly in agreement. He asked her to play it again and again until he was finally embarrassed by his boldness. She continued to play one piece after another, never showing signs of fatigue. It was satisfying and peaceful and enchanting, being an audience of one as if he were a prince or something. His thoughts wandered away from the music to admire her many attributes: charm, discipline, grace, and boundless energy. She was a woman with spirit. He liked her immensely.

Joining him on the sofa, she asked if she might see his work. "Helen and Charles are quite enthusiastic about it. And so is Mr. Schliemann.

He's my benefactor, you know. At least one of them. His daughter is a student of mine."

His spirit shriveled at the thought of showing his own creation after hearing her performance. "You mustn't expect to be entertained as you have entertained me," he warned. "I haven't reached the plateau you have."

"You're too modest, I'm sure. You've heard me at my best because I've been on tour, practicing every moment either alone or before small audiences. Now that I'm back home, I shall have to begin teaching again. Teaching has endless value to the concert artist, but it's time-consuming. I'm not complaining," she quickly added, "because I know I wouldn't be where I am today without my students. I can't tell you how many times I've solved a problem for myself while demonstrating for them."

In total awe, Emil hung on her every word, almost with the same zeal of Henri's lectures.

"Of course the biggest advantage in teaching is in having the students pose as my audience. Performing before an audience is my nemesis." The confession seemed to dampen her spirits. "You don't have to worry about that, do you?"

"Absolutely," he quickly admitted. "You've no idea. Even the instructor's critical eye devastates me. I've only one experience exhibiting my work. It was torturous," he assured her.

"Really? Well, we can conquer it," she said with confidence. "I practice, or exhibit my work, if you will, by inviting my own audiences here to the apartment. We have a lot of fun. Sometimes others in the group play, and sometimes two of us play together. Maybe you'll join us next time?"

She gave him no chance to object. Not that he wanted to, but he had hoped for a repeat of the same wonderful evening with just the cozy twosome. Joining the ranks of a roomful of Riverside Drive residents would put him through a rigorous test of fortitude. He wasn't at all certain he could handle it.

Seeing his hesitation, she added, "If you enjoy the society's programs, you should enjoy this. Forgive me. I didn't mean to brag. It's my guests you'll find stimulating. People from Russia, Austria, and Germany. Schliemann you've met already. Fascinating man, don't you think? Of course I hope Helen and Charles Isaacs will be here as well. Oh, and

Muller, an Austrian ambassador who escaped when the war broke out. You simply must meet Muller."

"No, I couldn't," he blurted. For the first time that evening, he was rigid. The idea was preposterous. It was different at the society where the group was so large no demands were made of the individual conversationally. But a private home with a small gathering was out of the question.

Stunned by his outburst, she nevertheless spoke calmly. "It was just a thought. You really would like them," she said, tactfully focusing on *Capricio* again. "Delightful people," she added, smiling that same gracious smile that seemed a part of her.

He hated himself. "If they're friends of yours, I'm certain I would like them." He tried to sound casual, but his uneasy smile betrayed him. "Please understand it's not your friends that worry me. I'm afraid they would find me a bore."

"Nonsense," she replied, dismissing the idea as just that. When their evening together ended, he gladly accepted her invitation to return the following Sunday.

The hours and the days dragged by slowly, reminding him of the torturous days in Schwabisch-Gmund when he and Karl had planned their first sketching trip to Lauterburg. When Sunday finally arrived, he spent the day painting at the school and found that he was quite fatigued when darkness set in. But thoughts of the previous Sunday with Marcy invigorated him.

When he arrived at the apartment, Marcy welcomed him in the same gracious manner that had entranced him the Sunday before. He was not, however, to enjoy the cozy twosome, as the parlor was filled with people, all strangers except for Schliemann.

"Please forgive me," she begged. "I was afraid you wouldn't come if I told you. They're only my students and a few friends. Come, I'll introduce you."

Reluctantly, he followed her, his movements stiff and unnatural. "But I'm afraid I'll offend your guests. All this turpentine odor and—"

"Oh, nonsense. It's just a casual gathering."

Laughter came from all areas, guests having spread throughout the sitting room in groups of two to four, chatting. Most of the women wore dropped-waist dresses or similar straight, unbound attire. It may have been casual, but there was no mistaking its quality. Marcy stood out from the rest in her soft pongee dress in luscious sea-green. The fitted waistline drew attention to her sensuous body. The trim on the contrasting hemline fell six or eight inches above her white chunky-heeled shoes, revealing slim ankles clothed in white hose that completed her delicate and alluring look.

Smiling nervously, Emil apologized to each new face about reeking of turpentine and oil. When Marcy began to play, he shuffled awkwardly toward an unoccupied corner, safely away from anyone who might wish to carry on a conversation with him.

Marcy played several selections, sometimes accompanied by other musicians, sometimes solo. When another pianist took her place, she playfully sought Emil out, peeking through this group and that, and finally spotting his hideout. "Come, come. Join me here," she motioned, pointing to an occupied armchair. Seating herself side-saddle on the chair's arm, she left space for Emil behind her. He followed her lead but not before checking facial expressions for disapproval. Seeing none, he perched himself on the arm, scarcely making contact with the chair, and with both feet planted firmly on the floor. He appeared ready for a quick departure.

"My students think you're quite handsome. You should hear their comments," Marcy whispered. A sharp, convulsive smile was his only outward reaction. Marcy couldn't have known of the pervading spirit lurking within him, a spirit that yearned to fit in with these talented intellectuals.

"You're not serious?"

"Cross my heart," she teased. She squeezed his hand gently.

He could only laugh a bit, a nervous, unknowing chortle. Katy had done a great deal to erase the image he held of himself, but since Katy, there had been no one to reinforce, or to deny, her idealistic notions. He tended, on this occasion, to cling to his original idea of himself, that of rather a dull figure.

In truth, the shock of dark brown hair, already tinted with white strands here and there, instead of maturing him, gave him a youthful countenance, as if he were still a playful boy emerging from a light snowfall. His bright blue eyes begged for tolerance, if not acceptance. The strong jaw suggested strength of character, the full sensuous mouth, passion. His sun-browned skin gave him a healthy glow and contrasted favorably with the light sprinkling of white hair. All in all, he was a winsome man, as much for his humility as his appearance, for his shyness was well received by the opposite sex.

"You're not angry with me?" It was more of a plea than a question.

"No, of course not," he assured her. "It's very nice just as you promised. And you were right. I wouldn't have come if I had known. I'm glad you didn't tell me." Somewhat comforted by the lack of attention from others in the room, he smiled, almost without effort. He did worry that the situation might change at any moment, and he wondered what might be expected of him when it did.

"We won't have them every time," she promised, squeezing his hand again. "Oh, here's Muller," she said, rising to greet a short, stocky man. "Come, let me introduce you."

"No, please. Just let me sit here for now," he begged. He couldn't help noticing Muller's attire as he was meticulously dressed in a Norfolk style jacket, a loose-fitted coat with waistband and vertical sewn-in pleats. His cuffed pants touched the top of his matching spats. Except for Emil, he was the only man in the room who wore a tie.

The similarity of the two ended there. Protecting his coat at school had been easy for Emil as he hung it on a rack, but efforts to keep his white shirt clean with an apron always failed. Several unconscious swipes of his hands across his pants' legs didn't do a lot to enhance his appearance either. Only his tie and the detachable collar remained clean as he had kept them wrapped in a cloth until time to head for Marcy's.

Everyone moved about, laughing, talking, and drinking. Everyone except Emil. He clung to the edge of the chair-arm, wondering if he should return to his isolated corner. He cowered noticeably when one of Marcy's students approached him. She was a German girl whose name was Anny. Though fluent in English, Emil still found a certain security in the use of his native tongue, especially among intellectuals.

Anny dived right into the subject of socialism, apparently convinced she would find a willing listener, if not an advocate. Muller joined them, seemingly for the purpose of discounting her idealistic philosophy. His peppered hair was as carefully groomed as were his clothes. While most of the guests towered over him in stature, his presence commanded a certain aura of respect, or so it seemed to Emil.

He argued with Anny. Emil listened. The conversation continued in German but that alone was not sufficient for luring him into their net. The truth was, he had never given the topic a single thought. Anny, on the other hand, if not experienced, was well-read on the subject of socialism, rolling the theories off her tongue with voluminous detail.

"You're obsessed," declared Muller. "Mere theory, my child. Mere theory." The bridge of his nose, though narrow, led to a bulbous end, a fate that might have been disconcerting except that it epitomized his stocky, thick-set body.

"You're a capitalist," she accused, though she didn't appear angry.

Just then, a thin man they introduced as Adolf Weins stepped in. Emil remembered him as the bassoonist Marcy had accompanied earlier in the evening. He too, spoke German. Emil wondered if there was anything these people hadn't done, or couldn't do if they wanted to. He particularly remembered Adolf, who had moved from bassoon to violin to piano during the course of the evening. "We're all capitalists, my dear," declared Adolf. "You're looking at a proud one." In marked contrast to Muller, Adolf was thin and willowy, a towering young man well over six feet in height.

"Ah, but Marcy is playing," Muller noticed, shushing them.

"To have a teacher like Marcy," he remarked, directing the comment to Emil. "I'm afraid my students didn't have it so good." Muller seemed more interested in changing the subject than halting conversation.

"You're a music teacher then?" Emil asked.

Everyone in hearing distance laughed, including Muller. Emil's face was crimson, though nobody seemed to notice.

"Only a bit of tutoring," Muller laughed. "My student dreaded the sight of me. Hated discipline. You know the type. Spoiled rich kid." He paused, but Adolf urged him to continue.

"Well, I had always gone to the front door of this boy's house, but one day nobody answered my knock. I walked around to the back and I heard the boy praying. I looked in, and there he was on his knees, praying to God not to let Muller come that day." Most of the guests were already laughing, including Marcy who had rested her hands on the piano.

"With fervor he never showed in anything, no matter the subject we studied," Muller continued, "he implored God to grant him this one favor, in return for which he would be a very good boy, of course. I stood for a while and finally decided to return home without giving him his lessons.

"The next day he asked why I hadn't come the previous day. With all the sincerity I could manage I told him something from above, some power greater than anything I had ever encountered, had taken hold of me on my way to his house and wouldn't let me come."

Everyone roared, including Emil.

"Did you ever tell him the truth?" someone asked.

"Oh, no. I think that little devil prayed every day from then on that Muller might not be allowed to come. And he was so certain of the success of his prayers that he was totally unprepared in his assignments as well as shocked at my arrival each morning."

Though not the story Emil expected from an Austrian ambassador recently escaped from the war zone, his story-telling prowess captured the attention of everyone in the room. When the laughter died, Marcy claimed the small audience as hers with her sparkling and subtle fingerwork in Debussy's *Afternoon of a Faun*. With incredible accuracy and finesse, she held her guests spellbound until the last note was played. She was then mobbed with praise by her benefactors and students alike.

Emil applauded vigorously but remained silent, still awed by it all. What an education he was getting, one that Henri declared a necessity for the maturity of any artist. He wished he might listen without being listened to.

What was he doing there, he wondered. The haunting question had surfaced all through the evening, and the answer frightened him immensely. It seemed impossible even to him but the truth was, he had fallen in love.

Marcy and Emil saw each other every Sunday evening after that, sometimes with friends but more and more often, just the two of them. Saying goodbye each Sunday became painful for both of them, with neither willing to let go. He began to stay longer and longer.

With less than two hours' sleep, Monday mornings would have been morbid except for the memories of the previous evenings spent with this passionate and charming woman. The hours that once had dragged on Sunday evenings seemed to disappear before they had begun.

There had never been anyone in his life who appreciated the finer things as Marcy did. He envied her lifestyle, so much akin to his own idea of how things should be, filled as it was with creativity. Her world appeared to him a dream world with make-believe characters.

And yet, Marcy was genuine. She returned his love with great passion and desire. He often thought how wonderful marriage to her might be, but he hadn't the courage to propose. *Why would a woman like her marry a coxcomb*? he asked himself repeatedly.

One Sunday evening, Marcy asked if there were any way they could see each other more often. "Maybe after class?"

If she only knew what little time he had between class hours and factory hours as it was. On many occasions, he left her apartment too late to catch the last train and was forced to spend the night at the Turkish bath. It meant rising even earlier the next morning to catch the train back to the Newark factory and grab a bite somewhere along the street.

"I could meet you at the studio," she suggested.

Nothing short of giving up his art studies would prevent him from being with Marcy. The idea appealed to him.

Almost nightly, Marcy began to appear in the classroom doorway, sometimes early enough to visit, but more often at closing time. And every Sunday she prepared dinner for the two of them just as she had the night they met. The maid, he learned, usually did the cooking, but Marcy always gave her Sundays off so she and Emil could be alone. He remained a captivated audience of one, delighted beyond belief that he had been singled out. She always began the evening by playing *Capricio*, his favorite piece. One evening he joined her on the piano bench, his back to the keyboard.

"Forgive me for interrupting, my darling. I just had to hold you," he said. They embraced for several minutes, both vowing their love. It was a scene they had been through countless times, and yet, each time was more special than the last. They each felt it.

"Dear God, I hate to leave you," he whispered.

"Then why not change things?" she asked.

"You mean?"

"Yes, darling. Why not?" she whispered. Both left "marriage" out of their conversation, though it was foremost in both their minds.

"Darling, if you only knew how much I've wanted it."

"Then why didn't you say so?" she scolded.

"Fear of rejection," he admitted. "It's more than that, my darling. I have so little to offer you."

"Nonsense. You have everything to offer. Don't we love each other? And we both love the artistic things. I think we would make a great couple."

"I'm afraid you don't understand. In my work, I'm associated with boring, unrefined people. I'm just a..."

"I won't listen to such talk," she interrupted. "You're a sensitive and gracious and talented man. And never boring," she added warmly.

The remark startled him. This passionate and desirable woman, so sensitive and talented herself, was much more than that. She was a woman with deep understanding.

"Darling, you amaze me," he said passionately. "But I—you see, well, my salary is—"

"Please, Emil," she interrupted. "I don't want to marry you for your money."

"But it'll never change," he warned her. "If I were willing to give up my art, I could work up to a managerial position in the factory, but art is my life."

"And that's how it should be, dear. I'm pleased with your work. So modern. I'm certain you can sell it some day, and then you won't have to work in the factory."

The comment changed his mood without warning. "Don't count on it. Why do you think Henri teaches for a living? He told us many times not to expect to make a living with our work. Most of us can't even finance an exhibition. No, I'll always be a factory worker, believe me."

Marcy was shaken by the outburst, but quickly decided it was prompted by insecurity. "You're only twenty-seven. Given a chance, you can make a name for yourself before you're thirty. You'll love painting at my cottage in New Hampshire. Isolated and excluded, just the thing for an artist." Her dark eyes glistened. Her face was illuminated by their splendor. He wondered anew how this fairy tale could be happening to him.

She refused to listen to further arguments, though he had a string of them. They were married on Christmas Eve at the city hall in New York City. It was a simple ceremony, with Helen and Charles Isaacs as their only attendants.

Mr. and Mrs. Emil Holzhauer returned to the elegant Riverside apartment where Marcy's students surprised them with a decorated Christmas tree. It was Emil's first.

Only one thing marred Emil's happiness. Living in New York City posed a problem for a man whose work days were already long and tedious. It meant spending a great deal of time commuting to the Newark factory. But the wonderful new life he shared with Marcy made it worthwhile.

Many of her colleagues from the New York Institute of Music were regular visitors in their apartment. Emil listened closely to their discussions and the execution of the music in an effort to distinguish between the subtle differences in tone and technique, but success was painfully slow in coming. Marcy continued her custom of Open House every Sunday evening. The conversation and entertainment were not only stimulating, but also the gathering of knowledgeable people, some of international recognition, gave Marcy a chance to practice before an audience. Several evenings a week, she and Emil attended concerts and recitals or Open Houses in other musicians' homes, often including that of her sister, whose husband was a well-known conductor. Emil's new wife was always prevailed upon to play at the gatherings, and she gladly obliged.

There was no getting out of updating his puny wardrobe with an extra white shirt, silk ties, and a traditional black cutaway coat of cheviot, which he wore with matching trousers, a white vest, a silk foulard tie and spats. It pained him to spend the money, but he couldn't embarrass Marcy.

There remained a problem for which he had no solution. With all the activities and entertainment, there was precious little time to paint.

When summer came, Marcy urged him to quit his job and concentrate entirely on painting. "You simply must give yourself this chance. All those hours at the engraving desk take their toll on your concentration. Probably ruining your eyesight, too." He didn't like the idea. It would mean depleting his savings to pay his half of their living expenses. With all the entertaining they were obliged to do, it wouldn't last long.

It had been a topic of conversation from the beginning of their marriage. His emotions ran hot and cold, believing it possible one moment, and knowing it wasn't the next. Finally, he exploded. "You know nothing about painting. You and your fine friends and your lavish apartment! It's all a waste of money."

Marcy was stunned by the outburst, but she wouldn't give up. "With your talent, you won't need another job. Your paintings will sell once you give yourself a chance. Everyone says so."

He loved Marcy for reinforcing his own high hopes but he hated her for believing in something totally unrealistic. "Even Henri has to teach for a living," he reminded her again. He forced a smile in spite of the fact that his upper lip still trembled with anger. Inwardly, he was ashamed for lashing out at her.

Marcy sensed his shame. "Nonsense. Given time to paint, you'll see I'm right. You have the touch, but you need time to develop it. Your work will sell. I'm certain of it. My friends can get publicity for you."

Reluctantly, he gave notice at the Newark factory. In an effort to appease the factory manager, he recommended Felix as his replacement.

In her quest to boost Emil's art career, Marcy proposed a trip to Monhegan Island. Life with this selfless, and loving woman had been fulfilling beyond anything he had imagined life could be. As busy as she was with her own career and her constant drive to conquer stage fright, her devotion to him and his career never wavered. Faced with grueling practice sessions and nagged by constant fear of failure, she brushed her own priorities aside in favor of his.

Neither of them wanted to part, but they agreed that shipping her piano to Monhegan would be too extravagant. They said a sad, but sober, farewell.

The primitive island off the coast of Maine could only be reached by ferry. The quaint village's narrow winding road was used by only one or two service vehicles. Emil quickly took in the terrain, with its combination of rocky coast and sweeping cliffs, surrounded by the sea; with its variety of calm waters tinged with light blue, or dark when a northeasterly wind blew; and by crashing waves spilling over the soaring cliffs of granite.

The spectacle of Maine fishermen with their nets and their catch quickly caught his attention. He watched them lounge in their shacks, passing time in a card game. He needed little encouragement to capture their faces, their easy, unassuming manner, pride in their catch, and indolent approach to life. Gradually, he added names to the faces. Frank, Stanley, and Mandel he painted most often, arriving at their shacks occasionally with a bottle of applejack as an incentive for them to pose for him.

Their shacks were marvels in themselves with crab traps hanging from the open rafters, half-barrels filled to capacity in chaotic fashion, buckets, nets, and raingear scattered here and there, and whole barrels stacked against the walls of the tiny structures. There was scarcely space enough for the artist, much less his canvas.

Emil was possessed. Not since Schwabisch-Gmund had he seen such natural beauty. Romantic pathways led him through thick forests of spruce and fir to the rocky cliffs along the two-mile stretch of island glory.

He quickly secured a room on the ground floor of the local inn for twelve dollars a week, which included two meals a day, much more than he usually found time to partake in, and was off at sunrise to choose from the endless array of subject matter. He raced around the island as if time were running out.

Gradually he became known as “the artist”. Even though other artists roomed at the inn and trekked the island, brush in hand, there was a noticeable difference. While others took long breaks or even a whole day lounging around, especially during inclement weather, Emil painted. The worst days saw him painting still life, or other willing subjects, inside his primitive abode or capturing an outdoor scene from his tiny window.

One such day, Raymond Scheffield, another artist from New York City, knocked on his door. The two had exchanged greetings in the dining room, but nothing beyond that.

“It’s no wonder everyone here calls you the artist. You never put your brush down,” Scheffield joked. “Excuse me for interrupting. It’s such a dismal day, I was hoping you'd consent to pose for me, but I see you're busy." He remained in the doorway, Emil still clutching a brush in one hand, the doorknob in the other.

"Why not pose for each other?" Emil questioned. The idea had suddenly presented itself and he gave it breath without thinking. "I paint you painting me?" He laughed at himself, suddenly viewing the notion as silly.

Scheffield was intrigued by the idea. "Be right with you," he announced, then stopped abruptly. "Or maybe you'd like to join me in my room? It's quite large and it has a big floor to ceiling window."

It was agreed. Side by side they painted, each using the other as subject matter. When evening came, they shared background stories over a beer and then supped together. According to Scheffied, his studio apartment in New York overlooked the Brooklyn Bridge.

"That must be wonderful. It's so time-consuming," Emil complained, "getting permission to climb on someone's roof or even to paint on the bridge walkway."

"Ah, you have an open invitation to paint it right from my apartment window," Scheffield told him. "Any time." To show his sincerity, he pulled out a pad and pencil and wrote down the address.

Emil could scarcely wait to write Marcy of this new friendship. With his work schedule and painting excursions, there was never an opportunity to make friends on his own. He met the next day with anxious and inquiring eyes, stopping to answer the call of an abandoned boat that had been cast haphazardly along the island shore. He had become quite rooted to the spot when he heard a familiar voice calling to him.

"Marcy?" he questioned. Glancing toward the narrow pathway that led the islanders through a cathedral forest, he caught sight of her.

A faint cry emanated from his throat. For a moment, he mistrusted his eyes, thinking perhaps it was an apparition, a deep longing within him having created it. When she called to him again, he cast doubt aside and broke into a joyous grin.

"Marcy! How did you manage this? Why didn't you tell me?" He piled question upon question even before she was in hearing distance. They smothered each other with passionate kisses and a warm and lengthy embrace.

"Darling, you should have told me you were—"

"And spoil my surprise?" she interrupted. It was a glorious moment for both of them, but it was only a moment. Marcy's smile faded. "I'm afraid I lack your discipline, my darling. I just had to come."

He tingled with delight as he gazed intently into her warm inviting eyes.

"I'm sorry. I didn't want to disturb your work for one second. And here I am doing just that," she said. "It was your letters. They were wonderful. You were writing poetry without even knowing it. I knew something new and wonderful was happening to you and I just had to be with you. I know it was foolish of me." She searched his eyes for signs of forgiveness, and hopefully, understanding.

He squeezed her hand affectionately, and offered his own apology for smudging her clothes, then assured her she had done the right thing in coming. He paled, however, when he remembered her concert.

"But darling, you won't be able to practice. I don't want you to give that up for me. We'll stay another week here and then go home."

Marcy shook her head. "No we won't. This is God's Island and you're doing grandly on it. I won't let you leave so soon," she declared. "I'll send for my piano and we can spend the rest of the summer here." Again, they embraced, solidifying their love as well as determination.

If it was a dream, he wished never to be wakened. And yet, there were so many things to be considered. There was the primitive lodging and the absence of an audience for Marcy's practice. She needed that above all else. She quickly discounted all his concerns.

"Don't worry," she assured him. "If you can live there, I can. And I have recently spoken with Schliemann. He and Muller are coming to the island soon. They'll make a fine audience."

As it turned out, almost everyone on the island became her audience. Sometimes Emil remained close enough to the cabin to hear her practice, but mostly he went beyond the village to paint, all day, every day, never tiring and never ready for the setting sun. He was inspired as never before. His paintings began to show it.

Marcy seemed equally inspired. Emil was astonished by her fortitude, her unfailing energy, her dogged determination to be the very best and to overcome her stage fright. Large crowds gathered outside the cabin to listen to her music, and soon she was prevailed upon to give a benefit concert for the Polish Relief Fund. Word of the show traveled fast. "The artist's wife is a concert pianist," the islanders advertised.

When the big night arrived, crowds quickly filled the inn to capacity. Others filled the empty boats, perched on lobster traps, or sat on the ground. Marcy performed with ease for the informal audience. She needed little persuasion to repeat the performance the next Sunday, and the next.

Muller was one of her most ardent admirers. He spent much of his time in the tea room, from the veranda of which he could enjoy Marcy's music and view the Monhegan Harbor at the same time. Schliemann and Raymond Scheffield were also captivated by her performances, but Schliemann seemed to have endless business to take care of, and Scheffield spent most of his time painting. Muller was unique among the island guests in that he seemed to have no occupation, or even a hobby. Emil had long since learned that Muller's story about giving piano lessons had been just that—a story.

Emil wondered who supported him. He mentioned it to Scheffield who was often seen chatting with Muller, but Scheffield dismissed it with a shrug of his shoulders. He questioned Marcy, but she had no notion of any occupation.

"But how does he exist?" Emil asked.

"Darling, the man obviously has an income from somewhere," she answered. It hardly satisfied Emil's curiosity. Muller remained an enigma. He was like an intricate wiring system furnishing power to everything in need of it as he obtained visas and passports for those who couldn't obtain them, found odd jobs for the unemployed and untrained, executive positions for the trained, and acted as marriage counselor and more. He never seemed to collect anything for his work. Emil ached to know his secret of survival without punching a clock. He was convinced it was a good stock investment through their mutual friend, Schliemann. As long as Emil had known the stockbroker, he had never drummed up the courage to ask for his assistance in investing. The problem was his new lifestyle called for depleting his savings rather than adding to it. He wouldn't give Schliemann a chance to laugh at the small pittance he had in the bank

As always, Marcy commanded attention wherever she went, but on Monhegan Island, Emil was king. He was still known as "the artist," not the "pianist's husband" as in New York City, and Marcy took a back seat as the "artist's wife". Teasingly, Muller introduced her as such to Eugene Merks, the well-known New York banker, and Mrs. Merks, an art patron and dealer. Emil cringed with embarrassment until he learned the Merks were already acquainted with Marcy and her background in music.

In the presence of Mrs. Merks, Muller admonished him not to be embarrassed. "You deserve the praise the islanders are giving you. And I should think Mrs. Merks would want to hang some of your paintings." It was a bold hint only Muller would have made.

Mrs. Merks appeared startled by the remark. She spoke coldly of the many exhibits they had scheduled, pointedly mentioning well known artists who would be featured, all without making eye contact with either gentleman. They had been snubbed.

As soon as they were alone, Muller apologized to Emil. "Don't be discouraged. She has someone else running the salons. Messiahs, all of them. They still cater to the sophisticated things—you know, all that sugary prettiness." His voice rose gradually as he spoke, revealing a growing irritation as the snobbery began to sink in. "I thought she might be smart enough to see the error in that or I wouldn't have mentioned it. But come, I want you to meet my friend, Huffstetler. He's an art dealer, and I know he'll show your work."

"No, please," Emil begged. "Don't do it. I—." He turned to Schliemann for assistance, but received none.

"I insist. Don't worry. I can assure you he'll be glad to."

Sure enough, Huffstetler promised to give Emil an exhibition as soon as he returned to New York. The idea of showing his work in a Fifth Avenue gallery frightened him. Certain he couldn't go through with it, he had begun a mild argument with Muller on the subject when suddenly, a stranger appeared on the scene and thrust a business card in their direction.

"I'm an intelligence agent," he explained rather arrogantly as he flashed his credentials in Muller's face. He then directed all four of them to follow him into a private room for questioning. "What does this mean?" Emil asked. He searched Muller's face, then turned to Schliemann, and finally Marcy, for signs of comfort. Their own shocked expressions offered no comfort.

"We have had some complaints on the island about you people," the man began.

"Complaints?" asked Muller. "About us?" Creases formed in his wide forehead as his eyes pierced those of the intruder. He appeared startled, but not intimidated.

"Of course," responded the officer, quite matter-of-factly. "Seems you have been plotting your course on the rocks at night. I'll have to take you in."

"Take us in? Where?" asked Emil.

"Oh, I see," said Muller. "Spying, no doubt?"

"You admit it, then?" asked the officer.

Emil eyed Muller in astonishment. He opened his mouth, but Marcy stopped him with a quick elbow in his side.

"We have been observing you in your secret meetings at night. Always conducted in German, of course." At the request of some of the residents, the agent had been called to the island to investigate a German spy group which was deemed to be planning a submarine base there. The intelligence officer seemed quite certain of his catch.

"My friend, don't embarrass yourself by arresting a few innocent people who have been singing on the rocks at night in open view of everyone," said Muller, quite irritated. "Surely, you've heard of Miss Didrikson, the concert pianist? And this is her husband, an artist, who came to paint the beauty of the island. And Mr. Schliemann, a well-known stock broker from New York." Muller was curt and testy with the officer who seemed convinced, as well as intimidated.

He let them go, but issued a subdued warning that he might have to return for more questioning.

"He would have taken us in if not for you," Emil told Muller. He was ashen-faced, a trick indeed for a deep-tanned face like Emil's.

"You may as well get used to it as long as the war lasts," Muller warned.

Emil was suddenly grateful that it had happened at the end of the summer, rather than the beginning. It was time to say goodbye to their beautiful summer home and return to the city.

Just as he promised, Huffstetler called on them soon after they returned to New York. He liked Emil's work, and he chose fifteen paintings for exhibition, even promising to frame them himself. "All you need to do is come in the gallery as often as you can. Having the artist in the studio is always helpful in selling the work." Grinning, he added, "Even if he is a German spy."

The remark irritated Emil, who kept a sober countenance. The story of their "arrest" had made its rounds on the island. "We were only singing German songs," he protested sharply.

"Emil," Marcy scolded. "He was only joking."

"You Americans," he fumed. "The officer didn't even apologize after he realized we were only singing. And his tone, so insinuating. How can you people laugh it off so easily?"

"Oh, never mind that now," Marcy implored. "This is a happy occasion."

When Huffstetler left with the paintings, Marcy squealed with delight.

Unable to put Huffstetler's comment aside, Emil continued to rave against the man, even reprimanding Marcy for minimizing it.

She refused to be drawn into an argument. "Didn't I tell you?" she bragged. "All you needed was a chance to concentrate on your work. It'll sell too. I just know it," she glowed. She raced to the piano and played *Capricio*. As always, it reminded Emil of the night he met her. With her own exhibition drawing near, she had continued to give freely of her time in helping him reach his goals.

The next morning, Emil stood outside the Fifth Avenue gallery where some of his Monhegan Island scenes made up the window display. When the art dealer motioned him inside, he opened the door, but found himself quite rooted at the entrance. "Please," he moaned, "take it down." Huffstetler stared at him in disbelief.

Emil wanted to grab the paintings and run away with them before anyone else had a chance to laugh. Instead, he burst through the door and made his way quickly into the oblivion of the crowd on the street. For Marcy's sake, he returned to the gallery time and again, attempting to make an appearance as Huffstetler had requested, to mingle with the prospective customers, but the result was always the same. He was appalled by his own work, and was unable, and unwilling, to admit to anyone it was his.

When Huffstetler called at their apartment, he was clearly annoyed. "What's the matter with you? Don't you like the framing? The display?"

"No, please, it isn't that at all. It's my work. I should never have allowed you to show it." His voice sank as he spoke, clearly signifying the depths of despair he found himself feeling.

"My god, man, if you don't have confidence in your own work, how do you expect to ever sell it? If you would only come in and mingle with the customers." He was clearly agitated.

Marcy was as irritated as the art dealer. "You may never have another chance like this," she said. "Don't spoil it. A sale to the right person could mean a real beginning but the customers want to see and talk to the artist, especially if he's unknown."

Emil bristled with anger. He felt like a small boy, unjustly accused of wrongdoing.

"Don't you people understand?" he fired. "It's awful work. I don't want anybody to buy it. I don't even want them to see it." He marched determinedly toward his studio and slammed the door in their faces.

Marcy's own temper was at its peak. As soon as the art dealer left, she stood at the locked studio door and answered with her own eruption. "I'm afraid we've no time for childish tantrums, Emil. Perhaps I should go to the art gallery and make excuses for your absence." It was the first time Marcy had deliberately insulted his intelligence. It wouldn't go unnoticed.

Emil remained secluded in his studio day and night, never seeing her except at meal time when he addressed his only words to the maid. As for Marcy, he gave her a silent treatment even his father would have been proud of.

For weeks, silence prevailed in the apartment. When Marcy could endure it no longer, she opened the studio door a tad and left it slightly ajar. "Listen, darling. It's our tune," she called. "I shall play it just for you." Sounds of Brahms' *Capricio* drifted through the apartment, but the only other sound came from the slamming of the studio door. Night after night, she tried again, always with the same results. It was weeks later that he allowed the door to remain open.

"Are you listening, darling?" Marcy called cheerfully. Finally, he emerged, but it was days before things returned to normal.

When the month of exhibiting ended, Huffstetler returned all fifteen paintings. "Not one sale, of course," he said, casting an irritated glance in Emil's direction. "If you had only made an appearance."

Emil felt Marcy's animosity even though she remained silent.

When Huffstetler left, he lashed out at her. "You have only yourself to blame for your disappointment. I tried to warn you."

The whole ordeal wrecked the romantic atmosphere they had once enjoyed in the apartment. The gloom was monumental, and the change took its toll on both of them emotionally, often ruining Marcy's practice sessions and Emil's artistic efforts. One day he caught Marcy studying the paintings that had been on exhibit at Huffstetler's.

"Still harboring thoughts of selling those drab things?" he grumbled. "I tried to warn you. Why do you think Henri teaches? I'll tell you why. Because he can't make a living selling his work. And I'll tell you something else. That's why I learned a trade. I'm going back to work," he announced angrily.

Ignoring his ugly demeanor, Marcy sat down to the piano. But he was in no mood for her whimsical little Brahms. To his surprise, she played a different classic. "Listen, Emil It's Ravel's *La Mer*. Listen to the dawning of the day and you'll hear color. Yes, color!" She had his attention, though he wouldn't admit it.

"To color music, you have to blend it together instead of pounding out the separate chords." She played *From Dawn to Noon on the Sea*, the first movement of La Mer.

"Painting should be melodious just as music has color," she added. "They're one and the same." She played the piece in its entirety even though he marched out of the room and into his studio. When she finished the piece, he stuck his head in the doorway and complimented her on her musical talent, then added an icy comment. "Don't tell me how to paint and I won't tell you how to play the piano." He couldn't have seen the anguish in her usually warm and animated eyes.

She responded with disciplined voice. "I meant no harm, darling. I was only trying to point out the need for harmony and balance in your work." Rather than send him into another silent spell, she put Debussy aside and played their little Brahms' piece.

When he finally relented, he was exhausted, his eyelids drooping heavily over strained eyes. "Please try to understand. I have to go back to work," he said weakly.

"Give yourself time for painting, darling," she pleaded affectionately. "Get a part-time job?" He agreed, reluctantly.

The short work-week was of little use during New York's short and bitter winter days. There were times when Emil defied the elements, but he often suffered frostbite to his fingers and toes, making progress virtually impossible. As days began to lengthen and temperatures rose a bit, he searched for new territory, and discovered bountiful subject matter along the Hudson. With four days a week away from the factory, he sketched along the Palisades, and roamed into other communities and villages along the Hudson.

For the summer, he found nice, though primitive, lodging in a farmhouse in Fort Montgomery. It was to be a repeat of their summer on Monhegan Island, except that he would have to commute three days a week to and from the factory. He explored the majestic Hudson River from West Point to Haverstone.

Meanwhile, Marcy had become interested in Christian Science. It was supposed to assist her in curing her stage fright. In further preparation for her next concert, she had her piano delivered to the Fort Montgomery bungalow. She was well aware of her position, as they both were. One more failure at the concert hall would probably end her career.

At the end of the summer, they returned to the city well pleased with their accomplishments. Timidly, Emil peddled his work from gallery to gallery, almost giving up at times, but finally persuading the Braun and Cie gallery to accept the challenge of showing his work. Somewhat more confident, he assisted Mr. Kelly, the art dealer, in the framing and arranging of the show. Taking part in the display seemed to reinforce his confidence.

When he arrived the following evening for the show's opening, the whole exhibit took on a new look. Staring him in the face was a wall of atrocities. He begged Kelly to take it all down before anyone could see it. "Please. You're making a fool of yourself by hanging it."

"What's wrong with you?" Kelly asked. "First you beg me to show it, and now you beg me not to. Take it down, indeed! A newspaper man has already been in. The gallery's getting publicity. You have no right—"

"I have every right," Emil insisted, but stalked out the door without further comment. He cursed himself endlessly on the way home, thinking what a fool he had been for allowing the work to be viewed by the public. As for the newspaperman, he wondered what he would say, then quickly decided he didn't want to know.

The mood of the evening was a somber one, Emil dejected and irritated, Marcy pensive. Conversation was impossible, as it led inevitably to heated arguments. They retired in silence. Emil spent the night in sleepless anguish.

When morning came, he ignored Marcy's warm greeting and directed his only comments to the maid. He missed the animation in Marcy's face, the sparkle in her eyes, the spirit that burned to be released. When she began reading aloud from the art pages of the *New York Sun*, he left the breakfast table in a huff.

"It has taken a foreigner to show us the beauty of our own country. Emil Holzhauer, a young German artist, has captured the beauty of the Hudson," she read. Her voice trembled with excitement.

Emil peered over her shoulder in an effort to verify her words, then thought better of it. Marcy continued. "Mr. Holzhauer doesn't discriminate between the majestic and the homely. He sees beauty in all of it, whether it's the awesome orange cliffs or the Dyckman Street ferry landing many consider an eyesore."

Marcy's excitement for his accomplishments made him ashamed of his behavior. He often felt remorse for the pain he caused her, but found it difficult to admit or express. His tantrums and ensuing silent treatments always left him drained. While he harbored anger, she quickly brushed it aside.

Seeing her caught up in the moment, he felt his heart soften. "How much more?" he asked, managing with some finesse to catch a glimpse of his name in print. Inching his way closer and closer to her, he finally took the paper out of her hands.

A second article covered the exhibit later in the week. The writer praised him for his ability to express the quality of his subject without false appeal. He had rhythmically incorporated the Hudson with the dignity and force of the Palisades, something other artists had been unable to do.

The reviews gave Emil the courage to make an appearance at the gallery, but he still agonized at the sight of his work. "It's all so dark and drab," he complained. "Been that way since Monhegan. I don't know what it is. Probably this damn war," he told the gallery owner.

Smiling, Mr. Kelly waved his concerns aside. "You shouldn't complain. Two of your paintings have sold," he announced proudly.

The news was good, and yet, it was bad. The work was so appalling, he disliked knowing it would hang on anyone's wall. Given the opportunity, he would have refunded their money even though it was sufficient to cover the expenses of the exhibit, a milestone in itself. As confused as he was, he felt some pride in taking the news home to Marcy.

Plans to delay the news, nonchalantly mentioning it later in the evening, dissipated the moment he walked into the apartment. "I have some good news, my darling." He smiled that winsome smile of his, a coquettish thing that always set the stage for good humor between them.

"I can't wait to hear it." She seemed exhilarated, as if she already knew. "I have some news myself, but you first."

"Two of my paintings sold."

"Oh, Emil!" she cried. She threw her arms around him and begged to hear everything. "Which ones? Who bought them? What did they sell for?" She took it all in, totally forgetting she had news of her own.

"But what about you? What's the news?" he asked.

"Oh, you have a letter," she said. She smiled warmly, anxiously he thought, as she handed him the letter.

"An art dealer?" he asked hopefully. "Karl? Postmarked New York City? Well, well, the devil didn't get caught in Germany after all. But how did he get my address?" His attempt to sound irritated failed miserably. Marcy saw the eyes, filled with longing.

"Well, I don't know, but why not open it? I'm anxious to know what he has to say." She had heard the stories of how Karl played havoc with Emil's emotions, but she had always sensed that her husband still held a special place in his heart for his old Schwabisch-Gmund friend. The letter bore a short message: "I must see you to discuss an important matter. Please answer."

Emil laughed. "Broke again no doubt," he grumbled, tossing the letter aside. "I won't give him a chance to bring strife into my life again." His voice was a mixture of anger and excitement.

"Maybe he's changed," Marcy offered.

Emil laughed mockingly. "Not a chance. How many times have I thought the same thing?" he asked as he retrieved the letter from a nightstand and fingered it thoughtfully.

"You won't have to become involved just because you see him. It's different now, because you're on your way in art. Perhaps you could help Karl get started. And I would like to meet him after all I've heard about him," she pleaded softly.

Marcy made it easy for him. The truth was, he couldn't resist answering the note. He invited Karl to call at their apartment, but only after a solemn promise to himself not to be taken in again.

Karl was noticeably thinner and his sallow skin seemed to be pulling away from his impoverished face. Emil fought an urge to embrace him, and he was certain Karl expected it as well. When he extended his hand in a formal greeting, he noted that Karl's once long tapered fingers were bent and ugly. Karl quickly withdrew his hand and shoved it in his pocket. In a cold gesture, Emil moved aside to accommodate Karl's entry into the apartment without their coming in contact. It was a welcome he might have extended a stranger.

Marcy was shocked by the formal greeting and the strained conversation that followed. "Well, if you two aren't silly," she finally injected, "talking of nothing when you're such good friends." She was ignored. In an effort to ease the tension, she settled at the piano and began to play softly.

Karl was obviously impressed by everything he saw, registering surprise when the maid brought them refreshments. Emil watched in amusement as Marcy's music painted still another picture of wealth and accomplishments. His eyes wandered over the paintings that filled the walls throughout the apartment as far as he could see. Emil knew he was misinterpreting the whole scene, imagining that they were wealthy, but he decided against telling him it took most of their earnings to keep the lavish apartment which was essential to Marcy's career. He rather enjoyed watching Karl squirm with envy.

"Aren't you going to show Karl your studio?" asked Marcy.

"Don't know if he wants to see it."

"Oh, yes," Karl hastily assured him.

In the spacious studio, Karl seemed astonished by the paintings that filled the wall space and lay in stacks throughout the room. "You've really been working. When do you have the time? Don't you still work in the factory?"

"Yes, but only three days a week."

Karl's eyes canvassed the room, studying the paintings and admiring the view from the large picture window. "I've seen notices about you in various papers. I guess you're really on your way now." His tone was a mixture of admiration, disbelief, and envy.

"It's only a small beginning, I can assure you. I was lucky enough to have someone praise my exhibited work. How about you? Painting?" He knew better than to ask but he couldn't resist.

"No." Karl squirmed uncomfortably, but offered nothing further.

Emil didn't push. Instead, he picked up a stack of paintings and filed through them. "These are some of my latest, but I'm not too pleased with them. My canvases always turn out somber. I think the war has affected my work. It's an awful slaughter."

"Yes," Karl agreed. "I was in Germany when the war broke out. I thought I was trapped, especially since I was not an American citizen. You should have seen me rushing to get out of there."

For the first time since his arrival, they both laughed heartily. When the laughter died, so did the conversation. Emil was suddenly reminded of his mother's plight. Karl had known of it, but had made no effort to assist her in getting to America. "What brings you here?" He was abrupt.

It was with some hesitation Karl finally revealed his reason for coming. "I'm getting married."

"Oh? What has that to do with me?"

"Why, that's wonderful," Marcy injected. "Who is the bride?"

Somewhat relieved, Karl spoke freely. "She's a nice German girl. You'll like her, I'm sure." He directed his words to Marcy for want of knowing what else to do. "Frankly, I came to ask you both to be witnesses at our civil ceremony."

"Why not ask your good friend, Felix?" Emil asked. A grim smile parted his lips.

"But you're my best friend," Karl reminded him.

"No," he said. "I don't want to get involved with you again. Here today, gone tomorrow, always without notice. I'm tired of it." He was shocked by the words that spewed from his lips as if they had been imprisoned there and anxiously awaited release. The relief he felt was short-lived. He wished immediately he could retract the whole thing.

Karl's tiny mouth turned purple and began to twitch perceptibly. He pounced to his feet and made a dash toward the drawing room where Marcy had begun to play again. He stopped abruptly in front of her, but said nothing before marching determinedly toward the door. Once there, he paused long enough to vent his anger. "It was her idea anyway. I was never in favor of it." He slammed the door and was gone.

"I knew he wanted something," Emil told Marcy. "He read my name in the paper, bragged of my being his best friend and had to prove it to his bride with my presence at their wedding. Probably heard about my being married to Miss Didrikson, the concert pianist. His ambitious bride wanted to have what she considered a prominent couple at her wedding, so Karl was persuaded to mend the torn ties of his friendship." He paced the floor, gesturing angrily as he spoke.

"What of it?" Marcy asked. "I don't mind. I shall be happy to attend their wedding."

"No. It's best this way."

"Just as you say," she acquiesced.

The meeting with Karl haunted Emil though he never admitted as much to Marcy, who seemed to put it behind her and concentrate on her upcoming concert. Her interest in Christian Science had boosted her confidence, and she had been playing at larger and larger parties that Schliemann and Muller arranged. Everyone agreed that, if she played as well on concert night as she had played at these informal gatherings, she would be an overnight sensation.

Again, it was not to be. From the moment she stepped on the stage, she was gripped with fright, her hands so paralyzed she could scarcely get through the program. She was so upset with her failure that Emil prevailed upon her to see a doctor. Neither of them had confidence in what the doctor might tell her, but they hoped she would be comforted by talking about her problem to an outsider. He was in the studio when she returned from the visit. Humming *Barcarolle*, and moving rhythmically with the song's imaginary gondola, she entered the apartment in a joyous state. "Guess what, darling. We're going to have a baby!"

"A baby!" he shouted. "It can't be. How did it happen?" he demanded. A baby was the last thing he wanted and he had taken every precaution.

"Oh, you misunderstand. I'm not pregnant."

Comforted by the revelation, he asked, "What are you talking about then?"

"Our friends think we should have a baby, and the doctor agrees it might be just the thing to help me relax. Maybe a woman should bear the pangs of childbirth and know the joy of motherhood before she's a complete woman." She continued to dance around the room in joyous anticipation.

"That's ridiculous," he belittled.

"What's wrong with having a baby?" she retorted.

"Nothing, if you want one, but I don't. I certainly don't intend to have one just because others think I should."

"You don't want a child, then?"

"Not especially," he admitted. "I don't like bringing children into the world without preparing for them. I don't feel like taking on that responsibility. It wouldn't be fair to the child."

"Well, I had no idea you would be opposed to it," she said icily.

"Don't point a finger at me when all the while it's only your career you're thinking of, not the desire for motherhood. I suppose the doctor suggested relations with a man would aid you in your career. Is that why you married me?" The remark was meant to arouse her anger, nothing more.

"No, my friends did that. But, as you can see, it didn't work!"

He waited for an apology, a retraction or something comforting. But her flushed face told him it was the truth. *Was it Schliemann*? he wondered. *Muller*? *Surely not the Isaacs*? *At any rate, all of them knew I was only a seed they planted in hopes of bringing Marcy into full bloom*. Nothing could have been more devastating to his ego. The conversation came to an abrupt end.

He stayed to himself for weeks, refusing again to speak to Marcy. Through a closed door, she assured him time and again she married him because she genuinely loved him and that she still loved him. She admitted that some of her friends had urged their union as the answer to her stage fright, but that she had fallen in love with him.

"Do you really think I'd have a baby fathered by a man I don't love?" There was no answer, not then, or for nerve-wracking weeks. Time and again, *Capricio* failed to soften him.

Marcy wouldn't give up. She continued to plead for understanding until he finally yielded. Cautiously and skillfully, she convinced him of her unceasing love for him as well as her desire to have his baby.

Against his better judgment, he agreed. They planned the arrival of the baby for early autumn so that Marcy wouldn't miss too many of her classes at the institute. Also, it would enable them to spend another summer at Fort Montgomery.

Their plans began to materialize. Marcy became pregnant, the baby due in October. Emil continued his work with a jewelry concern in Newark where he worked three days a week, leaving the remainder of the week free to join her. He began to look forward to welcoming a new member to their happy family.

Then one day, a neighbor summoned Emil at the Newark factory. Marcy had been taken ill and was hospitalized in Newburgh, not far from Fort Montgomery. Emil left the factory in distress, his mind racing with thoughts of a dangerous miscarriage. Marcy was in her sixth month.

When he arrived at the hospital, she was unconscious. The gardener, he learned, had heard moans coming from her cottage. Upon investigation, he had found her on the floor, convulsing. She suffered another convulsion at the hospital. The doctor feared a third attack would be fatal.

Unconscious most of the time, she had lucid moments only occasionally when she talked rationally for a while, then dropped back into unconsciousness. Emil paced the hallway floor until the nurse summoned him into the room. "I'm sorry, Mr. Holzhauer. The doctor says your wife is dying. You may come in if you like."

A doctor and several nurses worked with her, trying to feed her oxygen through a tube. She gasped for breath, and with each gasp, she suffered agonizing coughing spells.

"Unless we can administer the oxygen successfully, there's no hope," the doctor told Emil. "We've been working like this for over three hours without success, I'm sorry to say."

They continued their efforts but even Emil could see the uselessness of it. In her unconscious stupor, she was not able to cooperate with them, and without that, it was impossible to administer the oxygen. They tried talking to her during her moments of consciousness, hoping that she would understand the necessity of helping them. Emil stood helplessly by, watching. Finally he asked permission to talk to her himself.

"Maybe a familiar voice?"

"Of course," agreed the doctor, handing him the tube.

Sitting on the side of the bed, he began a conversation in German. "Marcy, Darling, listen. I will count, *eins, zwei, eins, zwei*, and then again, *eins, zwei, eins, zwei*. Now you try to breathe with my counting. Ready? *Eins, zwei, eins, zwei*," he counted rhythmically. Repeating his pleas, always in German, he continued to count.

Marcy gave no indication that she had understood or even heard. She continued to gasp and cough. Emil refused to give up. The thought of losing her was too painful. Finally, in a moment of consciousness, she tried to follow his lead, failing at first, but her breathing eventually took the regular cadence of his count.

"Thank God, she heard me," he whispered, crossing himself.

The doctor warned him the battle hadn't yet been won, not until her breathing was normal without the aid of the oxygen tube. Hour after hour he counted, because the moment he paused, she began to gasp for breath. In her weakness she was totally dependent on the rhythm of his words to guide her breathing.

It was noon the next day before her breathing was normal. "As soon as she gains her strength, we'll take the baby," the doctor announced.

Emil was horrified. "Oh, my God. Take the baby?" In the night vigil to save Marcy, he had forgotten about the baby. "But how will she survive such a thing after all this?"

"We have no choice, Mr. Holzhauer. Your wife is filled with poison, and the baby is dead."

Thirteen

The year was 1917, nine months since Marcy's near death experience. As spring approached, Emil looked forward to a summer away from the city. But the events of April seventeenth of that year would make a significant change in his plans. Congress had declared war on the German empire.

Antagonism toward Germans in America, already raging, grew by the day. Anti-German feeling, whipped up by propaganda agencies, went as far as to ban Beethoven from symphony concerts. The papers were filled with anti-German sentiment, with word that Germans preached their domination of the world because of their superiority. German U-boats had all but wiped out the entire merchant tonnage, taking thousands of innocent American lives in their quest for battle. All Germans were seen as warmongers who gloried in killing.

Emil despised the German leaders for bringing the catastrophe, not only to America, but to his homeland. Strangers on the streets who heard his heavy accent yelled obscenities, and often made threats against him. He feared constantly that no factory manager would be willing to give him employment.

Fortunately, there had been no finger-pointing among the independent artists, most of whom were former Henri students. Emil had been exhibiting regularly with them, and his name, although submerged in small print along with dozens of others, appeared occasionally in the newspapers. Still dissatisfied with his work and humiliated at the sight of it on the gallery walls, he found it bearable by virtue of its being hidden among the work of others.

Since Marcy's battle for her life, things had not been the same between them. She had neither the stamina nor the zest of old, her spare time spent brooding instead of practicing. More and more she clung to her Christian Science friends who had all but replaced the musical gatherings.

Meanwhile, Emil continued to grieve over his lifeless canvasses. The colors in his palette grew dimmer and dimmer with everything a combination of grey and black. He forced himself to use bright colors, but always, dark depressing colors dominated the paintings before he brought them to completion. He often voiced his concern to Marcy, but as her suggestions in the past had not been graciously received by him, she declined to comment.

"It's this damn war and the slaughter that's taking place. Everyone points a finger at me as if it were my fault."

Marcy, who had always loved the German people, sympathized, but she had apparently grown tired of his constant complaints. "Perhaps we would feel the same way if we were born here. The thing that worries me is the draft. I just hope you can avoid it," she sighed. Emil was thirty, an age included in the required registration. Rather than add a new worry to his growing agenda, she quickly changed the subject. "Why don't we go to New Hampshire when I finish my classes? Get away from the city." She spoke with forced animation, an emotion quite distinct from the one she felt.

Emil answered with a satirical grunt. *Is it a reaction to the draft or to New Hampshire*? Marcy wondered. In the past, she had used the cottage on the lake, which was surrounded by the woods and isolated from all but a few distant neighbors, for her grueling practice sessions. This trip would be different. She had no scheduled concerts to prepare for.

Her own misery went unnoticed by her husband who had second thoughts about the trip. "You know, I think I might like getting away from the city at that. Yes," he contemplated. "Away from everybody and their accusing fingers and their filthy mouths," he pouted.

He wasted no time in carrying out the plan. As Marcy was unable to leave immediately, he opted to go in advance of her. The bungalow was in need of repair, a task he welcomed as a change in lifestyle. He gladly assisted local farmers with their chores as help was scarce and more food was in demand. By the time Marcy arrived, he had finished painting the bungalow and other repairs and had begun planting a garden.

Unlike in previous summers, Marcy idled away her time, taking short walks or lying lazily around the water's edge. Although she had begun to play again and to entertain in their home on Sunday evenings, she was still far from the healthy, robust girl she had been. She was no longer physically able to carry out the programs she had done with ease in the past. As her music suffered, so did their relationship. She seldom played *Capricio* unless he requested it, and then it lacked the enthusiasm of old. He blamed her health for the change, and he welcomed an opportunity to pamper her.

Then it happened. When notice of his draft arrived, he blasted everyone responsible for the war. "Imagine me serving in my adopted country's army. Forced to kill my own countrymen!" he raved. He kicked at the door, breaking the very lock he had only recently repaired.

"That may be a bit dramatic," Marcy suggested quietly.

Her soft-spoken demeanor, usually well received by Emil, irked him when he was enraged.

"Oh, sure. What do you care?" he said accusingly. "You and your Christian Science friends will be very happy without me around, won't you?"

"You know better than that, Emil. Why must you say such things?"

He was ashamed for the outburst, but he couldn't bring himself to apologize. He did attempt to soften the blow. "But it's just when you need me. You've been a very sick girl."

"Don't worry. I can take care of myself, really I can. We must think positively. Just imagine what a brilliant palette you'll have once this dreadful war is over."

After their tearful farewell, Emil reported to Columbia College where he and the other draftees were marched to the subway, taken to Penn Station and sent to Camp Meade, Maryland. Along the way, he sat by himself, thinking. Looking back, he realized he might have prevented Marcy's debilitating illness, as well as the loss of their baby.

When her pregnancy brought on severe constipation, Sue, her closest Christian Science friend, had challenged her to prove her strength. She was to begin by ignoring her doctor's orders to elimate her bowels with medication. In accepting the challenge, she filled her body with poison that led to the severe consequences at the Fort Montgomery bungalow. "Poor girl," Emil moaned to himself. He grieved to think what she might try next.

The men had scarcely arrived at Ft. Meade when some of the other recruits began pointing at him, whispering. It wasn't long before their remarks became audible, and it was soon established among the enlisted men, and many of the officers, that he was a German spy.

"Poses as an artist," one young man announced. "Don't they all? Always drawin' pictures of our secret buildings," he accused.

Emil yelled at them in the beginning, but he soon learned he was outnumbered.

Things looked a great deal brighter once they began the vigorous exercises. While others perspired heavily, gasped for breath, wilted, and a few collapsed, Emil was invigorated. He loved being outside in the sun even on the hottest days, but many of the men couldn't bear it. He watched in amazement as many of them collapsed day after day from physical exertion.

He tried to assist one poor fellow who had fallen to the ground, but with his last bit of strength, the fallen boy slapped at Emil. "Get away. I don't need the help of a goddamn German."

"I'm an American citizen," Emil protested.

"You're still a goddamn German," another boy said, gasping himself for breath. "You're not impressing anybody with your stamina. It's that urge to kill that keeps you standing when the rest of us fall. You're a goddamn spy!"

"What would a spy hope to learn from us?" The comment came from a Jewish boy. Emil remembered him from the train ride to camp. Only the sergeant's command for silence prevented him from getting the same tongue-lashing Emil had.

His new friend's name was Ed Weins. He advised Emil to ignore the troublemakers as much as possible.

Every night, he poured his aching heart out to Marcy, writing her of all the humilities he was made to suffer at the hands of "these barbarians". He went to sleep each night thinking about her and her music, wondering if she were recuperating, or if she had taken up a new cure. He longed to hear her play *Capricio*, or anything for that matter, and to be a part of her life. Much of the time she didn't seem real, and it was as if the wonderful life he had known with her had only been a dream.

Her letters did little to reassure him as he sensed a certain reservation, a change in her that he couldn't explain. In the beginning of the war she had been pro German, and had been a comfort to him in regard to the anti-German element. But in her letters she referred often to the "Germans' war," and she seemed insensitive to his complaints. Instead of commiserating with him, she filled her letters with her own complaints, citing financial problems, of being unable to bear the expenses of the apartment alone. In order to keep it, Sue had moved in with her to share the expenses. She filled her letters with Christian Science pamphlets, urging him to read them. He had no interest in them. She wrote enthusiastically about the parties and other activities she and Sue engaged in, making him jealous that she could enjoy herself without him.

As the burden of military service had to be borne, he vowed to give it his best effort and hope for an early return home. While serving on K.P. duty one day he was elated to find Ed Weins would be sharing the assignment. Their paths hadn't crossed since the day the young man had intervened for him. As they worked, Ed hummed something that caught Emil's attention.

"Brahms?" Emil asked. It wasn't *Capricio*, but it was a whimsical little piece he had often heard Marcy play.

"I'm flattered you could tell." Just under six feet, Ed towered over Emil, though physically he was a mite thinner. Accustomed to long walks through hilly country in his native New Jersey, he nevertheless lacked the stamina exhibited by Emil during the daily camp exercises. A boy of spirit and apparent intellect, he seemed as happy as Emil they had found each other. "It's very difficult to hum classical music, you know. You must play an instrument?"

"Oh, no," Emil scoffed, "but my wife is a concert pianist. Maybe you've heard of her. Maresa Didrikson?"

"Of course!" he yelled. "Years ago I attended the Sunday evening get-togethers in her home. But she was single then. Recently, I've been studying in Germany, so I've missed the gatherings. But you must know my brother, Adolf?"

"Adolf Weins? Ah, Adolf," he exclaimed happily. "Yes, of course. Plays the violin and the bassoon?" Like so many of Marcy's guests, Emil had envied Adolf for his musical talent and his apparent freedom to travel. But for the most part, Emil had listened and marvelled, rather than taking part in their conversations, so he could hardly claim a personal relationship with any of their guests.

Emil rejoiced at meeting someone with character and talent, someone who was sensitive to others' feelings. "So this damn war interrupted your studies too?"

"Yes, but I plan to return to Germany and continue my studies in theory and composition as soon as it's over." The thought lifted both their spirits.

They became good friends, a fact that made military life more bearable for Emil. Consciously and tirelessly, he drilled to perfection, never stepping out of line. In the beginning, the sergeant called on him to demonstrate how a soldier should march, for the benefit of those who showed less skill and energy, but the sergeant was soon ordered to stop flaunting "that goddamn German's skills". It ended Emil's hopes of becoming a drillmaster.

When assignments were made to regiments, Emil was placed in field artillery in charge of the horse-drawn guns. It was Ed's assignment as well.

Neither were horsemen. Almost daily, their horses threw them and ran away. One day, when the three teams had been hitched to the guns, Emil's team broke the reins, raced through the camp and shattered everything in their way. Already the butt of the men's jokes, his ineptitude on the field team only added fuel to their fires. Ed suffered nearly the same fate because of his friendship with Emil. Officers and enlisted men alike issued warnings if he didn't stay away from the "Kraut," and once he received a death threat. Ed, however, remained a loyal friend.

When Emil was summoned by the general, both of them thought all was lost. It was, however, an advancement of sorts, as he had been appointed orderly to General Stern.

"You should know the damn fools are saying the general wanted you in his service so he could keep an eye on your spying activities," Ed told him. "Sorry. I wanted to tell you before they did. I can assure you the general is smarter than that. He probably did it to put an end to all the rancor," he added.

Emil was appalled by it all, but a more pressing problem had begun to surface. He felt feverish and his body ached all over. There had been a lot of talk about the flu epidemic and many of the boys at the camp had contracted it, but as he had escaped illness all of his life, he considered himself immune to such things. He finally collapsed on the floor of the general's living quarters. He awakened during the night to find himself in the infirmary, surrounded by others who had the same symptoms, many of whom were on their deathbeds.

The next morning, those who could walk were ordered out of bed and told to get dressed. Emil was certain he couldn't do it, as were others who begged to remain in bed. He heard an orderly scoff at their pleas. "Lay there and die. Somebody'll come get you then," he warned.

Nausea and dizziness he had known from the boat and the trolley rides, but never weakness, never aches. It took a great deal of effort to sit up and get a shirt around his shoulders.

"Move it, move it, everybody get dressed. Hurry now, you're going to the hospital," the orderly yelled. A few were trying, Emil among them, but several lay dead.

While struggling to work his pants on, he felt a jolt to his cot that bounced him in the air. Another patient had been thrown into the bed while Emil sat tugging at his pants leg. He wasn't at all certain the man was breathing. Once on his feet, Emil caught a glimpse of the corpselike face lying there. It was Ed Weins.

"Wait in the hallway for the ambulance," the orderly barked. "Rush it up. We need your beds."

With his last ounce of strength, Emil dragged Ed into the hallway with him, cradled his head in his lap, and collapsed on his friend's chest.

It was after five that afternoon when the ambulance, a horse drawn covered wagon, arrived. They were given cots on the hospital porch as all the beds were filled. There were hundreds of patients in all, and only one doctor to attend them. An orderly told the newcomers, "If you want to eat, you'll have to get the food yourself." Most were unable to move, but Emil managed to fend for himself and Ed. As time went on, he noted that a few who showed only slight improvement had been returned to the barracks so he pretended to be sicker than he was in order to nurse Ed back to health.

Nine of the men from Emil's battery alone had lost their lives in the epidemic. The odor of death lingered with him long after the ordeal had ended. The only enjoyment he had left was the exercise, the drilling, and marching. That at least kept him from decaying physically as he had mentally. He had just made a beginning in the art world and, small though it was, at least he had been brought to the attention of the art-conscious society. Now those few gains had been cancelled out. When he added that to the mockery and the bitterness directed at him by the others, and the lack of sympathy from Marcy, he felt as though he had been dealt too harsh a blow. While performing his duties for the general, he languished silently in self-pity.

He was polishing the general's shoes one day when he heard joyful screaming and singing on the complex grounds. "Freedom! Freedom!" they shouted. The war was over!

Emil and Ed traveled part of the way home together, discussing with great humor their army experiences. Mostly, they looked ahead, anxious to begin anew.

"I hope you'll join us at our Sunday evening get-togethers," he told Ed. His own spirits rose just thinking about it.

Ed promised he would be there. When they said goodbye, they both vowed to continue their friendship in a much more civilized life.

At the apartment, Marcy welcomed him home with open arms, seemingly as thrilled as he was that they were together again. Gleefully, she pulled him close and pushed him away for inspection, then pulled him close and pushed him away again. "Darling, I was so worried when I heard you were ill, but you look wonderful. So robust and healthy, and so very handsome in your uniform. Oh, my, would you look at that broad chest?"

"All those exercises, my darling."

"But your tan? Don't tell me the army allowed you to paint?"

"Hardly," he laughed. "The exercises kept me outside in the sun." He could thank the army for his new physique, but he wondered if it would compensate for the mental decay. As short as he was on patience, he had to muster enough courage to wear the dreadful uniform until he could purchase larger clothes to fit his new form.

Sweet as it was, one thing in particular marred the homecoming. Sue had no intention of leaving, nor did Marcy desire it. Seldom alone with his wife, he began to feel like an intruder in his own home.

"Sue and I have become very good friends. She has continued my training in Christian Science which has been a real comfort to me," she told him.

"Marcy!" he bellowed. "You still believe in that after almost losing your life? I'm home now. We don't need her anymore. You seem to have regained your health."

"Yes, that's true, and I'm indebted to Sue and Christian Science for that. Did you read the literature I sent you?"

"Of course. I can't argue with their basic belief. I've always been an advocate of looking within yourself for strength, but you and Sue have taken the idea too far. Refusing to take a laxative? You damn near killed yourself. Can't you see that?" He was enraged.

"You say all the things Sue warned me you would. Look what happened to me when I depended on the medication at the hospital. I should have been strong enough to overcome the illness without medication."

"You're a damn fool! You would have died without the medical attention. You almost did as it was." He vented his anger with occasional smirks.

Marcy was not intimidated. "No, you're wrong. It was your strength that saved me. You have it, but I don't. Sue explained it all to me."

"Sue, Sue. I'm sick of Sue. Don't you see what's happening? You're losing contact with reality. Get rid of that woman!" he demanded.

"I need the money she pays me," she responded sharply. "I can't run the apartment alone."

Emil was infuriated by the cutting remark. "I have every intention of getting a job and helping with the expenses." Before his army days he might have stalked off and closed himself in the studio, but the situation with Sue had to be solved. While contemplating his next move, Marcy intensified his ire.

"You could make a living with your art if you wanted to. Think how much more elegant it would be, too. Not like working in a factory."

"Commercial art?" he bellowed. It was the last straw. "After all the years of pain and suffering, you would have me shuck my life's plan to become an artist?" Marcy had changed. He no longer knew the woman who shared his bed. After all that time, she seemed ashamed to be married to a factory worker.

He found a job in New Jersey at Henry Kohn and Sons, a jewelry manufacturer. Resigned to the fact that he would work in the factory, Marcy tried to persuade him to work part time again, leaving time for painting and exhibiting as before.

Every day they argued. Christian Science and Sue finally took second place in their daily arguments, moved down the scale by Marcy's insistence he paint with a commercial appeal. "At least your name would be thoroughly entrenched in the art world."

"Never!" he shouted. "Anybody can do it. I wouldn't think of telling you to forget your dream of becoming a successful concert pianist. Are you satisfied with playing for friends at home? Don't tell me how to paint, and don't tell me how to conquer my stage fright when you can't even conquer your own." It was the most cutting remark he could have made and he knew it. Maybe everyone had humored her too much for too long, he reasoned. He followed the remark with a silent treatment.

When he returned from the factory the next day, he found a note on the piano: "I want a divorce."

His first thought was to run after her and beg her to come back, but he couldn't bring himself to do it. He thought of the baby and the religion, both straws she had grasped in her fight to overcome stage fright. All night he lay awake, waiting, listening for her footsteps. He thought she would surely return if only to say goodbye. She never did.

As soon as possible, he left the apartment and took a studio on Forty-Second Street. He took nothing, not even his part of their savings. The nine hours he spent each day bent over a drawing board helped free his mind of her, at least until he went home at night to a drab and lonely studio apartment.

Fourteen

The divorce had been final for months, but Emil remained despondent and very bitter. Looking back, he saw the union for what it was, a plan for curing Marcy's stage fright, all without his knowledge.

Even though Schliemann was her benefactor and should have been number one on his list of culprits, Emil couldn't believe he had taken part in the sham. He had always shown a genuine interest in Emil's work, and had purchased one of his paintings which hung on the walls of his lavish home. Recalling this, Emil swallowed his pride one day and called Schliemann at his office.

"I've been wanting to ask you," he stammered. "I need to invest my money and I—"

"Why didn't you say so?" Schliemann scolded.

"Well, I thought you'd laugh at my—"

Schliemann didn't wait for Emil to embarrass himself further. He assured him it was the right thing to do. "But don't expect too much. It takes a while to realize a profit."

Emil exulted. Frugality became his lifestyle again. With his salary increased to seventy-five dollars a week, he began to harbor thoughts of saving enough money for a prolonged European trip. He made do in a tiny studio apartment in Greenwich Village, and limited his meals to one a day in an inexpensive restaurant or a quick substitute from the street vendors.

It was a lonely existence. He hungered for news of his classmates, but the war had apparently ended that relationship along with his marital one. While returning from the factory one day, he saw a familiar figure sitting on a park bench, his head drooped to his chest. A folded stool and easel lay on the ground beside him. It was Lamberty.

Anxiously, Emil quickened his step. "Lamberty," he called. He extended both hands, much as he might to an invalid who couldn't rise to the occasion. Indeed, Lamberty looked the part, his thin body speaking of the awesome hunger it had always borne. "Good to see you, my friend," Emil said warmly.

Lamberty stared at Emil with unfriendly, dissecting eyes. As his hatred for Germans coursed through Emil's mind, his own smile was reduced to rubble, the warmth in his hands dissipated into the chilly air. He was about to excuse himself and move on when Lamberty's cold stare showed signs of a pervading spirit of friendly recognition.

"Emil?" he asked. Flashing an eager grin, Emil nodded. "Ah, Emil!" he shouted. "I didn't recognize you. Your hair, it's—"

"All that fighting I did in the army, *mien Freund*. It turned my hair white." He laughed purposely then, uncertain if Lamberty would understand the joke. They grasped each other in a warm embrace, then shook hands vigorously.

"The army? Say, I didn't know you were in the army." He spoke with a slow drawl, between sputters, almost as if he didn't know there had been a war. "Tell me all about it." He cleared the bench of his belongings and brushed it meticulously before motioning Emil to the best spot. Emil had a strange feeling that Lamberty spent so much time on the bench, or one like it, he thought of it as home, the only one he had to offer.

Gesturing toward the battered easel, Emil asked how things were going. There was only one painting, and, just as in the old days, he had worn the paper thin with changes. "I see you've been painting?"

"Only now and then," he said, without offering excuses. Emil sensed that time had stood still in his mind, as if it were still yesterday and they would soon gather in the Henri classes. In the middle of their light conversation, his mind seemed to click, bringing with it a touch of reality. "Say, did you hear about Tiny?" Emil shook his head. "Died of influenza during the epidemic."

"No! Tiny? Poor devil," Emil moaned.

"Died with a broken heart. He was hopelessly in love, you know." He was like an old woman, delighted to be first with the news, but saddened by its reality.

"Not with Vamp?" Everyone knew he had a crush on her.

"No, not Vamp." He hesitated as if he had forgotten who it was. "It was, you know, another student."

"But there weren't any other—" He stopped in mid-sentence, uncertain if another female had enrolled after he left, or if Lamberty was simply confused. "Tell me more," he pleaded.

"Ah, you should have seen him. Got a job singing and bought himself some decent pants. Spent all his money on the girl, and then she left him." He seemed caught up in the story, unable to connect with other classmates and school events Emil mentioned. Emil wanted to take him by the hand and treat him to a decent meal but he knew Lamberty would be insulted by such a gesture. As poignant as Tiny's story was, Lamberty's was worse. He was obviously living as if it were ten years earlier when he had first started sketching. He had not yet accepted the fact that he would starve if he depended on his art to support him, and had continued to live from day to day in hope of becoming an overnight success. He looked like a beggar, in shabby, ill-fitting clothes that hung on him in extra folds, in need of a good cleaning. He was thin, almost skeleton-like, actually bringing to Emil's mind the bony creature Boss had used as a prop for building the muscles in the classroom so many years before. Emil walked away, saddened by the whole encounter, knowing that Lamberty would return to his shabby quarters for a bowl of thin potato soup just as he had done so many nights in the past.

He struggled to free his mind of it all, but it lingered with him well into the evening. When his housebell rang, he knew it was Lamberty, for he never had visitors. The poor miserable fellow must have followed him home, and then have stood outside, perhaps drumming up courage to ring the bell, he thought. Emil was in a quandary as to what to do, but he knew he couldn't turn him away.

It was Ed Weins.

When Emil heard the familiar voice, he ran down the stairs shouting his name. "How did you find me?" The two embraced, then broke out in laughter, as the sight of each other brought memories they never thought would be funny.

"You old horseman," Ed teased. "How did I find you? It was a chore, believe me. You should be ashamed of yourself for not getting in touch."

His feigned outrage only intensified the joy Emil felt just knowing Ed cared enough to call on him after all these months.

"But I thought you'd be in Germany by now. Really," he insisted.

"Don't try to change the subject," Ed implored playfully. "I've wasted my otherwise good Sundays searching for you along the Palisades. You told me you used to go there often."

"Sorry. Haven't been there since the divorce." The revelation dampened the spirited atmosphere, but only momentarily. Soon they were laughing again, each anxious to hear the other's story of life since the war.

"Ah, Germany. You know of course the war left such a mess," Ed moaned. "But that won't stop me from going. I hope to join a musical group to help pay my expenses."

"One thing's in your favor. The American dollar," Emil said. "My aunt tells me you can live on it a week."

"Exactly. I may never come back to the USA." They laughed but it was hardly a joke. Ed was miserly. He gladly accepted Emil's offer to share a meager meal, a sampling of the cheapest cold cuts and only water to wash it down.

They reminisced through much of the evening, each reliving their army days and contemplating their future. Before leaving, he invited Emil to dinner. "The entire family is anxious to meet you. Next Sunday. Come spend the day. It's family day at our house."

He looked forward to having a real friend again, especially a warm, sensitive, intelligent one like Ed. He gladly accepted the invitation and looked forward to it all week.

Almost immediately, the Weins family became Emil's family. In addition to those he knew, Ed had two sisters, Geena, and the youngest member of the family, fifteen year old Clarle. Mr. Weins, their father, was an accomplished bassoonist and clarinetist who had previously played with the Buffalo Symphony Orchestra. Emil remembered the stories Ed had told about the boys' strict upbringing, and of daily violin and piano practice from the time they were six.

Their mother prided herself, and rightly so, on her homecooked meals. She, along with her older daughter, spent most of her time in the kitchen on Sunday morning, while the others gathered around the piano, singing German folk songs.

The weekend visits with the Weins family soon became a ritual. After dinner each Sunday, Emil joined Ed, Adolf, and Clarle, the hardiest members of the Weins family, for long walks along the Palisades, where he had spent many happy hours painting. Sometimes they went along the Hudson, from Peekskill into the hills and woods, and took the train to Riverview, a quaint little village on the river. Situated in a valley and sheltered by mountains overlooking the Hudson, it featured mostly foreign born shopkeepers who shunned the crowded and unfriendly city.

Emil was introduced to the Riverview Hotel, whose friendly owners also ran a delightful German restaurant across the street. The entire village was an artist's dreamland, but one he had little hope of painting. It was past noon by the time they arrived and they were obliged to begin the return trip in a matter of hours.

Clarle, though much younger than any of the others, seemed to prefer the company of her older brothers and their friends over that of her schoolmates. Emil was enchanted by her creamy white skin and light-brown hair, fashionably bobbed on the sides, and tucked into a soft bun at the back of her slender neck. It was Anna of Lauterberg's hairstyle, a fact that didn't escape him. The aquiline nose, sensuous lips, and inquiring blue eyes completed the picture, a look of royalty Emil ached to paint.

During his marriage to Marcy he had been surrounded by beautiful young girls, students mostly, but none compared with Clarle. He longed to paint her, but never broached the subject for fear of rejection.

When Geena caught Emil making strange motions with his hands in the air, she jumped at the chance to initiate a private conversation. "What were you doing?"

"I was thinking what a great model your sister would make," he told her. Geena slumped in her chair. For want of knowing what else to do, Emil continued the explanation. "We use the head as a standard of measurement in drawing. You know how in some things you use the foot, or the mile? Well, the body can be pretty well thought of in terms of how many heads each part is composed of."

"Why not Geena?" Mrs. Weins asked. Geena lowered her head to conceal a deep blush. Emil had given little attention to the older daughter, much to her mother's chagrin. The purpose of her frequent references to Geena's homemaking skills soon became obvious to him. Geena had passed her prime and had failed to attract a husband. While Mrs. Weins stewed, her sons wriggled uncomfortably in their seats.

Embarrassed by his wife's effrontery, Mr. Weins came to the rescue. "Have you a regular model?" he asked.

"Heaven's no. I couldn't afford one," Emil laughed. "But I used to have the models at the Henri School, and, of course, there were the fishermen on Monhegan Island."

"Fishermen!" yelled Clarle, thinking it a joke. It was with some embarrassment she learned otherwise.

"Yes, of course. Fishermen. Everyone has something to offer. With you, of course it's youth. And beauty," he added with a blush.

Clarle blushed too, though it appeared she rather enjoyed the attention. Geena slumped further in her seat, unable to hide her disappointment.

"You mustn't take this old horseman seriously," Ed warned them all. The two of them had long since entertained the group with their tales of horsemanship on the army's wheel team. "He got so used to walking like a duck, I expected him to start quacking," he added, sending everyone into a jolly spin.

"Look who's laughing. You had to stand up to put your boots on because you couldn't sit, not even on a soft pillow. One morning I had to lace his boots," Emil declared.

When the laughter died, Ed turned to his younger sister. "Say, why not pose for him? Should be interesting."

"Yes," agreed Adolf. "You should hear the stories my poet friend tells about living in Greenwich Village. He lived high in a garret where he could witness all the village activity below. I visited him there once. Most intriguing."

"The building I live in faces Sheridan Square. Lots of activity there," Emil added.

"Interesting perhaps, but not safe," said Mrs. Weins who still held a grudge. Emil lowered his eyes to the floor. *What have I done*? he worried. His boldness in bringing up the subject might be construed as arrogance, perhaps alienating the whole family. He was about to apologize when Mrs. Weins surprised him. "If Clarle wishes to pose for you, she has my permission, but one of her brothers must accompany her. She's only a child you know."

If the remark was made to puncture Clarle's ego, it was successful, the triumph of being chosen over her sister shoved aside by her mother's remark. She prided herself in being much older than her years, and choosing older friends over her classmates, to prove her maturity. Geena, on the other hand, recoiled, her tongue silenced. Mrs. Weins let out a low moan as she tried to come to grips with the inevitable: Geena was destined to become an old maid. For Emil, it was a bitter victory, but one he savored, nonetheless.

When he returned to the studio apartment that night, sleep wouldn't come, but he didn't mind. Before his marriage, bedtime had always meant planning time, a time when the future was drafted, whether it meant plans for a day, a week, or a lifetime.

On this particular night, the problem of time surfaced. It remained the curse of his life. And yet, working part-time was no longer feasible if he intended to save enough money for traveling to Europe, to Monhegan Island, or anywhere for that matter. Suddenly, an idea came to him. If he could peddle his samples, take orders for jewelry designs, then fill them in the evening, it should leave several days a week for painting.

He decided to give it a try. The first week, he solicited trade after working hours. The response was good, because the jewelry season was at its height and new designs were the order of the day. Once it was established that he could do quite well freelancing, he quit his regular job at the factory, and for the first time since before his military service, he was free to paint a few days during the week. Unfortunately, it was exhausting, the day and night work, despite unusual stamina.

It did, however, leave Saturdays free for painting Clarle. When the day finally came, Clarle seemed reticent, even in Ed's company. From a box of paraphernalia, Emil pulled out a wide-brimmed hat. "Would you mind holding this, just so," he said, giving some instructions. "What do you think, big brother?" He almost danced with pleasure just watching her struggle with the wide brim, her wide-set eyes wandering aimlessly around the room as if searching for something.

It was clearly not what she had expected to find in an artist's studio. No elegant framework, no frilly-curtained windows, nothing by way of decor, unless one could count stubby brushes, empty cans, jars of crayon and pencils, all spent and dusty, and a lone can of smelly turpentine.

Ed, however, cast a vote in favor of the whole thing. Emil had promised to treat them to lunch, a fact that he made frequent references to. As time wore on, Clarle relaxed, if not in acceptance, at least in quiet vexation.

Ed soon excused himself, leaving the two alone. With him out of the room, Emil felt obligated to make small talk though he had always been a failure at carrying on a conversation during work. "What are your schoolmates doing today?"

"I've no idea." It was clearly not a topic she wished to discuss as she had questions of her own. "How long will this take?"

"How long? I can't say. I'm still working on the outline. There are so many things that enter into painting a picture. The dominating color and the focus, and so much more. And I might get into one idea and change my mind. Depends on what I see," he added, as he studied her. When she took a different position, he pleaded warmly, "That's perfect. Can you stay like that?"

"Of course."

By noon, the portrait was well underway, and Clarle and her brother were given a chance to see it. While she grimaced in silence, Ed found her reaction amusing.

"Looks like a Belgian refugee to me," he teased. The remark gave Clarle the courage to speak her own mind. "I look so desolate. Is it finished?"

The two men laughed. "Give the artist leeway, my dear," said Ed. "He's not painting a photographic likeness you know."

"As to whether it's finished, I can only say that depends on you," Emil told his somewhat reluctant model. "I'm afraid an artist is never `finished', as you say. Why don't we have lunch? I'm afraid this has been too taxing for you."

"Then what?" she asked. Clarle had taken on the desolate look she saw in the unfinished portrait. Emil was cautious, afraid she had tired of it all, though his own mind was racing with ideas.

"What do you think? Is she up to another session?" Before Ed could answer, Emil visualized yet another scene. "Ah, my dear," he gestured excitedly. "I should like to do a sculpture of your head one day."

She said nothing. Emil was certain it would be the last of his youthful model, as she was obviously disappointed in the whole process. While answering a nature call, he overheard Ed trying to console her.

"Don't concern yourself. The man still broods for his wife. His gloom is made manifest in the work he does. Come now, he has invited us to lunch."

"No!" she wailed. "I want to go home."

Emil was bitterly disappointed. He had envisioned a lovely luncheon followed by a fruitful afternoon in the studio. Fortunately, he hadn't the leisure for dwelling on the episode as he had design orders that must be completed before morning. Once delivered, he would have to canvass the jewelry concerns for more orders, a time-consuming job. On good selling days, he could steal a few hours for painting within the city, where he had begun to concentrate on the intricate steel wires that made up the Brooklyn Bridge, approaching it from every angle imaginable, from beneath its arch to a position obtained by permit along its right-of-way. Sometimes he took advantage of Sheffield's open invitation to paint the bridge from his apartment window. The two often supped together at a nearby restaurant, then returned to the apartment for portrait work, using each other, or their mirrored selves, as models.

In the beginning, freelancing had seemed a miracle cure for lack of time, but catering to the whims of the factory managers who couldn't make up their minds proved to be too time-consuming, not to mention economically unsound. Such waffling on the part of the jewelers meant he had to return the next day, and perhaps the next. In half a day he could create designs that would bring in fifty to seventy dollars, an amount that would easily meet his needs, but the time it took to sell and deliver the work nullified the gains.

There was a positive side. It left Saturdays free, and as time went on, he became quite intertwined with the Weins family, a member in good standing, as it were. Mr. Weins, along with his bassoon, was an excellent model himself, as was Mrs. Weins whose needlework intrigued Emil. Gradually, Clarle became an excellent model too, and she was allowed to pose for him without the accompaniment of her brother.

Emil used the opportunities to develop his skills in sculpting as well as portrait work; and in an effort to hold Clarle's interest, he reduced the sessions to half a day, giving them both time to relax and get acquainted away from the watchful eyes of the family. Once he introduced her to the Weldschloss Restaurant, it immediately became her favorite, not only for its excellent cuisine but for its orchestra and dance floor.

Dancers had always fascinated Emil, who envied them their obvious pleasure. Caught up, he watched the couples move with ease across the floor, and admonished himself time and again for not being able to join them.

Clarle was a grown-up seventeen before she aired her own feelings on the subject, revealing a long-time urge to get him on the dance floor. "Nothing to it," she assured him. He was skeptical. At thirty-seven, new movements of the body didn't come so easily. When other men began to ask his lovely companion to dance, he knew it was time to act.

"Could you teach me?" he asked. He lifted his thick brawny eyebrows, revealing a ray of hopefulness in anxious blue eyes. "I don't know," she admitted, "but you can probably do it if you try. All you need is rhythm and coordination, and desire."

"I'm not so sure about the first two," he admitted.

Clarle took over, burning with pride and anticipation that she could teach him something for a change. In no time, he was, by his youthful teacher's own admission, an excellent dancer. He loved holding her as she had gradually become much more than a model to him.

She had developed a keen interest in art, and wanted to know everything he could teach her. Clarle, a fascinated student, and Emil, a proud and dedicated teacher, left the apartment at noon Saturday after Saturday, enjoyed lunch, and proceeded to Fifth Avenue and Fifty-Seventh Street and the art galleries.

"If you really want an education in art, you'll need to spend many hours in each section of every gallery," he told her. She gladly did. She looked up to him, entirely dependent on him for her art education and they both began to love the arrangement.

Meanwhile, she had become an excellent model. Saturdays, with their painting opportunities, cozy luncheons, dancing, and gallery tours, were the highlight of the week. Emil felt like a youngster again, anxious as ever to move the hours along during the week, making way for a fulfilling day with her.

Freelancing hadn't been the answer to his quest for time, but part-time work had freed him for Clarle's companionship on Saturdays. The arrangement, however, ate into his savings, his only hope for that long-awaited European trip. He began looking for full-time work.

Finding a job proved to be more difficult than it had ever been. There were so many well-trained European steel engravers in the country that he was no longer superior to most. His past record enraged the factory managers, who delighted in telling him, "I don't need you," and many emphasized the "you."

It was months before he found a job, a frightening experience he never wished to repeat. Having secured a job one day, he had taken a rare moment of leisure, just standing on the stone steps outside his apartment building, taking in the sights and sounds of Greenwich Village. He loved it there in the artist-filled village, especially since Marcy's memory no longer haunted him. He hadn't achieved the success he wished for, but he was exhibiting again, and he was full of energy and zest for painting and living. Taking in a deep breath of satisfaction, he turned to enter his apartment when he saw a man ringing his housebell.

"Did you wish to see me?"

"Mr. Holzhauer?"

"Yes."

"I'm a neighbor of your friend, Karl Ott. I'm sorry to tell you he has suffered a stroke."

"Karl? No! Is he dead?" The fist he made with his pocketed hand was so tight, his toughened nails dug into his palm, making him wince with pain.

"No, but he has been hospitalized in critical condition, apparently dying. He has been calling for you."

"Where is he?" His voice was hollow sounding, almost as if it had abandoned his body.

"He lives in Bridgeport, Connecticut. Here, I'll write the address for you."

The next morning, Emil was on his way to Bridgeport. Thoughts of their whole relationship raced through his mind, jumping from events in Schwabisch-Gmund to disappointing times in New York City, and returning always to the last time they had met. He grieved as he recalled Karl standing in their lavish apartment on Riverside Drive when he had turned him away, refusing to attend his wedding. Seven years had passed since then. "Poor devil," he mumbled. "What a mess. It must be the syphilis. Not even forty yet." He had finally overcome the power Karl had over him, but there was no satisfaction. His old friend was dying, perhaps dead already, he thought.

Lacking the courage to go directly to the hospital, he went to the home address first. If death had already come, he preferred hearing it from his wife or perhaps a friend, not some indifferent hospital attendant. A woman in her late thirties answered the door. She was masked in heavy makeup, almost reminiscent of a clown, or at best, a garish actor. Her body was laden with cheap jewelry. It dangled and clanked with the slightest movement of her body.

"Oh, Emil! You came," she cried. "I told Karl I would recognize you. I'm Mala, Karl's wife. You have no idea what this means to us to have you come. Please come in. Children," she called, "this is your Uncle Emil." Two youngsters came in, very close in age, both obedient to her command. "Now say hello to your Uncle Emil. Give him a nice hug. He's a famous artist. He's come to see your father. Isn't that wonderful?" She required no answers, and she left no time for them.

She rattled on, never pausing. He wondered if she was hysterical because her husband was dead or if this was her usual demeanor. He pitied the children who were told to say something, then given no opportunity to do so before receiving yet another order or admonition. A third child, the youngest, was not included in welcoming the new uncle. Emil noticed him immediately, not only because he had been ignored, but because he was crippled. With a great deal of difficulty he dragged his deformed leg across the floor to take a look at the white-haired stranger everyone seemed excited about. Each time he did, Mala ordered the oldest, a girl, to take him back into his room.

Meanwhile, she continued her discourse, repeating herself mostly, and proclaiming her joy at his coming. "You were constantly on Karl's tongue, you know. You hurt him deeply when you refused to be a witness at our wedding, but never mind that. You've come now. Let's go in and see him."

"He's at home? Well, he must be much improved."

Ignoring the comment, she led him down a narrow hallway and into a low-ceilinged bedroom darkened by drawn window shades. Emil shuddered to think Karl's final moments might be spent in this closet-like atmosphere, depleted of sunlight, nature's gift to the artist. "Karl," she called excitedly, "look who's here." Her husband gave no indication of being conscious, though his eyes were wide open, fixed on the ceiling.

As gruesome as the scene was, Emil forced himself to speak. "Karl, my old friend. I'm sorry you're not feeling well." His voice sounded strange even to him.

Karl turned his head only slightly, and answered with an empty stare, the same one he had focused on the ceiling. Emil tried again to talk to him, mostly repeating his name, until Karl finally responded.

"Emil?"

"Yes, yes, of course, old friend." Karl reached out to him with the eagerness of old. Tears flooded Emil's eyes.

"Wonderful to see you, Emil."

"And you, my friend. They told me you were very sick, but I knew the old healthy Karl of Schwabisch-Gmund days was only fooling them. They didn't see you climb Lauterburg and Hohenstaufen as I did, eh?" he asked, though his heart wasn't in his words. Karl appeared to be dying.

"I'm fine now. I'll be going back to work soon. You'll see," he mumbled, then lapsed into semiconsciousness.

"Karl? Karl?" Emil repeated anxiously. Just then, the little girl came in and sat on the bed beside her father. "Do you like my daddy, Uncle, Uncle Emil?" Her words had obviously been memorized after heavy prompting by her mother, for even as she spoke, Mala stood in the doorway motioning to the child.

"Yes, of course I like your daddy. We've been friends since we were your age. Do you help take care of him?"

Before answering, she checked the doorway for instructions, then shook her head affirmatively.

Suddenly, Karl sat upright. When he saw the child, he thrust his hand in her crotch with eager lecherous mien. "What is that? Eh? What is it?" he asked, running his hand inside her panties. Fighting to get away from him, the child screamed and ran to the arms of her waiting mother while Emil sat horrified. Almost immediately, Karl screamed out in disgust at what he had been doing, then sank into unconsciousness again.

"Lecherous beast!" Mala screamed, her metal bracelet clanging noisily as she raised her arms in protest. "The minute he got home from the hospital, he attacked me, and now he has molested his own daughter. It's too much. You must help us, Emil." She grasped his arm in a tight grip and looked him directly in the eyes. The lone tear she had been successful in wringing from her left eye splotched her thick layer of makeup.

Emil stepped away from her, but she held on. "But what brought this on? Did you discuss it with the doctor? What can be done for him?" he asked.

"The attack came on suddenly," she said. "Before that, he was always well since I've known him. The stupid doctor says he won't live six months. Two years at the most. That's ridiculous, of course," she added haughtily.

She had revealed one thing in her admonition of the doctor. She had sent a message of Karl's imminent death when in reality he had been sent home from the hospital. "I would like to talk to the doctor myself," Emil said.

It was exactly what Mala wished for. Karl's doctor told the story, none of which came as a surprise to Emil. Karl had contracted syphilis and the end was in sight, the doctor explained. Another stroke would most likely kill him. As Emil listened, he pictured the youngest child dragging his crippled leg along the floor. Karl's disease had been responsible.

When they returned to the Ott house, they found Karl much improved, sitting up in bed and able to carry on a conversation. "Emil!" he exclaimed, as if seeing him for the first time. "I'm so glad you came. I've been reading your name and seeing your paintings on the art pages. You're constantly exhibiting your work." He seemed to reel with vicarious pleasure. "I have all of your articles right here," he said excitedly. He pulled out a handful of newspaper clippings. "Your Monhegan Island oils, watercolor shows at the Martin Gallery—"

"Every time he sees your name, he gets his own sketch pad out," Mala interrupted. "I'll show you some of his drawings. They're really good, too." Karl held out his hand, objecting weakly, but he was ignored.

"That goddamn woman has been my ruin," he declared the minute she left the room. Sensing his anguish, Emil reached for Karl's hands, but almost drew back in horror. The once shapely hands and long thin fingers were gnarled and stubby, far worse than Emil's had ever been. Tears stole from Karl's eyes in a moment of self-pity. He obviously wanted to spill his emotions, but Mala was back in an instant with a stack of his sketches.

They were simple drawings done in much the same vein as those of their Schwabisch-Gmund days, and all in ordinary ink on a poor grade of paper. They both watched eagerly for Emil's reaction. Not one to pretend, even during the worst of times, he rebuked Karl for not trying another medium, perhaps watercolor, oil, or even charcoal, anything other than plain ink. "And the paper," he protested. "Why didn't you—"

"We couldn't afford anything else," his wife moaned pitifully.

Karl's smile faded as did the ray of hope that had momentarily revived his withered countenance.

It was obviously a subject Mala was determined to pursue. "They're good, aren't they, Emil? What does the paper matter? You can still sell them for us? You know the art dealers in New York City. It would be easy for you. We need the money for the hospital bill."

"I'm afraid you have no idea how impossible it is to sell a painting. Maybe if Karl's name were known, but even then, believe me—"

"But your name is known," she interrupted. "You can sell them if you want to. They should bring at least a hundred dollars each." Her gaudy lips, swimming in fresh paint, wobbled endlessly, again bringing to Emil's mind a noisy clown who kept his mouth moving, but had nothing to say.

Her ignorance on the subject made reasoning with her impossible. If Karl were in his right mind, he would tell her how impossible. But a glance in Karl's direction told him the poor fellow was no longer capable of rational thought. "Why do you think I work in a factory if paintings are so easy to sell?"

"Because you're greedy, just as Karl said."

"Shut up, you little bitch," Karl warned. His eyes flashed with anger.

"I think he's afraid you'll get more attention than he does, Karl. Isn't it true he always envied you your talent?" Again her husband shouted obscenities at her, demanding that she keep quiet. She finally snatched the sketches up and left the room.

"Believe me, old friend, I would be happy to sell the sketches if I could. Yes, I exhibit, and I have my name mentioned in the paper occasionally. Sometimes I'm lucky enough to sell a painting, but it's a rare and exciting occasion when I do. Even then, the money it brings rarely does more than cover the cost of framing the work and renting the gallery."

"I know. It's that goddamn crazy woman's ideas. She's responsible for my downfall," he repeated bitterly, then broke down and cried convulsively. Emil wanted to comfort him, but he knew nothing would.

Mala soon returned to the room with a new tactic. She reached out for the clasped hands of Emil and Karl, patting them softly. "Isn't it wonderful, Karl? Your best friend has come to see us through this crisis. I'm sure his wealthy wife shared her fortune with him and he'll share it with us."

Emil jumped to his feet. "My wife was not rich!" he protested. He looked to his old sketching friend for assistance, but Karl responded with downcast eyes. Emil realized that both of them had harbored thoughts of Karl's wealthy friend helping them escape their dilemma. Clouding Karl's memory was the lavish apartment with its elegant furnishings, maid service, spacious studio and the like. Emil had been his last hope.

In a final effort to shame Emil, Mala shook her fist in his face, a move that clanged a barrage of bracelets against gaudy ropes of necklaces. "Karl's doctor is willing to take one of your paintings as payment. He told me so. Why would he if your paintings are worthless?" The single tear she'd harbored earlier had long since dried and left a mottled spot on her cheek. Emil suddenly saw it as the epitome of Karl's life, a weakness that marred his life and finally ruined it. It was with some difficulty he was able to force his thoughts away from Karl's tragic life and respond.

"People often accept my paintings as gifts, and occasionally they buy them, but not often."

From Mala's throat came a gaudy gasp of contempt. Emil made up his mind to leave, as it was obvious nothing could be done. Visiting was a chore, as the only emotion he felt for Karl was pity.

Mala followed him to the door, blasting him for his callousness one moment, and embracing him the next. When he reached the door, she grabbed a stack of Karl's sketches and thrust them in his arms. "You can do this one last thing for your best friend, can't you?"

Emil let go a deep sigh of disgust. He returned the sketches to the table from which she had taken them, and headed for the exit. When he reached the door, he pulled out a wad of bills from his pocket and handed them to Mala. "Use this toward the hospital bill."

Hastily and greedily, Mala counted it while Emil made his way down the street. "Two hundred dollars? Ha!" she screamed at him. "You think that makes up for a lifetime of friendship? You cheap bastard!" She followed him, shouting obscenities. Neighbors peered out the doors and windows while passersby stared in disbelief. "Look at him," she screamed. "He's rich, but he won't help his best friend. Look at his crooked hands," she yelled. "Jealousy, jealousy, that explains it." Block after block she taunted him, finally turning back when exhaustion claimed her emotionally and physically.

Emil quickened his pace.

The episode with Karl lingered with Emil week after week after week. He wanted to get away somewhere, perhaps Monhegan or anywhere for that matter, but leaving a new job would be risky. If he took a vacation, a long-term employer might hire him on his return, but only with a substantial cut in salary. A new manager would only laugh in his face. Given his state of mine, he felt he had to do something. He decided to try for a five-day work week, an arrangment that would enable him to paint, and to visit the Weins family again.

Timidly, he approached the manager. "If you please, sir, I would like Saturdays off. I mean so that I can, well, you see, sir, I—"

"Anything you say, Holzhauer," the irate manager bellowed. "Perhaps you'd like to begin your day at ten in the morning?" In spite of the cutting remarks, the manager finally agreed to a five-day work week.

With the job secure, he was quick to call on the Weinses and was welcomed like a member of the family. Ed was pursuing his musical career in Germany again, and Clarle had recently graduated from high school. Geena mothered him, mending his clothes and serving his favorite foods. Clarle would have none of the domestic chores, but she talked excitedly about continuing their gallery tours. Much to Geena's consternation, the two made arrangements for Clarle to pose the following Saturday.

He soon received a request from the Boston Art Club for an exhibition of his most recent work. Such requests were not uncommon for anyone who exhibited with any regularity, as he had been doing with the independent group. He usually did not respond to the requests because of the expense involved, but this time, he selected several works and shipped them immediately. It would be a one-man show, but one that he would not be required to attend. That was the best part.

In the *Boston Herald*, he read:

> *Hudson River Before Sunrise*, a most unusual composition, possesses much distinction, shows a strongly patterned landscape of hills and winding river, in a cool, luminous light...

It was a boost to his morale. On Saturday, he began a bust of Clarle in Plasticine. After lunch, they continued their gallery tours, saving the Weldschloss for the evenings, where they waltzed the two-step and hesitation waltz as long as the orchestra played.

The age difference of almost twenty years seemed less and less important now that Clarle had blossomed physically and intellectually. Emil continued to tell himself she was a mere child, but he no longer believed it. As she modeled week after week it became more and more difficult to keep his mind on the canvas, but the desire to paint her always overcame his emotions. One Saturday they were in the midst of a session when there was a knock at his door.

"Mr. Holzhauer, Mr. Holzhauer," the landlady called. "There's a telephone call for you."

"Must be someone from your family," he told Clarle. "I never get phone calls."

Downstairs, the shrill voice of an hysterical woman greeted him on the phone. "Oh, Emil," she sobbed. "Our beloved Karl is dead. He's dead," she repeated through choking sobs.

Emil clutched the receiver in a tight grip as the morbid scene in Karl's bedroom four months earlier took over his thoughts. There hadn't been a word of correspondence since that day.

"Emil?" she asked. "Emil! You must help us. We're Karl's family!" she screamed.

"I can't believe it," he said more to himself than to Mala, "Karl dead?" Mala calmed herself long enough to acquaint him with his responsibilities. "He was your best friend. He needs a new suit. You can bring him one when you come."

"A new suit? What for?"

"Why, to be put away in, of course."

"But he had a closet full of suits when I was there. In fact, he boasted about it."

"The idea!" she shrieked. "Bury our Karl in an old suit? You're a goddamn miser just as Karl said."

He missed most of her ongoing rebuke as thoughts of what to do bombarded him. With Karl dead and beyond help, he wasn't at all certain he wanted to go back to Bridgeport. His own agenda ran through his mind, the Martin Exhibition in less than a week and framing yet to be done, and the artists' ball only a week away. Clarle had been looking forward to it and her mother had made a dress just for the occasion.

Everything clamored for his attention, but Karl's dead body seemed to take priority. Walking into the studio, his announcement surprised him as much as it did Clarle. "My best friend has died. I have to leave right away."

At the Ott house, he was duly welcomed by neighbors who worked in the kitchen.

"We have been expecting you," one woman said. "Mrs. Ott is out, I'm afraid. Shopping for funeral clothes."

"Shopping? What time is the funeral?" He asked anxiously.

"Tomorrow at ten."

"Tomorrow! She told me it was today! I can't possibly stay overnight."

"Why Mr. Ott's still laid out on the bed. She's been waiting for you. Said you were bringing a funeral suit."

"But didn't you say she's shopping for funeral clothes?"

"For herself," the woman explained.

Emil crossed himself. It was an unconscious reaction he couldn't account for. "Dear God," he moaned, a reaction brought on by frustration and genuine grief. *What a waste.*

As much as he hated the thought of seeing Karl, he hated not seeing him more. As others arrived, the women became engaged in their work, leaving Emil alone with his private thoughts which quickly put him in a state of tumult. Finally, he walked with uncertainty toward Karl's bedroom. Pushing the door slightly ajar, he peered in the gruesomely dark room, but quickly jumped back, his hand over his mouth, his eyes closed, his mind a jumble of emotional turmoil.

Determined to go through with the ordeal, he opened the door wide and walked in. A quick survey of Karl's dead body revealed a lifetime of memories to the unwilling artist in him. It had been a horrible death, as witnessed by the gnarled fingers clutching the bed post, a desperate attempt to hold onto something, as life had been squeezed out of him. Emil tried releasing the long fingers Karl had once boasted of, now crippled from his disease. He tried placing the once talented hands in a peaceful pose on Karl's chest, but he was ill prepared for the task.

With his own body stripped of its usual strength and vitality, he began to feel weak and nauseous. He raced out the door in agony, barely making it outside before he began heaving convulsively. When a semblance of normalcy returned, he entertained the idea of going back inside, but the mere thought of it sent him reeling again. He left a message of regret with the women and made his way wearily toward the train station, the scene permanently carved in his memory.

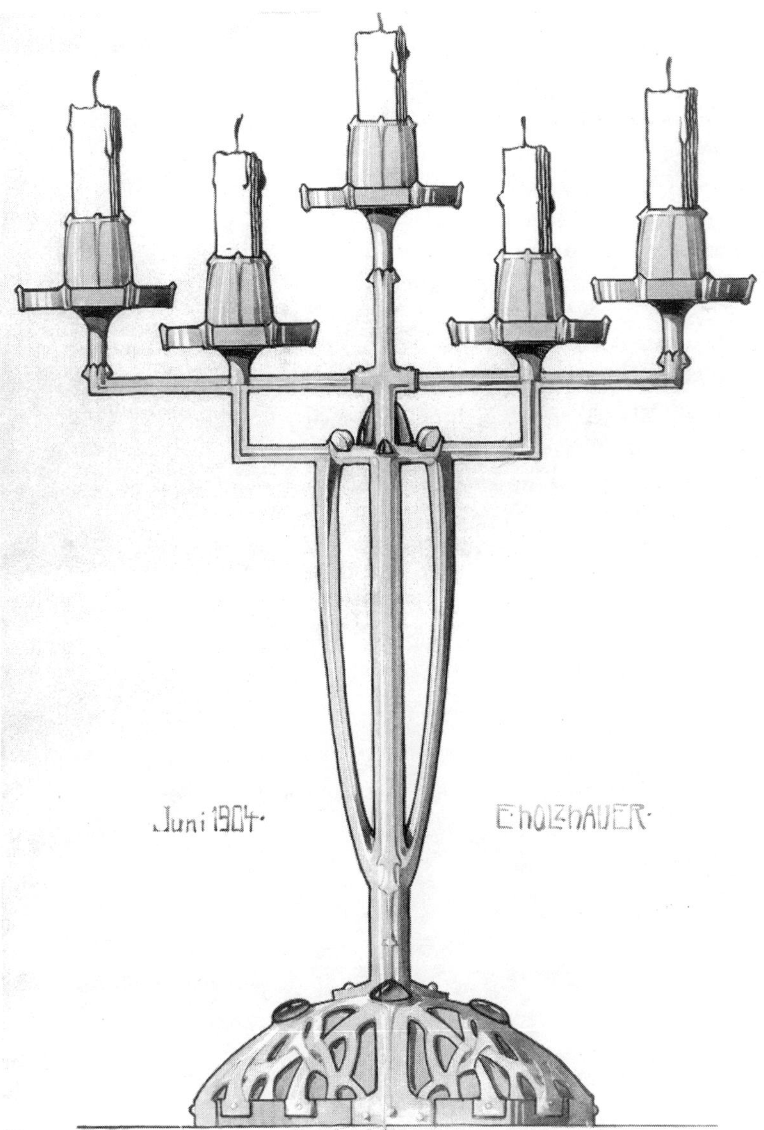

Watercolor, 1904.
Courtesy Museum fur Natur & Stadtkultur,
Schwabisch Gmund, Germany

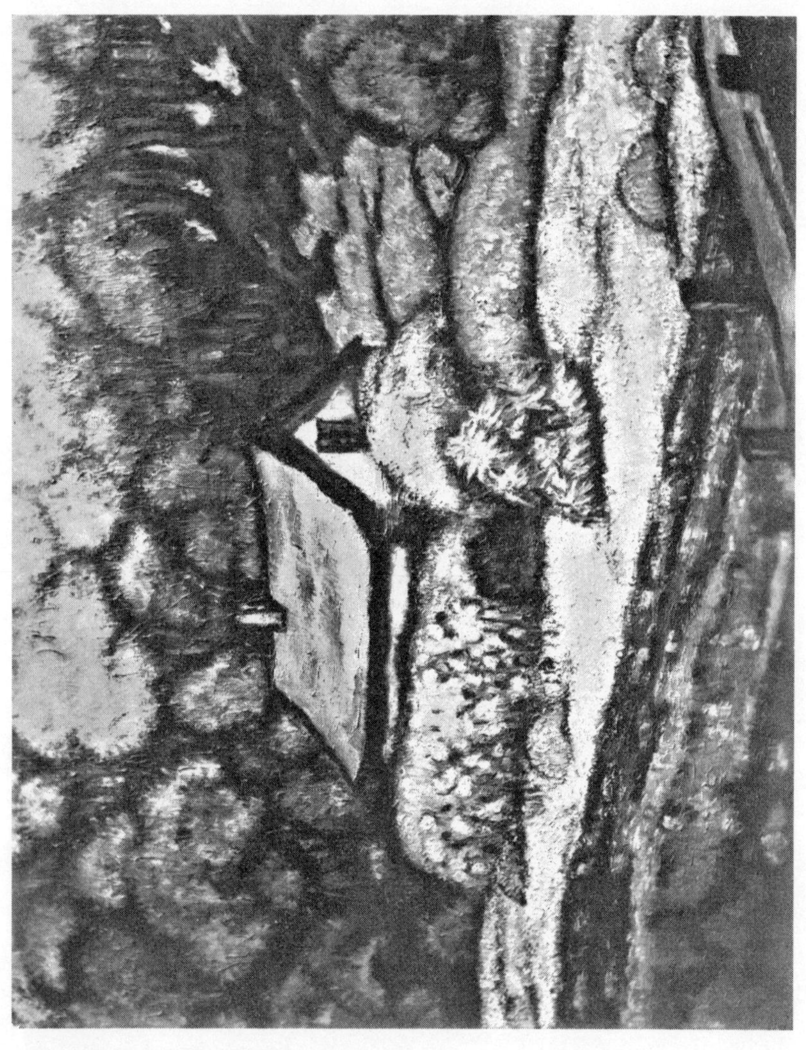

The Englishman's Farm. Oil. (about 1913).
Courtesy Okaloosa-Walton Community College

Still Life, Watercolor, 1927.
Courtesy Lee Ann Wayland-Funk.
Photographer: Jack Gardner

La LSande, South France, Oil, 1925.
Courtesy Ed & Deborah Scofield.
Photographer: Jack Gardner

Cribbage Players, Monhegan Island, Maine. Oil, 1928.
Courtesy Ed & Deborah Scofield.
Photographer: Jack Gardner

Brooklyn Bridge Through the Window. Watercolor, 1928.
Courtesy Edward & Kristie Scofield.
Photographer: Jack Gardner

Patricia Watercolor
Logan Medal Winner, 1930.
Courtesy Institute of Art, Chicago

Main Street, January, Watercolor, 1939.
Subject of NBC Radio Show, 1940.
Courtesy: Okaloosa-Walton Community College.
Photographer: Jack Gardner

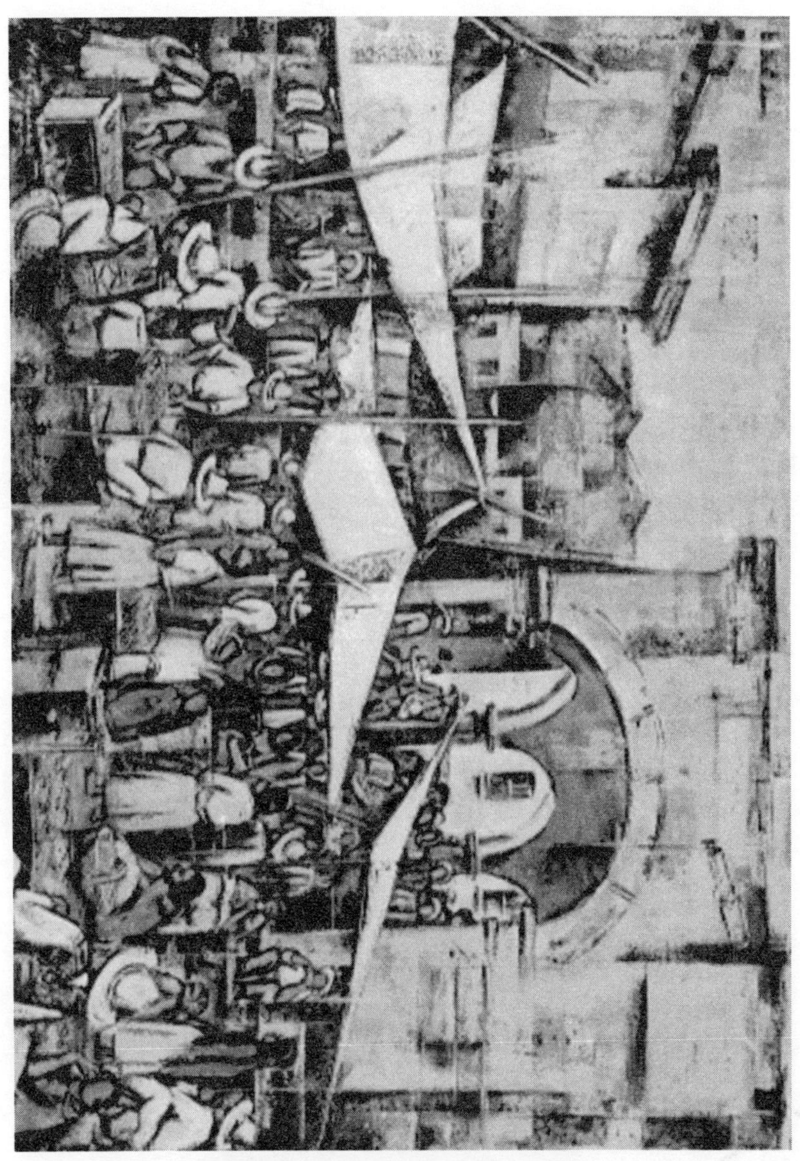

Market Place, Mexico, Casein, 1950.
Courtesy Ed & Deborah Scofield.
Photographer: Jack Gardner

Reflected Reflections, (Holzhauer Self-Portrait).
Macon, Georgia. Oil. 1943.
Courtesy Ed & Deborah Scofield.
Photographer: Jack Gardner

Spence Boats. Oil. Niceville, Florida, 1960.
Courtesy Ed & Deborah Scofield.
Photographer: Jack Gardner

Fifteen

On the return trip from Bridgeport, Emil tried to focus on happier days when he and Karl had roamed the Schwabisch-Gmund streets, the valleys and the countryside with their sketching materials. For the first time, he realized those early days in Germany were the only fond memories he had of Karl.

As difficult as life had sometimes been in Schwabisch-Gmund, he remembered it with warmth and longing. With Karl gone, nearly everyone close to him in the little village was dead. There was, however, his Aunt Rose. It was through her he had learned of the plight of his countrymen since the war.

It was a source of much concern for Emil. For months, he had received requests from former acquaintances, fellow employees, and a few strangers for monetary assistance. For that, he could thank Aunt Rose. Assisting her gave him great satisfaction, for it was a means of repaying the many loans his father had negotiated, and never repaid. But like his parents, she couldn't keep the source of her funds a secret. Sharing her joy usually meant sharing her nephew's address.

When he returned from Bridgeport, he was greeted by a handful of letters from home, none of which were from his aunt. Many begged him to find them a "life job" in the United States, or for passage money loans or outright monetary gifts. One letter captured his full attention, escaping the wastebasket as had been the fate of the others. Anxiously, he opened the one from his old *Fachschule*. It was written by Herr Kreisel.

The old professor began with praise for his former student, both for his dedication as a young student in Schwabisch-Gmund and for the recognition he had received in his adopted country. To Emil's dismay,

Herr Kreisel was asking for financial assistance just as the others had, not for himself, but for the school.

"The school will close if we don't get financial aid very soon," he wrote.

Most of the previous requests had touched the former Schwabisch-Gmund boy, some of them bringing tears to his eyes, but as he couldn't help them all, he answered none of them. The plight of the school was quite another story. He wanted to reach out to the young boys who, like him, would have no other source of inspiration for learning art. Taking on the entire finances of the school would deplete his savings, even the investment Schliemann had going for him. That he couldn't do, but for the moment, he opted to send two hundred dollars with a promise of more to come.

Walking back from the post office, he mulled over the possibilities. Felix had the money. He was not noted, however, for his generosity, but he might be persuaded to donate in hopes of advertising his own success.

He made arrangements to meet with Felix at his own factory. Emil was acquainted with the factory and most of its employees, as it was the one he had worked in all the years he attended the Henri School. When Marcy had persuaded him to quit, he had recommended Felix for the job. Later, when the owner of the factory was forced to retire from active work, Felix stepped into a managerial position that paid handsomely.

It was with a great deal of satisfaction that Felix welcomed Emil into his private office. Only a manager, or the owner himself, would have been allowed to carry on a personal conversation during factory hours.

"I heard you went to Bridgeport," said Felix. His tone was one of mockery.

"You going to the funeral?" Emil asked.

"No, no, no," he rattled, as if the idea were preposterous. "Crazy devil. What a mess he got himself into." Anxious to know the reason for Emil's visit, he jumped to conclusions, one after the other, uninterested in discussing Karl. "You need a job?"

Emil was appalled by the lack of respect he showed their dead friend. "I thought you and Karl were good friends."

"He was a damn fool," he said without feeling. "Hell, you know that."

"You've met Karl's wife?" asked Emil.

"Yes, once," he said. "And that was enough." His body stiffened. "So that's it. Raising money for the widow? You won't get any here," he said, jumping up from behind his desk and pounding it with his fist.

"Don't worry," Emil laughed. "I didn't come about Karl. It's the *Fachschule*. I received a letter from Herr Kreisel, who says the school will close unless they get financial help."

Felix broke out in raucous laughter, apparently relieved to know Emil's purpose in coming. "I get letters every day begging for money or a life job," he said in obvious scorn. They both laughed at the mention of a life job and, the German people's illusion that such a thing existed.

"My father had one of those life jobs, you know. Superintendent of the factory for life. Then the factory closed and all my troubles began," Emil reminisced.

Felix would have no part of Emil's gloom. He opted instead to laugh at the past. "What about Wulz?" he guffawed, his big lips engulfing his face. "He lived in fear one of us would take his life job."

Emil enjoyed the laugh and joined Felix in further bantering, but soon rose from his seat, purposely changing the mood. "I should like to support the school, but I can't handle it alone."

"Who're you kidding?" he laughed. I've seen your notices in the paper. Reproductions of your paintings. Why not spend a little of that money? Join the Schwabisch-Gmund gang at the rathskeller. I can't remember the last time you did. After all, you're responsible for all of us being here. Say, why not ask all the Schwabisch-Gmund boys to contribute? We could form a club," he mused, finally taken by the idea.

"No!" Emil snapped. "No social clubs. If you're not willing to contribute, just say so." He headed for the exit, but Felix stopped him.

"I'll give what you give, and not a nickel more," he said.

It was obvious to Emil that he had no real interest in assisting their old school, but neither did he want to give the impression he couldn't afford it. Emil was sent home to determine the amount they would contribute each week.

Meanwhile his thoughts centered on the coming artist's ball. Not since the formal evenings as Marcy's husband had he donned his cutaway, and that had been before the Camp Meade exercises expanded his chest. While women's styles changed like the hands on a clock, menswear had remained basically unchanged, especially formal wear.

Luckily, Emil's irregular eating habits had relieved him of a few extra pounds, which enabled him to squeeze into the outfit. The fitted waistcoat offered the most resistance to his broadened chest but once buttoned, it seemed to give a tad, allowing him to breathe normally. The cutaway coat with its one button near the waistline posed no problem, as his waistline was one area unchanged by the army's exercises. Completing his outfit were pointed calf oxfords and spats. The lengthy coattails gave him the appearance of being taller than five feet, eight inches, and diverted attention from the snugness of the front portion. All in all, he cut a handsome figure with his broad chest, flat stomach, and slender hips.

Clarle was elegant in a satin and lace gown with a fluted, dropped waistband, and ankle length skirt of soft lace tiers over satin. Though loose-fitted in the waist, it failed to hide the waspy waistline beneath.

"Clarlekins," Emil whispered passionately. For a moment at least, he felt as if his life were in its beginning stages, that he had returned to Lauterberg and his beautiful Anna.

Clarle smiled knowingly. She knew his passion for her beauty. At the ball, everyone seemed as captured by her as her escort, who stood a bit taller than usual. Her periodic blush only added charm to her already graceful visage.

She looked to Emil for guidance only to find him staring at her. "Forgive me, darling. You amaze me. Such zest, energy, and intellect," he bragged. "How can one girl have all that and beauty too?" he marvelled. It was all a fairytale he was caught up in and he wished it might never come to an end.

Virtually everyone attended the ball, including former Henri classmates, Homer Boss, and his colleagues. Other students, teachers, name artists, and art patrons were in attendance, and it seemed to Emil that every man there danced with his Clarle.

As for himself, he tried dancing with others, but found it boring, as did his partners. It was impossible to take an interest in their conversation, as his mind was constantly on Clarle, his eyes always searching for her whereabouts. He was glad when the last waltz was played so he could have her to himself.

Parting became more painful as their relationship grew, a fact that both exhilarated and worried him. She returned his affection and seemed as anxious to be with him as he with her, but no amount of rationalizing on his part seemed to ease his mind about their age differences.

In spite of admonitions directed at himself, he never said good night without making plans for their next meeting. This night was no different. They each looked forward to the following Saturday when she would pose for him again.

When the day came, Clarle seemed restless. She put her book aside and left the makeshift model stand on several occasions. In the past, she had been content to sit for hours with hardly a stir. She had learned to ignore his outbursts, his grunts and groans, and his seemingly careless jabs at the canvas, having recognized them as unconscious noises emanating from the artist in him.

"Let's walk along the Palisades," she said. "It's past our lunch hour."

"Oh, forgive me," he begged, tossing his brush aside. "You must be very tired."

"Not at all. Let's go to the galleries, and then to the Weldschloss for dinner and dancing."

"Dinner? Dancing?" he questioned. "Darling, you amaze me with your energy." Truly, it was quite equal to his own, which in itself was extraordinary. Later that day, he watched her on the ferry, silently taking in the scene before her, the churning waters, the Palisades behind them, and the city's skyscrapers stretched out before them. Her exhilarated countenance of earlier in the day had dissipated.

"Anything wrong?" he asked.

"I was just thinking I'll miss all this when I go to college." She eyed him closely.

"But can't we see each other even so?" he asked.

"I don't see how. Not often anyway. I'll be going to Boston you know. September isn't that far off. I won't be able to pose for you or, or anything," she said, avoiding his gaze.

"Boston!" The news shocked him. His involvement with Karl and the Schwabisch-Gmund school fund had taken him away from the Weins family too long. Without Clarle's companionship, life in New York would be quite boring.

They took the ferry on 130th Street and walked along the Palisades to the Weldschloss on the Jersey side of the Hudson. There, in the joyous atmosphere of mixed nationalities and background music from the small orchestra, they enjoyed dinner and an evening of dancing, never pausing except when the musicians took a break. Yet, they had both become taciturn.

Finally, Emil broke the silence. "Darling, I can't stand in the way of your education. I've been planning a trip to Europe for a long time." He laughed at himself, a derisive sort of snicker. "Been planning it for twenty years now," he admitted. "Maybe I'll take the trip when you begin your studies. I'm afraid I would find it hard to think of life without you if I stay here."

Clearly, it was not what Clale hoped to hear. "I don't want to go to Boston," she said, her eyes cast downward. Her comment had apparently called upon all the courage she could muster.

"Darling, what are you thinking?"

"I should like to go with you," she said.

Emil felt a restrained euphoria, a kindling of his soul held at bay. Her soft, creamy-white hands called attention to the rough ill-shaped hands that held them. She was pacified by his gentle touch and warm, reassuring smile. "Sweetheart, nothing would please me more than to take you with me as my wife, but you're so young. What would your parents say?"

"We mustn't tell them." He knew at that point she had thought the whole thing through.

He raised her soft hands to his lips and kissed them gently, then gazed into her troubled eyes. The whole episode had been emotionally draining for her, a fact that spoke for her sincerity.

"Darling, I can't tell you how happy this has made me," he confessed, but fell short of giving in to her. A lengthy silence ensued.

"All right, my darling," he whispered, embracing her gently. "But first, you must have a chance to be with others your age. You go to college, and then, if you still want to be with me, well, I'll send for you."

The idea appealed to her. While she attended college, he worked and saved his money, adding most of it to the trip fund. The fund had grown considerably as had his stock market investment even though he had contributed handsomely to the Schwabisch-Gmund school. With Clarle's letters assuring him of her love and the long-awaited trip to his homeland coming to fruition, factory life became bearable as never before.

For some time, gratifying letters had been pouring in from Herr Kreisel and other professors at the *Fachschule*, but along with them came numerous requests for personal loans for their own pet projects. Even Herr Kreisel was guilty of it. Emil, incensed by their pettiness, courted the notion of dropping the whole project. But with Felix contributing equally, he had no authority to do so.

Sixteen

Emil's long awaited return trip to his homeland became a reality. More than ten years had passed since the death of his mother, but he fully expected, and dreaded, being required to relive the whole episode of her death with her only surviving sister.

Aunt Rose was in her eighties. She looked it, with her deep-set facial wrinkles, thin grayish hair, and curved spine. She was, however, still very much in the know, especially about the price of things. After the war, survival had become her main concern, and like most Germans, she especially feared not having enough to eat. In their minds, those who had not lived to see the war and its aftermath were the lucky ones.

"Your mother, God rest her soul," she said, making the sign of the cross, "I'm glad she didn't live to see this." No tears, no dwelling on the subject. "You brought her ashes?"

"Yes, yes," he said anxiously. "I'd like to attend to that right away."

"We'll see to it soon enough," she said, nervously jumping from one subject to another, seldom demanding much from her listener. "The German mark is useless, Emil. Useless!" She quickly added that she was in need of nothing because of his generosity. "I'm one of the few who has plenty of food," she declared. "You must be starved, Emil. I'll prepare your dinner. Because of you, there's plenty."

He watched as she arranged a one-place setting and directed him to take his seat at the tiny table. "Eat to your heart's content," she told him proudly. "Sit, sit," she directed when he made no effort to move toward the table.

"Me? But what about you?"

Ignoring his question, she pulled his chair out and motioned him to sit. "I'll eat soon enough. There's plenty," she kept repeating. While he ate, she kept insisting he eat heartily. The meal consisted of a few cold cuts, a typical German supper, and one Emil delighted in. Just as she insisted, he ate heartily, leaving only a few scraps on the table.

"You don't know how lucky I was to get the *Schinkenwurst*," she said proudly. "I had to tell them my rich nephew was coming from America. Ah," she gasped, "the cost of it. I couldn't have managed that many marks in my wheelbarrow. But of course I had your American money. You have no idea how far five American dollars will go. You could buy a piece of land with it. Course, who would waste it on land? Except the Jews."

"Jews? What Jews?"

"Any Jews. They came from Austria. They bought everything. All the land. All the property." Aunt Rose's voice reeked of hatred.

"How do you know?"

"Everybody knows!" She gasped at his ignorance. "Look around when you go into town and see for yourself. Now we have to buy everything from the Jews. The most they paid for anything here was sixty dollars," she groaned. Her brow, already deeply creased, formed extra convolutions as she spoke.

"But why do they sell it to them?"

"You can ask why? For money! For sixty dollars I could live a lifetime."

God, what a revelation, he thought sadly. Excusing himself, he walked outside. There it was, stretched out before him, his beautiful little Schwabisch-Gmund. Unharmed by the war, at least in appearance, destruction had come to its inhabitants through hunger, debt, and loss of property. Strange, he thought, how the inward turmoil of the city and its people had no effect on its charm for the artist. He couldn't wait to begin painting. But first, he had to see to the burial of his mother's ashes.

Returning to the kitchen, he found his aunt devouring the few morsels he had left on the table. Only then did he realize she had put her entire ration before him not knowing whether he would leave anything. And he damn near hadn't, he thought, silently scolding himself.

When morning came, he was faced again with a one-place setting. "Nothing for me but coffee. I never eat breakfast," he lied.

Satisfied that he was telling the truth, she poured his coffee. Startled by its taste, he examined the cup's contents.

"How's the coffee?" There was no mistaking her countenance. She expected praise for her efforts.

"A little weak," he admitted. It was the best he could offer under the circumstances.

The creases in his aunt's mottled face seemed to grow deeper with every disappointment. Her smile had totally vanished. "I'm afraid you've been spoiled in your new country, my boy."

He almost objected, but held his tongue, a rarity, his thoughts often spouting from his mouth long before his mind agreed to them. The truth was, the coffee was only water, colored slightly, but unflavored. Plain water would have been more tasty.

The task of breakfast over, he went to see the *Rettenmayer*, the official in charge of the town cemetery where his father was buried.

"Next week," the *Rettenmayer* said. "Won't be easy finding a gravedigger in this weather."

"Gravedigger? For ashes?" he asked. "What can it require? I could dig it myself."

The graveyard official was clearly peeved by the request. "You have kept your mother's ashes ten years and now you can't wait another week? We have rules you know."

Emil persisted, finally persuading the *Rettenmayer* to send the gravedigger the next day. The weather was horrendous, a dismal day in more respects than one, and weather his aunt should never have been subjected to. At the grave site, the digger cursed the elements and everyone associated with the burial, quite outraged at being called upon. Suddenly, he reached down and pulled out a bone, one he and Emil recognized as a femur.

"Oh, no! Is that my father's?" He clutched the vial of ashes in one arm and put the other one around his aunt's shoulder, hugging her gently.

"Don't worry, Emil. It's not your father's bone. There are no clean burial grounds in this city," she assured him.

It reminded him of his youth when he had seen diggers excavate bodies, throw them in a pit and bury them all in one massive grave. He had been horrified by it all. But those graves were different. Their markings were half moons with a star inside instead of the cross as the locals had. "War prisoners," his mother had explained at the time, referring to the war of 1870 between Germany and France. She left the impression, purposely no doubt, that only the prisoners were treated that way.

"The truth is," offered the gravedigger, "all burial's only temporary. Eventually, everyone's thrown in the big ditch."

As soon as the grave was finished, the digger urged Emil to act hastily. "Be quick before it fills up with water."

"Watch your tongue!" Emil screamed at him. "Have you no compassion?" Turning to his aunt, he followed her lead with the sign of the cross. They bowed their heads for a silent moment before placing the simple vial in the watery hole. It was a dismal moment for Emil, and he deeply regretted his haste in performing the task at hand. He would have savored a few moments over a dry grave, reminiscing with Aunt Rose about his beloved mother. But the deed was done, and the two of them departed hastily for home.

Back at the apartment, they were greeted by a neighbor who told them Herr Kreisel had called on Emil. "The *Fachschule* is giving a dinner in your honor," the neighbor told them.

"A dinner! Just imagine," Aunt Rose beamed. "What an honor, Emil. Nobody gives a dinner anymore."

"It's tomorrow evening, and they want you to come early for a look around the school. You should have heard him praising you," said the excited neighbor. "He was quite disappointed that you weren't here."

The next morning, Emil slipped out of the house before dawn, saving himself the trauma of drinking colored water under the watchful eyes of Aunt Rose. With the Holzhauer dinner to attend, and the intermittent rain to contend with, he was confined to the city for his painting adventures. He spent most of the day packing and unpacking his painting paraphernalia in an effort to keep it dry. Exhausted and hungry at the end of the day, he looked forward to the dinner where he could eat without anguish. At his old arts and crafts school, he was treated as a celebrity by professors and students alike. He was shocked by the professor's fashionable attire, a direct contrast to others whose clothes bore signs of lengthy wear and outdated style. Physically, he was little changed except for the once reddish hair now turned to gray. He greeted Emil with a healthy grin and followed it with a bear hug, almost bouncing with delight. When the two took a tour of the school, the old professor pointed to materials and repairs he and Felix had been responsible for. In the watercolor studio, Emil was told to look around the room.

"Perhaps it'll bring back memories?" The old professor's puffy eyelids nearly concealed the gleam in his eyes.

"I can't believe it!" Emil yelled. Still tacked on the professor's wall after twenty years was Emil's childhood rendering of the pink crane. "I'm afraid I remembered it as much better than it is," he confessed, laughing heartily. Somehow, the sight of his early work didn't distress him like exhibiting in the States had, but he did wish for a chance to rework it or take it down.

At the banquet, the food and the ample supply of beer received more attention than the honored guest, at least until it was gone, but as he was as hungry and thirsty for a good meal and a bottomless stein of beer as the others were, he took little notice. Herr Kreisel made a speech in his honor, praising him highly for his achievements in the field of art and for his assistance to the school. The turnout was tremendous, apparently including all the professors and many former schoolmates, some of whom had been successful in their own pursuits.

Formalities complete, Emil was deluged by whispering professors who voiced their complaints about the way Kreisel had handled the money.

"He uses the money for his own pet projects," one accused, and others shook their heads in agreement.

"We need the money for supplies for our own classroom, but we never get a cent. Take a look at his new suit," offered another.

A former classmate of Emil's joined the bickering group. "You should have bought the school building and started your own. It wouldn't cost more than fifty American dollars." He laughed, but it was a mournful laugh, signifying his indignation. "The damn Jews bought everything in town," he added. "Herr Professor Kreisel should have bought it all in your name just to keep them out."

As other professors registered complaint after complaint against Herr Kreisel, Emil glanced across the room at Herr Braun who was hanging on Kreisel's every word, smiling agreement to all he said. As Kreisel spoke, Braun brushed the director's jacket with meticulous care, even though it needed no attention. Only moments earlier, Braun had initiated the criticism of Kreisel.

Emil felt like washing his hands of the whole affair. The beautiful image he had always harbored for Professor Kreisel and all the others was destroyed. He had always associated the title, "professor" with integrity, irreproachable conduct, and superior intellectual capacity. Like the pink crane on Kreisel's walls, the image had been greatly damaged.

He was glad when the affair ended.

He looked forward to painting trips into the mountains and the open country where the fresh country air would restore his zest for life. But the weather simply would not cooperate. He was lucky to get in a few hours' work now and then within the city's walls. One rainy day followed another with no end in sight. He would have left sooner than originally planned except that he was waiting for word from Clarle. When no letter arrived by the expected date, he decided to travel across the country.

Aunt Rose made one last effort to please him with the coffee. He watched from the doorway as she counted the customary number of coffee beans one at a time. Once the daily maximum had been counted, she removed five more from the container, carefully placing each bean in the grinder one at a time. At the last minute, she walked back to the cupboard, picked up the coffee container and pulled out one more bean, placing it strategically among the painfully thin layer already there.

The coffee was no better than it had been, but Emil complimented her on its good taste. She smiled contentedly.

At the train station, his aunt handed him a brown package. "Open it later," she insisted. They embraced in a teaful farewell. When he promised to return before leaving for the United States, they were both appeased.

On the train to Berlin, Emil took in the sights of his native country, sights he was seeing for the very first time even though he was nearing his fortieth birthday. He had traveled at night on the incoming trip, thus depriving him a view of the country. Basking in the glory of the thick green forests and quiet country villages, he enjoyed a rare moment of relaxation.

Traveling on Sunday brought to mind the days when he and Karl had been forced to attend Mass, a chore for the young boys who wished to be outside with their sketching materials. He watched as village after village presented its steepled churches, some already filled with worshippers, while others rang their bells in an appeal to the masses to heal their spiritual lives. He watched as parents led their children inside the awesome entrance doors. He wondered if they felt tortured by it all as he had.

He laughed as he recalled the thoughts of a young boy that were filled with momentary remorse for his sins, but thoughts that were erased by a burning desire to be elsewhere. For his mother's sake, he had tried feigning a desire to worship, but hatred for his father always overruled those tender emotions.

The awesome church doors had always symbolized imprisonment to him. Even his soul, the priest's favorite subject, had been incarcerated and made to flounder in distress while penned up inside the church's walls.

The scenery continued to overwhelm him, to bring back memories of the past, but also to suggest the future, one he hoped to fill by giving voice to all his yearnings for artistic expression. Thoughts of the future always meant thoughts of Clarle. He yearned for the comfort and stimulation of a close companionship again. From time to time, women had made overt advances, some peddling sex only, but even that kind of relationship proved to be too time-consuming for his lifestyle. The permanent relationship with Clarle had become his heart's desire.

He was hours from Schwabisch-Gmund when he became conscious of Aunt Rose's brown package still in his hands. Curious to know its contents, he loosened its tiestring and unfolded the paper. "*Schinkenwurst*!" he blurted. There must have been a week's ration. But he was famished. Except for the night of the banquet, it was the only time since arriving in Germany that he had had his fill.

As soon as he arrived in Berlin, he contacted Ed Weins, who was studying music composition at the *Akademie die Kunst* under Arnold Schoenberg. Since the early days when Karl had written about the art galleries in Berlin, Emil had longed to see for himself, and he relished the notion of sharing those experiences with his old army buddy.

Nudging its way into his thoughts was the notion that Ed would have to be apprised of his plans to marry Clarle. Rather than chance a confrontation, he opted to postpone the news. While Ed studied, Emil painted and toured the galleries. During evening meals, they shared the experiences of the day and mulled over events occurring at home. A young twenty-eight himself, Ed clearly saw Emil as a middle-aged man as evidenced by his comments.

"It must have been very difficult for you. The divorce I mean. At this time in your life?"

"I'm afraid an artist isn't easy to live with," conceded Emil. "I was immature. I take most of the blame for the breakup of my marriage. I would be a much better husband now," he added purposefully.

"I think you may be too generous. Everyone knew about Miss Didrikson's stage fright. Clearly, she lacked discipline. It must have been a dismal feeling for her, one that no doubt ate into your relationship."

"If you only knew the whole story," he moaned. "Marcy had tremendous insight. With no background in painting at all, she saw the need for me to make more use of color in my work, to soften the harsh lines. She saw the parallel of painting to musical impressionism, but I was too shallow and too stubborn to listen." His mood was one of regret. "She had tremendous discipline, believe me."

"For practicing perhaps, but she lacked the discipline needed to quell her insecurity, so she couldn't lose herself in her performance. Inner beauty comes from the soul, not the ear, not the eye. You won't disagree with that, will you?" As Emil made no response, he continued. "You should hear Schoenberg. Such freedom he advocates in music. As a Henri product, you would appreciate his attitude. Inner beauty doesn't mean traditional beauty. It may even result in dissonance."

Emil was impressed, as always, with Ed's understanding of things artistic. Nor was he in a position to argue, as he had spent years seeking that inner beauty, discarding conventional outer beauty in the process, and there were times he felt on the verge of discovering it.

"So far, it has eluded me except for fleeting moments," he whined. "What an education you must be getting with Schoenberg."

"Perhaps your dad's strict upbringing has had its rewards as well," he noted. "He must be very proud."

"Not proud enough to pay my expenses," Ed joked. Like Emil, he lived a frugal life, often forgoing comfort and proper nourishment. It was only with Emil's promise to pay that he was persuaded to dine in a nice restaurant in lieu of washing down a day-old meal in the dungeon-like basement he rented. He financed his studies by playing with a musical group, but judging from his lifestyle, the pay must have been poor.

Emil soon bade farewell to Ed and headed south toward Munich, still unable to broach the subject of Clarle. In Munich, he revisited the galleries he and Karl had marvelled at so long ago, then tackled the Bavarian foothills of the Alps as subject matter. Later, he sought German art classes at different studios, though most were closed for the summer, and others were spiritless compared with those in New York.

When a letter arrived from Ed, it lifted his spirits considerably. The group he had been playing with had disbanded and he was on his way to Munich.

As soon as he arrived, Emil asked him about Vence.

"Filled with artists," Ed told him. "And no wonder. I hear you can live there for a dollar a day." If anyone would know the price of things, Ed would. He took a long look at Emil at that point. "You're leaving your homeland so soon?"

Emil shrugged. "I've stayed about as long as I intended. I've toured the galleries and painted. Covered a great deal of territory, too."

Ed sensed disappointment. "Starchy people, the Germans. Don't you think so? Even in the beer gardens I found it true."

Emil admitted as much. "Maybe the war."

"Don't worry. You won't find it that way in France. Of course the French hate the Germans, you know. Speak English when you're in their presence. *Sale boche*, they yell. Filthy Germans," he translated, laughing. "But listen, I need a vacation from my work. I'll go with you to Vence and spend a few days."

Vence was not a disappointment. Artists from all over Europe and the United States and other parts of the world vacationed there. Emil was happy to learn that none of them fought wars, beliefs, or nationalities. They came to paint, not criticize. Guests in the inn and the small cottages gathered nightly in the Chateaux. There was always champagne available, and at ten cents a bottle, nobody quibbled over losing a bottle or two. Nobody but Ed.

"Who wants hot champagne?" he complained when it was his turn to pay. Cheap, but not chilled, the bottle's entire contents sometimes emptied in a spurt, but when someone else bought, Ed suddenly developed an unquenchable thirst. His penny-pinching soon became a joke among the group.

From the beginning, Emil painted in his newfound paradise. The little city offered an eye-catching view of the mountains that came right to the sea and held the cold north winds back. Even in winter, the whole Riviera was covered with violets and other perfume-making flowers.

He soon found himself using arbitrary color, kept almost to a monotone, and geometrically identifying everything from stone steps to floating clouds. If the objects weren't angular and he thought they had too many curves, he rounded them, geometrically simplifying them. Conventional objects such as clouds he saw as nothing more than elliptical shapes. White cloud shapes became the positive, dark the negative. Lines in buildings he tended to spiral and elevate to the sky. He found that he could make the whole thing solid by relating each part to the whole through the use of shape.

All of his training, experiences, and influences seemed to come together, producing a spiritual expression of the soul. He felt freer than he ever had, and his paintings showed it. He was so pleased with his work he shipped several pieces to Schliemann to be included in a Weyhe Gallery exhibition.

Finally, the long-awaited letter arrived from Clarle. Her letters had been returned from Germany, she explained. And just as he insisted, she had met other boys and had dated a few times, but nothing interested her. She wanted to marry him. He sent the passage money and made plans to meet her in Paris.

Meanwhile, news of his exhibit came from Schliemann:

> … your spiraling stairs have been well
> received by the critics. The *Post* mentions your
> aggressive brushwork which you accomplish without
> allowing forms to become too severe and your
> organization of planes as having an agreeable
> sense of space…

The idea of the stairs, spiraling, and circling had been good for him, but it had reached its peak, making his work stylistic again. His search for expression outside the bounds of convention sent him painting daily. Meanwhile, Clarle was on her way.

He was faced with the inevitable. Ed had to be told. Emil began by telling his future brother-in-law he planned to be married.

"Married! Why that's wonderful. Someone in the States?" Ed was taken aback. "Not a French girl? Say, did you meet someone out there?" He gestured in the general direction of the sea, a path Emil often took when painting.

Emil fumbled for words. Instead of answering Ed's questions, he asked if he would be a witness at the wedding. "I'll need a translator in Paris," he explained.

"Paris? You found a wife in Paris? But when did you—" Ed was clearly shocked and confused.

"It's Clarle, your sister," Emil blurted. "She's arriving on the train tomorrow." He gestured with flying hands as if to explain further, but quickly decided he had said enough.

Ed sat down heavily. With his elbows resting on his knees, he covered his face with his hands and remained in that position for a long moment.

Emil made meaningless gestures. "I know how you must feel. She's very young and I—"

Ed finally stood up and faced Emil, a confused look on his face. "I can't believe how blind I've been."

Emil was speechless. It was apparent to him that Ed would fight the union and Clarle would be sent home.

"You have my blessings!" Ed assured him warmly. "I won't have to support her anymore," he added. They laughed, then embraced.

The next day, they met Clarle at the Paris station. When she stepped off the train, both men stared at her with unbridled joy and admiration. They marvelled at her ability to travel alone and her commitment to the changes in her life. She was elegant in a soft grey calf-length suit with dropped waistline enhanced by tiny embroidered flowers. Her cloche was banded with the same soft grey and the same pink flowers, the brim framing her classic face. She appeared to have just stepped out of a dressing room instead of having traveled for days.

For a moment, it seemed to Emil he had returned to Europe to claim his beautiful Anna of Lauterberg. He finally broke the silence. "Darling, I was just telling your brother how beautiful you are. I should have waited and let him see for himself."

It was exactly what Clarle wanted to hear. They were married that day at the Paris city hall with Ed as their witness.

Clarle seemed in awe of it all, impressed by her new husband's worldliness; his command of two languages, and his ability to travel with ease in a foreign country, his knowledge of art and artists, and, of course, his own recognition in the art world.

In Paris, they toured the galleries, a world away from the New York galleries where Emil had first begun her art education. It was Clarle's first opportunity to see the post-impressionist work of van Gogh and Gaugin. Time and again, they returned to a Picasso/Matisse exhibit, often topping off the day's tour at the Cafe du Dome where they had the pleasure of seeing artists whose work graced the walls of the exhibition halls and museums.

As much as Clarle enjoyed the art galleries and exhibitions in Paris, she loved Vence and its countryside more. Her husband took her to Grasse to view the making of perfumes from the very flowers that had delighted her on the hillsides back home.

Clarle more than filled the void in Emil's life that Marcy had created. He took time out from his work to take her to other parts of France, Italy, and Schwabisch-Gmund, where mouths opened and tongues wagged about the union. Later, they returned to Vence and continued with their full schedule of painting all day and partying in the evenings. They amazed everyone with their tirelessness.

Eventually, the partying took its toll on Emil's artistic efforts. His work had steadily improved since his marriage to Clarle, but the day came when he was exhausted and stale. He made up his mind to return to New York and make a concerted effort to show his work.

Seventeen

When the newlyweds returned to New York, they found jobs plentiful again, for women as well as men. In order to take advantage of the situation, Clarle enrolled in a typing course. She was bent on earning enough money for a return trip to Europe, a place she had come to view as paradise.

Emil shuddered at the sight of the paintings he had shipped from France for exhibition, so thin and unsubstantial in his view. It was discouraging to think that was his best effort after months of daily freedom for painting and experimenting.

In spite of the negative attitude, he kept his promise to exhibit his work, shipping it to Milwaukee, Denver, Rochester, Philadelphia, and other cities. The out-of-town exhibits allowed him the pleasure of showing without appearing. When the twelfth annual independents' show came along, he was expected to appear in person. He fought a daily battle, raving first against his work, and then against himself, certain one minute of the superiority of the watercolors, and reaching the depths of despair the next because of their mediocrity.

Only the oils had been shipped to out-of-town exhibits because that was the medium he had been recognized for, as well as the medium galleries requested. In a vain moment, he made up his mind to show a few watercolors at the independents' show.

Clarle had to represent him at the pre-opening, as it began during factory hours. While she reveled in such events, he agonized over it. The gallery would close shortly after factory hours, but if he hurried, and public transportation ran on time, he could make the closing moments of the exhibition. Wearing his good clothes to work meant an exercise in fortitude, not only in keeping neat and clean, but in subjecting himself to caustic remarks from fellow factory employees. Most of them rarely read the art pages and wouldn't have known about Emil's recognition if not for the jealous manager who wrote "cheapskate" on his pay envelope, making certain everyone got a peek. It gave the crudest employees a source of entertainment at Emil's expense. "That rich son-of-a-bitch" and "goddamn miser" were common remarks, and many mocked him with insulting gestures of pretentiousness, a reference to the fine clothes he wore on opening days at the gallery. Fortunately, no conversation was permitted once the working day began, but they saved their remarks for lunchtime, when Emil, tense anyway at the thought of exhibiting, flared back at them, an act that only heightened the situation. By the end of the day, he was churning inside, a combination of factory agitation and exhibition woes eating away at him.

Clarle was a gracious representative for her husband at the pre-opening. With assurance she didn't feel, she told his former classmates and Mrs. Martin, the gallery director, that Emil would arrive before closing time.

"We never used to see him at all once he assisted with the hanging," Ms. Martin said. Clarle smiled acknowledgment of her own influence.

"It's just that he's never satisfied. No, that isn't it, either. He's satisfied until he sees his work exhibited," she quickly added. "But I think he's coming into his own, if only he could believe it. Come, let me show you what I mean. Do you mind?" On the contrary, Mrs. Martin seemed pleased.

"Look at all the details, and still, he gets monotone. Skillfully handled. And notice the grey porch? Has enough green and blue to make you look within. He shows you the important things that hold the building together, and it's not the stones."

Mrs. Martin was impressed. "Do you paint?"

"No, I don't have the patience." Grinning, she added, "Emil lacks the patience for little else. He would be happy painting every day of his life." She hadn't intended to reveal bitterness, but she had failed in that attempt.

Mrs. Martin let it pass. "What do you think of the other exhibits?"

"Very modern, all of them. But still individualistic. I don't know what they would have done without you, Mrs. Martin. Really. While others vowed they would debauch public taste, you gave so many a chance to show. You truly can take part of the credit for greater liberality in the art world."

When Emil finally arrived, he stood at the entrance a moment, searching the room for Clarle.

"Emil," a voice called. "Emil, I have been waiting for you. I was afraid you weren't coming." It was a familiar voice, but one he couldn't identify immediately.

"Lamberty?" he wondered aloud.

"Emil," Lamberty called again, unaware his identity had been questioned. "Ah, my friend, this is wonderful," he gasped, waving his hand in the air, an awkward reference to the exhibit. "Your work shows your French inspiration. I saw your exhibits at the Weyhe, too. Tell me all about it," he demanded, but failed to pause. "And you married in Paris. Ah, a French girl," he rejoiced. "Did you see Picasso? And Matisse? I shall be going there myself soon," he announced quite seriously. It was obvious the poor fellow had lived a vicarious life, totally dependent on others for his satisfaction. Emil suddenly felt a deeper than usual pity for the skeleton-like creature who never seemed to touch base with reality. But he had attended the show, an indication he had read the newspaper or at least made contact with someone in the art world. It had to be an improvement over the street episode that had lingered in Emil's memory.

"What about you? What are you doing these days?" Emil asked. He wanted to rephrase the question, or perhaps retract it, as it would no doubt lead to a dissertation about his upcoming trip to France, the one he had considered imminent for almost fifteen years. "Painting?"

"Oh, just sketching. Studying the muscles you know. One can never get enough of it. I still have the skeleton, but I want you to have it," he announced. He broke into an uncharacteristic grin, apparently pleased that he had something he considered valuable enough to offer his old Henri classmate. He peered into Emil's face, anxious to catch his reaction.

Having caught a glimpse of Clarle across the room, Emil stared for a moment, giving himself an opportunity to admire her firm, shapely legs in a new knee-length dress. Women's hemlines went up and down like a window shade, but it didn't matter. Clarle could wear them all, he thought proudly.

"Please excuse me," he told Lamberty. "I must say hello to my wife." He saw the hurt then, the expression of a hungry child who had been denied supper. "Come, I'd like you to meet her," he said warmly. He almost swaggered in her direction, Lamberty following close behind like a doting pet.

Clarle's glare spoke for her displeasure. "I thought you'd never come," she pouted. "Come, let's make the tour," she urged, ignoring Lamberty.

"Forgive me," Ms. Martin called. "I may not get another chance to ask. Would you be interested in gallery work, Clarle?"

"Gallery work?"

"Yes, for an art dealer. Selling. I'm sure you would be perfect for the job."

"She certainly would," Emil said. "She'd lend beauty to any art gallery too." The idea so entranced Emil that he forgot about Lamberty.

"Emil, please," Clarle scolded, though the remark was obviously well received. "I really would," she told Mrs. Martin.

"Good. I know of an opening in the Van Diemen Gallery on 57th Street. I'll recommend you."

The news lifted both their spirits, and for Emil, it made the ordeal at the factory all worthwhile. In order to remain presentable for the exhibition, he had removed his jacket at the factory and had worn an apron to protect his white shirt and pants. He didn't come away clean, but his suit coat hid most of the damage.

It was with some difficulty they escaped the grasp of Lamberty who followed closely behind them like a small child clinging to its parents. Flitting in and out of Emil's thoughts was the old skeleton Lamberty had mentioned. He couldn't help recalling the day it was purchased, a poorly put-together frame practically disintegrating before their eyes even then. It had to be chalky rubble by now.

His thoughts flitted from Clarle to the exhibition to Lamberty and the skeleton, making it impossible to focus on any one thing. Clarle had made her feelings clear. She scarcely nodded when introduced and had turned her back on Lamberty almost immediately.

Lamberty refused to be insulted. He attached himself to Emil like Spanish moss to a live oak tree, his every move dictated by those of Emil.

The whole scene ruined the evening for Emil who wanted to spend some time with Lamberty, perhaps help him escape the rut he appeared to be in, and take him to dinner. However, he longed to have a rare evening with Clarle as well. He knew the two wouldn't mix.

"You can get the skeleton anytime," Lamberty told him for the third time. "Here, I'll give you my address." Reaching into a raveled pocket, he pulled out a small piece of paper that had been folded and re-folded so many times it almost disintegrated in his hands, and he began to write something with a stubby pencil that apparently had never been sharpened.

"No, my friend," Emil insisted. "You mustn't get rid of the skeleton." Placing both hands on Lamberty's shoulders, he looked directly into his consuming eyes. "It has served you well all these years. You mustn't part with it." The gesture seemed to satisfy Lamberty, but it clearly agitated Clarle that her husband had touched what appeared to her to be a dirty beggar from the streets. Even as tears welled in her husband's eyes, she insisted they leave.

At the exit, Emil took one last glance in Lamberty's direction, hoping he had focused on something else, but the comfortless creature's hollow eyes remained fixed on Emil.

"Poor devil," he moaned again and again as the two of them walked toward the subway.

"Who was that creature? You hardly had a chance to see the exhibits," she grumbled. Emil's heaviness lingered but Clarle was soon energized by Mrs. Martin's promise of a job. The Van Diemen was one of the most prestigious in New York. A position there could have far-reaching advantages, as she would come in daily contact with influential people in the art world. Thinking of the possibilities raised her spirits. She felt an urge to do something different. "Let's eat at the Lorelei," she said.

"The Lorelei? It's in the opposite direction," he pointed out.

"So? We'll take another train," she said, quite insistent.

"It's not so elegant you know."

"Even so, I should like to go there. I want to hear the parrot sing."

It was the Cafe Bismarck she spoke of. Just three blocks from the Henri School, the group often went there on Sunday, though it was a rare occasion when Emil joined them. Not that he didn't like the cuisine or the atmosphere; it was the time and the money that kept him away. They served excellent German dishes, but the restaurant lacked the elegance Clarle had always preferred. "I should have invited Lamberty," he mumbled.

"What?"

"Oh, nothing."

At the restaurant, Clarle was childlike with her questions about the parrot. "Does she speak English? What is she saying?"

"She sings the Lorelei," he explained. "Listen," he shushed, joining the parrot,

Ein Marchen aus uralten Zeiten
Das kommt mir nicht aus dem Sinn

"What is she saying?" Clarle asked again.

"Let's see now. 'Why is it I feel so sad'" he translated.

Suddenly, they heard another voice, a familiar one, at least to Emil. "*Ein Marchen aus uralten*—" it mimicked.

"Felix!" Emil yelled. "When did you come in?"

"I was here when you arrived, but you never saw anyone except the lovely lady," he cooed. His eyes were planted on Clarle, his big mouth spouting praise. Clarle was visibly irritated.

"Felix, this is my new bride." He turned quickly toward Clarle, for he knew she would disapprove. "An old friend from Schwabisch-Gmund, Felix Smythe." Without an invitation, Felix took a seat at their table. Clarle glared at Emil, scarcely recognizing the intruder. Stirring in his seat uncomfortably, Emil began to grope for words. Suddenly, an idea presented itself. A report on the *Fachschule* would preclude a visit to Felix's office, something he dreaded.

Obviously taken by Emil's young bride and quite oblivious to her snobbery, Felix showed no interest in discussing their old school. Several times he brushed the sleeve of his suit coat, apparently for the purpose of calling attention to its quality. He was to be denied the pleasure of impressing Clarle, however, as she kept her agitated gaze glued on Emil.

"Why have you kept the lovely lady a secret from your friends?" His eyes remained focused on Clarle, his big lips moist and parted even when he wasn't speaking.

Emil ignored the personal questions. "You would have been proud to see the results of our contributions to the old *Fachschule*," he began. "The students have advantages we never dreamed of. Gallery trips to Munich, Berlin, and even Paris. Just think of it. What an opportunity. Their work is shipped all over Europe for exhibit."

"You're not serious?" he yelled. "And they call that in need?" He looked at Emil for the first time.

"No, you don't understand. They can do these things with our money because a little goes so far. But without our help, the school would have closed." He continued his spiel, his eyes catching Clarle's angry demeanor all too often.

"How did you like Schwabisch-Gmund?" Felix asked Clarle, but gave her no chance to respond. "I'm going back to the old Gmund one day soon. Invested my money in stocks. Put two thousand dollars in one day and had it doubled in a week," he boasted.

Emil almost laughed, but managed to stifle the urge. For the first time, Clarle looked at Felix, a stony glare that spoke clearly for the agitation he was causing her.

"Here, call my broker," Felix insisted. "I'll give you his phone number and the name of the stock." He folded the paper and placed it on the table near Clarle. "You won't be sorry, believe me," he added. "Gotta go," he announced, noisily pushing his chair back from the table.

His departure left a muddled atmosphere, the way a storm leaves scattered debris in its quiet aftermath. It was impossible to recapture the moment. Clarle finally lashed out at Emil who had picked up the folded paper and had torn it in half. "Who is that awful man?" she asked. "You and your dreadful friends," she pouted.

Emil wondered who had the worst manners, Felix or Clarle. He decided it was Clarle, since Felix was clearly under the influence of ignorance. Quite exhausted from the gruesome day at the factory and the stressful ordeal with Lamberty and then Felix, he felt like walking out without eating, but his empty intestines begged him to reconsider. "Let's try to forget we ever saw him. He's a tiresome braggart," he said.

"I'd like nothing better," she snapped. Silence prevailed then, each too irritated to converse. Clarle was first to bounce back, to focus on the parrot, to seek a translation, and capture a moment she had dreamed of. "I've always wanted to come here," she said. Her voice was humble and tempered, an unspoken apology for her part in ruining the evening. She was prepared to begin anew. Wiping the whole scene from his memory was not so easy for Emil. Too, the possibility that Felix's stock was really a winner monopolized his thoughts. He began to piece the papers together and memorize the information written there. "What if it's true?" he wondered out loud.

"Surely you don't take him seriously? You told me yourself he was a braggart."

Emil agreed with her, but he couldn't forget what Felix had said. An investment like the one he described could free him from the factory and place him behind the easel permanently.

The very next evening, he knocked on Schliemann's door.

He was familiar with the stock. "Yes, and there are others like it. Rich today, poor tomorrow. You have to be cautious about these get-rich-quick things," he warned. "You can lose everything in a week or a day. Even an hour, my friend."

"But Felix invested over six months ago, and he's still realizing returns." Emil was in torture. *What if it did keep on going up? I could leave the factory and be free to paint.* "Is there a chance the stock will continue to rise?"

"Of course, but there's a better chance it won't. It's a big gamble when you put your money in those volatile stocks."

For some time during the discussion, Emil had trotted around the room, making nervous, sometimes angry gestures. "Oh, for heaven's sake, Schliemann. Take that down!" he demanded, pointing angrily at one of his paintings on the wall.

As Schliemann made no attempt to comply, Emil snatched the painting off the wall and tore it out of the frame. In a final gesture, he tossed the pieces in a nearby wastebasket. All the while, Schliemann watched in astonishment.

"My dear fellow," he said, his voice giving way to a quiver. "You have destroyed private property."

"I'll give you a better painting."

"Better? That's for me to decide. I purchased that painting because I liked it. I don't want another one!" he shouted. Emil had never seen his friend so angry and out of control.

Instead of tempering him, it infuriated him more. "I painted it! A painting always belongs to the painter. It isn't worthy of me. I'll give you another," he repeated.

"I'm surprised you don't yank the work off the exhibition walls," Schliemann grumbled.

"You have no idea how close I've come," he admitted. The remark eased the tension somewhat, bringing a smile to Schliemann's face. "I want you to invest two thousand dollars in this stock," he said, handing Schliemann the paper bearing the name of the stock.

Schliemann shook his head. "It's your money. I'll give it to you, but I won't invest it in that stock. You can do it yourself."

"All right, then. I will."

Schliemann sent the money right away, and Emil invested it. In a matter of weeks, his money had doubled. Finally, he gloated, a chance had come to really build a savings account. He continued to invest in the stock from his salary, and directed Schliemann to release more and more of his funds for the same purpose. If things kept going the way they had been, he could retire from the factory and do nothing but paint.

While he held onto hopes of a secure future without the drudgery of factory work, Clarle was happy in her new job at the Van Diemen Gallery, where only the old masters were represented. On weekends, they began taking the train to Peekskill and hiking to Riverview.

They renewed their friendship with the proprietors of Rett's Farm, a hotel restaurant known for its tasty German-American delicacies. Paul Rett, the proprietor, welcomed them as old friends. He was a dealer, he said, in everything. Rett was a jolly fellow, always anxious to celebrate something with a drink from his homemade brew. He repeated stories of his days as a European motorcycle champ, but his paunchy belly and other expanded parts indicated it had been further in the past than he remembered.

"A dealer?" asked Emil.

"Yes. I'll buy it if you want to sell it and I'll sell it if you want to buy it." They both liked him immediately. He invited them to his home, where he had a cellar filled with odds and ends. Spotting a beautiful intricate wooden frame, Emil fingered it longingly, then returned it unwillingly to the barrel.

"Sell it to you for fifty cents," said Rett.

"You're joking of course," Emil laughed.

"Not at all. It came in a barrel of things I paid fifty cents for at an auction. Leftovers," he explained. "Things they don't sell. I wait around until the auction is over and bring barrels of things back." As much as Emil desired it, there was no way he could manage the large frame on the train back to New York City as he was already burdened with his painting materials.

"Don't worry. There'll be plenty of others," Rett promised. Opening a bottle of wine from his private stock, Rett filled their glasses and ordered them to drink. "*In vino veritas*" (In wine, there's truth), he beamed. "Let's drink to your coming to Riverview often." They gladly complied.

Hiking there from Peekskill became a weekend must for the Holzhauers. Emil delighted in painting Main Street, Hudson views, and the surrounding mountains. With jobs still plentiful, he often quit the factory and painted for weeks at a time in Riverview and Monhegan Island. The new freedom brought with it noticeable improvement in the quality of his work, especially his watercolors. He continued to exhibit every chance he got.

The reviews substantiated his own renewed belief in the individuality of his work. No copying, no stylization, no mimicking. A *New York American* critic wrote:

> Holzhauer's new canvases are solidly constructed.
> They have balance, depth and organization. The charm
> of subject interests him but little; he is
> preoccupied with good drawing, sound harmony and
> excellence of design.

Before the Martin Exhibition closed, a *New York Times* writer said his "design, with the suggestion of dimension, makes delicate drawing of homely landscape and simple people," and *The New York Evening Post* described him as "less rigid, less absorbed in intricacies of design, and more free."

More and more critics noted his strength of suggestion and freedom from consciousness of technique. They spoke of his mastery of the watercolor medium and uncanny success in eliminating clutter. Mention was often made of his ability to handle snow scenes by using the white of the paper to produce the white of the snow.

As much as he loved painting winter scenes, freezing temperatures often prevented it. Much of the time, his watercolor mixture froze, and once he suffered two frozen fingers. As both were on his left hand, he finished the painting before going home. There would be no more hiking to Riverview until the thaw, perhaps as late as March, or even April.

Winter in New York was an albatross around his neck. Without weekend painting, he felt cheated. Nights were taken up in entertainment. Through Clarle's contacts at the gallery, and with Emil's name appearing more and more on the art pages, they were constantly invited to parties, balls, exhibitions, and the like. It was life akin to what he had known with Marcy.

There were times when he would have preferred a quiet evening at home with Clarle, but it was still a thrill to show off his beautiful bride.

Weekly, his new stockbroker sought him out to share the good news and collect another contribution to the growing fund. When he didn't show one week, Emil called the broker's rooming house.

"Mike doesn't live here anymore," said the landlady.

"Then where does he live?"

"Can't say. They come and go," she said with disinterest.

"But surely he left a message for me, Emil Holzhauer? Please, I must get in touch with him."

"Can't help you," was the disinterested reply.

Emil refused to believe it. Felix, he thought. He would know where to reach the broker. He dialed Felix's apartment and waited an eternity while the landlady fetched him to the phone.

"Felix," he shouted. "I've been trying to get in touch with Mike."

"How much did you lose?" He laughed, a morbid sort of sound that might easily be mistaken for crying.

"Lose! Dear God," he moaned pitifully. "It can't be. I had over sixteen thousand dollars invested. It was my life's savings."

Felix spoke with a thick tongue. It was obvious he had been drowning his own sorrow in alcohol. Rather than try to communicate with him, Emil replaced the receiver, his glint of hope evaporated. Within moments, the truth invaded him. He was nearly as penniless as the day he had arrived in New York City twenty years ago.

The days that followed were almost unbearable. Factory hours dragged as never before. It wasn't unlike the imprisonment he had felt as an apprentice to the Buchhandler concern in Schwabisch-Gmund, the American factory managers scarcely a step above Wulz.

The constant partying Clarle insisted on complicated matters considerably. Emil had difficulty focusing on anything. He developed open sores on his buttocks, much like those he had endured in the artillery. It became almost impossible to sit, and yet, he had to sit nine hours a day, six days a week. His livelihood depended on it. Daily, the situation worsened, the pain excruciating at times. He finally saw a doctor.

Ulcers, the doctor told him. The medicine he prescribed didn't help. Nothing did. The raw ulcers bled, causing his underclothes to cling to his skin. The slightest movement pulled his clothes loose, ripping the temporary scab away and leaving the fresh wound to bleed again. All day, every day, it was the same. Bleeding, temporary crusting, tearing loose, and more bleeding. He would have to quit his job if something didn't change.

His life centered around the dilemma. He thought of nothing else, talked of nothing else. "Clarle, I need two books the same size," he told her one evening. "Place them so," he gestured, "and leave most of the sores free from surface contact." Just as he had done the night before, and the night before that, he was constantly devising methods for survival. "What do you think?"

"I don't think anything," she snapped. "Can't we talk about something else?" The subject of his rear bored and irritated her, especially as it had been the cause of their missing several parties.

The books worked, but one day after lunch, he returned to his desk to discover them missing. He searched the faces of other employees, especially the most vocal ones who had branded him "old sore ass."

"What did you do with my books?" he demanded, switching his glare from face to face. All of them bent over their desks in total submission to their work, ignoring his pleas. From the start, they had shown no sympathy for what they believed to be a well-to-do artist who was willing to suffer through daily pain for the sake of money they thought he didn't need.

Difficult enough with the books, it would be impossible without them. The manager was quick to notice Emil had not begun his work.

"I guess you didn't know the lunch period's over, Holzhauer."

"I don't have my books," he explained with a pitiful grimace. "Oh, you don't have your books," the manager mocked. "Well, you ain't here to read, Holzhauer." The factory employees nearly choked from holding back their laughter.

Emil waddled to his desk. It was either that or quit the job then and there. With no savings in the bank, and no growing investment, he could think of no options. By the end of the day, he knew for certain he could not go through another day like it. Before giving up, he saw the doctor once again.

"I'm afraid I can't help you. You appear to have nothing physically wrong with you. Perhaps your problem is mental anguish," the doctor told him.

With no hope for a cure and no options available, he wondered what Clarle would say to supporting him. Faced with acquainting his bride with the news, he headed homeward, his spirit as low as he could remember it. But Clarle had no time for discussing his dilemma with books, doctors, or the barbaric factory employees. She had her heart set on bowling.

"Have you no compassion?" he asked. "All you think about is partying."

"Partying?" she asked icily. "A simple game? Well, it's better than moaning and groaning about your butt and the money you lost. The doctor's probably right. If you could only learn to relax. You don't have to sit on your butt to bowl," she added. "Or for dancing or skating," she pointed out in a huff.

"Don't talk to me of bowling. Walking itself is a task. Those goddamn *Schweinehunde* at the factory stole my books." To her chagrin, he gave the details of the grueling day and was about to detail the doctor's visit when she interrupted him.

"If you could only learn to laugh with the factory employees, Emil. Learn to see the humor in the situation, then they wouldn't get such pleasure from teasing you. Laugh at yourself," she insisted, as she rummaged through their supply of books. "Here, these should do it," she said, thrusting two small books toward him.

He left for the factory the next day clutching his books. Once there, he held onto them during the lunch hour, snapping at those who needled him. He performed his work diligently, almost with a vengeance, in an effort to lose himself in the process. Each day had become a fight to survive, with no thoughts beyond getting off his sore butt. His usual brisk walk had slowed to an amble.

He made no effort to answer exhibition requests as they, too, were a chore. Matting, framing, and shipping were tasks he couldn't manage.

Day after day, week after week, it was the same. It was months later when the Rochester Woman's Club sent a representative to insist upon an exhibition of his latest work, a one-man show. Their enthusiasm brightened his spirits enough that he assisted them in choosing thirty landscapes, still lifes, and portraits, but beyond that, the women took care of everything.

Somewhat revived by the interest in his work, he thought to surprise Clarle one day. It would mean wearing his suit to the factory, but he was determined to pick her up at the gallery and take her to dinner, something he hadn't done since his attack with ulcers. It would be a treat just seeing her at work again.

He entered the Van Diemen with a rare smile on his face and greeted Clarle with the affection and charm of earlier days. "They should pay you more. Your presence adds so much to the place." He turned her around so as to get a good view of her in a peachy crepe dress with dropped waist and scalloped hemline which had plunged from her knees to mid-calf.

The compliment pleased her. "I'll tell them you said so. Does this mean you're going to the party?"

"Party?" he asked, then quickly slumped in disgust. "I should have known," he remarked icily. "You have no compassion at all, do you?"

"I forgot," she snapped. "You have a sore butt."

"Clarle, sweetheart, why not dine, just the two of us?"

"You dine. I'm going to the party. Everyone's going."

"Hogwash!" he belittled. "The same ones who're always there. Don't you ever get tired of it?" he moaned. "No, I guess not. You live to be seen, don't you? And being sought after on the dance floor. Nothing would induce you to leave before they close the doors."

He left the gallery in anger. At home, he grabbed a few tasteless bites from the kitchen before going to bed.

Eighteen

Perhaps the get-rich-quick broker hadn't done Emil a disservice after all, as nearly everyone he knew was as broke as he was, and most were jobless.

It was October, 1929. The stock market had crashed less than a year after Emil had lost his savings. Businesses, factories, and concerns everywhere began to close. Jobs were scarce as never before, especially those associated with the arts. Clarle's exclusive gallery was among the first to close. Emil's factory only cut production, leaving him with a few days' work a week. Except for the reduced salary, it was exactly what he wanted.

Gradually, his sores had become crusted enough that he could sit with relative ease. With the Woman's Club exhibition in Rochester bringing good publicity, things were not so bad for him, maybe better than for most. An art critic writing for the *Rochester Democrat* spoke well of him:

> Holzhauer is recognized as one of the leaders in this field of expression, and his work as represented here may to some extent, be taken as indicating the direction American art impulses in the last few years. His work is individualistic and not definitely associated with any group or movement. Although his use of water color is in line with the modern tradition which conceives of this medium not so much as for pictorial realization of actual structure and volume…

While life had grown better for Emil, it had become boring for Clarle. Parties were gradually unheard of, and dining out was considered an unnecessary extravagance. Arguments came easily now that she had nothing to occupy her time. Having survived his own private market crash, Emil found that he was too busy to worry about the national one. While others suffered through joblessness and poverty, he painted and he exhibited as long as there was a gallery in business. There were no sales, but he had grown accustomed to that even during the raging economy. Americans who did purchase art continued to buy European for the most part.

He entered the annual exhibition sponsored by the Hamilton Easter Field Foundation at the American Art Anderson Galleries in New York. Like the annual independents' show, the exhibits were accepted on a first come, first served basis as there was no jury. The *New York American* selected Emil's *The Cribbage Players* for reproduction on its art pages and called it, "One of the most noticeable paintings" in the exhibition. The painting, said the critic,

> ...arrests attention by reason of its technical ability. In color it is rather duller than need be, but among its intricate lines and forms there is a distinguished decorative balance. The manner of lighting suggests the abstractions of the cubists and the breaking up of the light finely assists the composition...

Holzhauer was a well-established name in the eastern United States art circles. Even the National Academy of Design chose some of his work for exhibition. From that opportunity came another significant honor, an exhibition of "Thirty Prominent American Artists," at the Memorial Art Gallery. The work was selected from recent exhibitions in four large American Art Centers, including the National Academy of Design from which Emil's work was chosen, the Corcoran Gallery of Art in Washington, the American section of the Carnegie International Exhibition in Pittsburgh, and the Brooklyn Museum.

The opening for such an event would be a celebration, and something Clarle would revel in. The art pages of the *Post*, *Sun*, *Herald*, and *Times* were filled with praise for the exhibition. The work of the thirty artists represented the most characteristic phases in American art.

The exhibits were hung according to two dominant points of view, one largely realistic and more typically American in type; and the other, which included Emil's work, more modern in spirit, with a cosmopolitan stamp after the fashion of Cezanne and the post-impressionists.

His *Apple Blossoms* was reproduced in one of the papers and captioned, "one of the most outstanding canvases on exhibition." As with similar recognition, this one brought no monetary returns. Indeed, the expense of matting and framing had cut deeply into his meager savings, an account that he had only recently opened. With Clarle unable to find work, it was nearly impossible to put anything aside from his part-time work. When *Fortune Magazine* commissioned him to do a tri-color illustration for their publication, he gladly complied and greedily added the money to his dwindling savings account. His haste in this caused much dissension at home. Clarle wanted a break from the boredom of frugality. She wanted to dine and dance, and take in a show. "Just once," she pleaded. A bitter quarrel ensued, closing communication lines for weeks.

Finally, Emil began to entertain the idea. With factory retirement out of the question, it was a mistake to deprive himself and Clarle of travel and other activities they both enjoyed, he reasoned. It was with much anticipation and compassion he announced his decision.

"Clarlekins, we should celebrate, don't you think?" She seemed startled by his tenderness, but receptive. He savored these rare moments when his playful guttural voice, so well received in the beginning of their relationship, still entertained her.

"What did you have in mind?" she asked.

"Monhegan Island. We could stay as long as our money holds out." He waited anxiously for the energized smile, the one that always pressed the dimples in her cheek and reminded him of happier days.

He was to have a long wait. "From what you tell me about Griesheimer, if you leave, you might lose your job."

Her response came as a shock. "I thought you'd be pleased," he said haughtily. "You said yourself we should enjoy life more."

"You have only part time work now. You'll soon have every manager in the city angry with you, and it isn't like it was in the old days before the crash when factories and jobs were plentiful."

It was a slap in the face, an undeserved put-down. "A self-appointed expert on keeping a job, are you?" he said icily. "I'll find a job. I always have, but right now, I'm going to Monhegan. Stay here if you like," he spouted angrily.

"I'm going to Europe," she announced.

"Europe! We can't afford to go to Monhegan and now we're off to Europe?" He laughed mockingly.

"I have my own money. I plan to go alone," she said.

Nothing had prepared him. His lovely Clarle alone on a trip to Europe? She, who had been dependent on him as a guide, a translator, and protector? It was a devastating, and humbling, blow to his ego. He sat down hard.

"I don't think you'll enjoy a trip alone," he said, but a glance at her determined countenance told him otherwise. He had been too busy to see it coming, but like it or not, Clarle had come into her own. From the time she began working in the Van Diemen Gallery, she had put her salary in a separate savings account, intent on returning to Europe. He had always assumed they would make the trip together.

He was wrong.

Fortunately, the trip to Monhegan freed his mind of Clarle. He pounced upon the fishermen as never before, filled with envy for their freedom in the outdoor life where one could always bask in fresh air. It should make their fight for survival a pleasure, he thought. No factory walls, no barbaric factory workers yelling obscenities, no sedentary lives.

With his new inspiration, he was able to take advantage of the scenery even on wet, rainy days. The fat sea captain engrossed in his game, so often his subject in the past, called to him on a rainy day in June. Inside the tiny, cluttered shack, he fought for easel space and elbow room, finally wedging himself among the disorderly assemblage of fishing equipment.

The captain and his fishing companion, absorbed in their cribbage game, inspired Emil to capture their salty characters. Occasional outbursts from the cribbage players were his only interruptions, unless there was the yell of "Mackerel!" With that, cards were quickly abandoned and all in the fishermen's path was dismantled, including, at times, Emil's easel. As often as he warned himself to be cognizant of such a turn of events, he never remembered, was taken by surprise, and was left to muddle in the aftermath.

He had been working in the cramped fishermen's shack for hours when a man poked his head inside. Emil was aware of the intruder but refused, as usual, to take his eyes off the canvas. The sound of a refined voice, so rare in these surroundings, got his attention, however.

"Isn't it rather an ugly day for such a large canvas?" the man asked playfully. Emil recognized him as an official from the Institute of Art in Chicago. He had seen Mr. Seligman on the island during previous visits, but only from afar. He had never spoken to him. "Mr. Holzhauer?" he asked.

"Yes?"

"I'm Jim Seligman. I've been looking for you." He surprised Emil with descriptions of his entries in the institute's exhibition the previous year. "If you promise to join me for dinner at the inn, I won't disturb your work any longer."

As it turned out, they dined together on several occasions, and before Emil left the island they had become good friends. Seligman gave him a special white card to send along with his entries to the next show in Chicago. The card would eliminate the pre-judging and possible rejection by the jury. It made the trip worth the expense if only for that.

Back in the city, he began immediately to choose paintings for the Chicago show. It was perplexing, as always, because so much depended on how the work impressed an individual on the jury. The white card eliminated him from pre-judging, but there remained a final jury to reckon with.

Settling down again in the city was difficult, especially with job-hunting facing him, and without Clarle's companionship. The job proved to be the easier of the two, as part time work was all he desired. Clarle's letters depressed him. She wrote about exciting activities and new friends, the Enger sisters, from Westchester County in New York. He was jealous that she could enjoy herself without him. If she missed him, she didn't say so.

Westchester was the society section of New York. Matt Enger, the girls' father, was an attorney as well as head of the Board of Education. The whole family consisted of university graduates. When Clarle returned, they were all made acquainted, and all showed great interest in Emil's work, especially Mr. Enger, who loved to sketch during his free time.

Emil's knowledge of art, artists, technique, and periods fascinated him, as did his artistic accomplishments. At Enger's insistence, Emil gave him private lessons. The enthusiasm with which Emil demonstrated his ideas led Enger to offer him a teaching position in the county school system.

"No, I couldn't teach," Emil declared. He tried to sound indifferent, certain it was a gesture made out of kindness.

"I know better," Enger argued. "Our schools have never had an art teacher with so much to offer the students. I've learned more from you in one lesson than I ever learned in all my schooling." Emil was humbled, but he knew it was impossible. He had no training or experience for such a position. Rather than entertain the glorious idea of thumbing his nose at oppressive factory work, he tried to concentrate on assisting his student. "Don't feel you have to fill in the space with lines or decoration. Think simplicity. If you think you need ten lines to say something, say it in one instead," he told his ambitious student. Again, Enger threw himself into his own interpretation of the still life Emil had arranged, but soon found himself reprimanded.

"Why ruin the whole thing with all that clutter in the background?" He grabbed Enger's brush and did away with the extra lines. "You're drawing 'things' now instead of making the background a part of the picture. See it as a whole first, not as individual pieces. That's how you simplify." He apologized then, realizing he had taken over Enger's painting.

Enger stood in awe of it all. "Don't apologize," he said. "That's what separates you from the others. Your enthusiasm. You are so utterly caught up in your art. You have proven again you can teach. How about it?"

Emil had difficulty believing such a chance had come his way, but Enger's own enthusiasm left no doubt of his sincerity.

"When would I start?"

"Right away. We always need teachers, especially in art. How soon can you leave the factory?"

"Leave the factory?" he repeated, with a titter. "Immediately," he said, with a broad, hopeful grin.

"Great. How about next week? Just send for your college records. We can take care of that anytime."

"I'm afraid you've been misled. I have no college records."

Enger was shocked. "That's a damn shame. I mean, you have more to offer than any college graduate we have in the system." He thought for a moment. "I'll see if we can get around it. Don't worry."

But standards for teachers had been set and they were not to be broken, not even by a man with Enger's clout. It was with injured pride that Emil returned to the factory, his hope of escaping it gone up like a puff of smoke.

He found no compassion at home. Clarle had her own problems. Unable to find employment, her spirit reached a new low, her boredom a new high. Arguments came often. While she brooded, Emil spent his free days painting the Brooklyn Bridge, the Palisades, or the streets of New York, where he remained until dark. During inclement weather, he turned to sculpting, or still life, or self portraits at Scheffield's studio apartment, where they often used mirrors to paint their own reflections.

One evening, he returned from a painting excursion to find a letter from the Art Institute in Chicago. Certain of its message, that his entry would soon be returned, he ripped the envelope open, tearing the letter in the process. He was obliged to piece it together in order to read it:

> I have the honor to inform
> you that the Committee on Painting and Sculpture
> of the Art Institute of Chicago has awarded your
> painting entitled "Patricia" the Mr. and Mrs.
> Frank G. Logan Medal and Purchase Prize of Five
> Hundred Dollars in the Tenth International
> Exhibition of Water Colors…

He read it again, and then again. No one had to tell him the significance of the honor. Artists from all over the world had exhibited, and only three out of more than 450 works had been given the honor, only one of which was a watercolor: his.

Much of *Patricia* was untouched paper; no fussing, no detail, almost like a descriptive abstraction. An extended moment of total absorption had freed him, allowing him fresh vision and the expressive means for conveying it while painting the portrait. With the genius of Lamberty, he had described with two lines the model's nose, and used only one small thick line and two strips of the brush to describe her mouth. Minimum use of soft shadow implied eyelid movement.

He stood virtually alone in his looseness, his blatant honesty, his failure to hide all the forms in the work. Apparently it hadn't gone unnoticed. The painting showed signs of discarding rules and methods he had previously ascribed to, of generous use of the abstract color field and geometric simplification he had successfully called upon in France. While making use of conventional beauty in his subject, he had injected it with his own idea of beauty.

The front page of the *New York Daily* art section carried a large reproduction of *Patricia* along with a complete story of the significance of the award. There was also a short biography of Holzhauer, the artist, including his training, schooling, and experience. The *Chicago Art World* gave a rundown of the entries, along with a list of countries represented. The honor included a purchase prize of five hundred dollars. Not a means of retirement, but it would look good in a savings account that was nearly empty.

The coveted Logan Medal and the recognition he often received in art magazines and newspapers gave Emil the courage and momentum he needed to answer as many exhibition requests as possible. By January 1931 he had shipped some of his work to Oberlin College in Ohio for an exhibition while exhibiting almost simultaneously at the Martin Galleries in New York in a one-man show. A letter from the Oberlin curator declared the students and faculty alike to have been most receptive toward his work. So much so that the practical arts department had plans for purchasing one of the paintings for their permanent collection. The curator referred to his work as having "very beautiful and suggestive line; {it is} the imaginative quality in the French which so perfectly expresses {this}".

From the Martin Exhibition, his work received good reviews, and one of his portraits was reproduced in the *Detroit Free Press* and the *New York Evening Post*.

Awards and complimentary words, Emil found, did not truly change his lifestyle. In order to put food on the table, he had to continue factory work and suffer insults from fellow workers who deemed him a miser, too stingy to spend the mass of money they assumed he earned from his art.

He had learned to divorce himself from the trauma of these daily struggles. He treated his subjects sympathetically, a fact that spoke for the inner beauty with which he viewed the world.

It was perhaps this attitude that sustained him through years of factory work where managers were of the same caliber, if not worse than, the employees. One day, he received a phone call at the factory, a rare event in itself, and even more rare for the call to be accepted. His heartbeat quickened as he raced to the manager's office, for he knew something terrible had happened to Clarle.

The caller was Matt Enger. "I found a teaching position for you at a girls' camp this summer. No college required," Enger told him. Griesheimer, the factory manager, glared at Emil throughout the conversation, and listened to every word on his end of the line.

"Let me call you after working hours, Matt."

"No, I'm going out of town. Sorry. I wouldn't have called you at work, but I ran out of time. I have to know before I leave. I'll explain later."

Emil committed the camp director's name and number to memory, then rushed back to his desk, the manager on his heels all the way.

"Ain't you the nice one? Calls from Westchester!" He made certain other workers heard the snide remark.

Enger's reputation as attorney and politician had probably been Griesheimer's reason for allowing the call. He lacked the courage to refuse such a man, but he would have his satisfaction through Emil. "Better tell your society friends you ain't paid to talk on the phone."

He rallied at the thought of teaching, yet he cringed at the same time. "A girls' camp?" he asked himself. All from Westchester families, no doubt. Spoiled, perhaps. He concluded, however, that nothing could be worse than factory life.

Cautiously, he approached Griesheimer the next day. A filthy man, obnoxious in manner, he was equally obnoxious in appearance. His filthy hands and dirt-encrusted fingernails revealed a life without soap and hot water, as did his breath and body odor.

Emil had lacked the courage to ask Griesheimer for the previous summer off for a trip to Monhegan, leaving no alternative but to quit the job and take his chances, as usual, on finding another. Rather than begin at the bottom again, he elected this time to ask for time off without pay.

"I would like the summer off. You see, I--" He had thought of a dozen ways to initiate the request, but he knew instantly he had chosen the worst of the lot.

"So would I," Griesheimer yelled. "I'd like the whole damn year off. Maybe you would, too," he threatened without giving Emil a chance to finish.

"You see, sir, I have a job teaching art at Camp Wah-na-gi this summer." The news got the manager's undivided attention. "It's a girls' camp at Lake George," Emil explained.

"I know where and what it is, Holzhauer!" he bellowed. "Monhegan, Lake George, always something. I don't like your work anyway," he growled.

He stormed out of his office and headed for Emil's desk. By the time Emil caught up with him, Griesheimer was fingering a ring design Emil had spent hours preparing.

"Look at this. You've lost your touch, Holzhauer. I can hire your kind anywhere." With that, he pushed the wax model out of shape with his filthy thumb. "You have your wish. The whole summer off. And take the other nine months, too."

His job lost anyway, there was nothing to hold him back. He took the job at camp.

It was a decision he would not regret. At Camp Wah-na-gi, he enjoyed respect and admiration which had been unknown to him in the past. Everyone referred to him as "mister," a show of respect neither age nor experience had ever gotten him in the factories or anywhere in his adopted country.

The camp director advocated outdoor painting and field trips, a euphoric assignment for Emil. To paint while he worked, and get paid for it was beyond anything he had ever imagined. The girls, who ranged in age from six to sixteen, seemed to be in awe of him and his talent, and to be inspired by his enthusiasm and encouragement.

He began their studies by teaching them to draw. "You can't paint if you can't draw. If you learn nothing else, you must believe in yourself. Express your ideas, not mine." Always, he talked while he painted.

After classes, he was free to paint. On Sundays, he hiked into the nearby mountains where he painted the illiterate mountaineers. They made him realize as never before what Henri had taught his students about the character to be found in the faces of common folk.

They welcomed him to their shacks, some of which were dangerously in disrepair. Once Emil fell through rotten boards on a porch and found himself wedged underneath where roosting chickens squawked at him. Again and again, he returned to the simple people for inspiration. He was never disappointed.

Back in the city, Clarle continued her quest for a job. With the Depression in full swing, the arts had suffered perhaps more than anything, but the state of New York had created its own art program which was designed, not to sell the artists' work, but to prevent the death of the art world.

Emil managed to secure a position in the program, which paid him a small weekly wage for taking part in easel paintings and murals to be used in public buildings. Meanwhile, Clarle's contacts from the Van Diemen Gallery finally paid off, securing a position for her with the College Art Association. She was to assist in selecting exhibits for the association's shows.

At her request, Emil had returned to his sculpting, exhibiting it along with his paintings now and then. One show at the Newark Museum brought praise in the *Newark Evening News* for his work: "His sculptures, mostly heads, show strength and individuality," he read.

This increased newspaper coverage led to more and more opportunities to exhibit. By 1934 he was exhibiting in major shows including one at the Whitney Museum of American Art, which led to the museum's purchase of a Holzhauer painting for their permanent collection. Though recognition brought no monetary returns, it led to invitations to serve on art juries, an honor, not a chore, except for the time it stole from his own work.

When summer came, he gladly repeated the exciting Camp Wah-nagi teaching job, commuting when possible, while Clarle remained in the city. At summer's end, he packed his belongings and headed for Hague, just a few miles up the lake, and home of the frail old woman whose porch had caved in with him the previous summer.

On this trip, he met Nat Yawn, owner of the area's only sawmill. Nat became a Holzhauer favorite with his patched overalls, shortened and faded from years of boiling-pot syndrome, and held up by one twisted gallus; a sweat-stained hat that had seen more life than it had been constructed for, and brogan shoes tied haphazardly with a broken shoestring laced lazily through less than half the holes. Emil followed him around the sawmill, catching him in various activities.

At the end of the summer, it was with regret that he returned to the city. Fortunately, exciting things were beginning to brew in Washington, where it had become apparent to President Roosevelt that some states could not carry the load of recovery from the Depression. A massive new agency, the Works Progress Administration, was created to increase employment that would benefit all of society, not only by creating jobs, but by creating services and useful projects.

Some of his former Henri colleagues signed up as muralists in this new program, but Emil preferred easel painting, as it could usually be done in his own studio without supervision, and, unlike the muralists who were expected to do the American scene, he was given free rein.

The new federal program eventually led to a position for Clarle in Woodstock, but with Emil commuting more and more from Riverview during the winter months, and Lake George in the summer, she played less and less a part in the new life he had gradually created.

In spite of this, Emil treasured the opportunity to teach. In explaining to the young minds the need to see the unusual, to be sensitive to colors, to be capable of reaching beneath the surface of things to obtain greater understanding, and to express those emotions individually, he reached a new awareness himself. This new power of vision begged to be utilized, and he was determined to answer the call.

One evening, he returned from the factory to find Clarle energized by an exciting promotion. She had been named assistant director for the new Art Projects of the Works Progress Administration. It was an exciting program, far superior to ones run by the state, she quickly explained.

She was radiant, her eyes afire with excitement, her vibrant body kindled with new life. Emil became caught up in her spirit, anxious to hear all about the new job. "Tell me everything," he insisted. "What are your duties?"

"It calls for a great deal of travel, but I shall enjoy that aspect of it. I'll be selecting artists' work for hundreds of shows throughout the country."

She explained that she would be in charge of nearly one hundred community art centers. Part of her job would be to travel across the country selecting works for various exhibitions. She looked happier than Emil had seen her in a very long time. He hoped the new position would put life in their deteriorating relationship.

"Clarlekins, sweetheart," he cooed, "I'm not surprised in the least. You have efficiency and charm, my dear. Rare qualities," he bragged. He surveyed her passionately, admiring the soft brown hair, the expressive eyes, the flawless complexion. At thirty-five, she was more beautiful than ever. "But how did this happen? Did you apply for the job?" He wished to know everything at once.

"You remember Mr. Holly. He offered me the directorship here in New York. At the same time, he told me I had been chosen by Washington officials as vice-director of the federal program if I wanted it. 'If I wanted it?'" she mocked. "Well, I couldn't turn it down."

"Of course not," Emil agreed. Again, he stared at her, this time with thoughtful eyes. Her intellect and charm had finally been brought to the attention of the culturally elite, and his full agenda had denied him the pleasure of watching it all happen. Regret absorbed him. He wished they might begin at the beginning, erasing all the unpleasantries from both their slates. For his part, he would gladly do so.

Thoughts of renewing their vows took precedence with him, almost drowning out the rest of her exciting story. Clarle remained energized.

"I received a call from The White House," she said. Emil regarded her wistfully.

"It was Harry Hopkins, a Roosevelt aide. Just imagine living in Washington right now, with Roosevelt's New Deal going into effect."

"Washington! Clarle?" His eyes pierced hers, searching for signs of jest, but he was denied that comfort. "Why, you'd have to live in Washington. You can't possibly take such a job."

"I have taken the job," she informed him. The gravity with which she spoke told him nothing would change her mind.

Her eventual promise to come home every weekend didn't ease his pain. His ego hit a new low, particularly as she had accepted the position without discussing it with him. As director of the state program, she could have stayed in New York with her husband, but that was obviously not a high priority with her.

A heated argument ensued. He finally grabbed his sleeping materials and headed for the sofa, following the action with a long, arduous silent treatment, something he had seldom been guilty of since his divorce from Marcy.

Nineteen

Six months had passed since Clarle began working in Washington. With her gone most of the time, Emil fought a familiar battle with loneliness. His work with the federal arts program helped fill the void her absence left.

For some time, he had made an effort to locate Lamberty. It had been a great comfort to him when the Museum of Modern Art began to exhibit the work of Cezanne, van Gogh and other French artists for it would offer Lamberty a long sought after chance to view the work of his idols without making that elusive trip across the ocean. Emil never attended a special event at the museum without canvassing the gallery long after he cared to, in hopes of running into his old classmate. He never did.

The federal arts program had brought many of Emil's acquaintances from the Henri school together again, but sadly for him, Lamberty was not one of them. Fortunately, Raymond Scheffield was. The chance meeting with Scheffield on Monhegan Island had paid off, not only in friendship with a fellow artist, but in opportunities. When Scheffield had been commissioned to paint a mural in a federal building in Washington, D.C., he asked Emil to assist him. It was not only an honor, it had put food in his mouth during some very lean months.

Daily, Emil searched the ranks for Lamberty, hoping he had taken advantage of the federal program. None of the former Henri students could help him. One day Scheffield overheard Emil questioning one of the men.

"You were inquiring about Lamberty?" Scheffield asked.

"Yes. You know him?"

"Yes, of course. Met him during one of my Steiglitz Gallery tours. But he's—"

"I should have known," Emil interrupted. "He must have gone there every day. Used to keep us all informed about everything that happened there," Emil recalled. "I've been trying to locate him. He needs to know about this program. He could sure use the money, pittance though it is."

Scheffield put his brush aside and eyed Emil with compassion. "I'm so sorry to tell you this, Emil. Lamberty is dead."

"No! Lamberty?"

"Yes. Died in the insane asylum."

Emil felt cheated. He had thought of himself as one of Lamberty's best friends, and now a man who was practically a stranger to the luckless devil was informing him of his death.

"How did you know?"

"Why I just happened to overhear one of the other artists talking about it. One of your former classmates, I think. Say, I understand Lamberty left you an old skeleton or something. Naturally, I assumed you knew all about it."

"His only possession," Emil mumbled. He was distraught. For days he tried to locate the man who knew the details of the story. When he finally found him, he was told that Maurice had been contacted by the institution where Lamberty was confined. But Maurice had been unable to find Emil, as the two of them had not kept in touch.

The news was depressing. He remembered the hollow eyes, the painfully thin body clothed in oversized hand-me-downs, and most of all, the yearning to be somebody, to do something with his life. The worst part was remembering the talent gone to waste. Lamberty's natural instinct for catching the essence of a subject, of leaving out unnecessary obstacles and incidentals that cluttered the canvas, was a talent every artist wished for, but few possessed. Unfortunately, he had tried living his life the same way, ignoring obstacles and hardships that threatened to clutter his life. His energies were spent on what he considered the essence of life, leaving none to cope with life's problems. For weeks after learning of Lamberty's fate, Emil was without comfort. When Clarle arrived for a rare weekend visit, he tried sharing this latest heartache, but they spent most of their time quarreling, each accusing the other of being selfish and self-centered.

As time went on, he learned with some bitterness that she had been returning to New York for regular weekend visits with her friends without his knowledge. Until then, he had harbored hopes of rebuilding their crumbling relationship.

Night after night, he lay awake, thinking about the nightmare of another divorce, of the heartache, the remorse, the regrets. In the middle of a sleepless night, he penned a note to her:

> ...I have decided to leave the arts program,
> begin freelance work in the city, and commute
> from Riverview. I find that single life here
> in the city is too depressing. I cannot keep the
> apartment in New York and rent one in Riverview
> too. Please let me know what you intend
> to do. You don't have to hide from me. I will
> give you your freedom. You name the conditions...

To obtain a divorce in New York, one had to prove adultery, unless, of course the couple in question had not been living together for five years. Emil had solved the problem for Marcy by arranging a sexual rendezvous for her detective. He offered to do the same for Clarle. Her quick response by letter was confusing. "I'm in no hurry," she wrote.

Meanwhile, Rett located a room for him above the Riverview butcher shop, complete with meager furnishings that matched the bleak exterior of the building. It was back to the austerity of his first days in America, but it was of no consequence to a man who put little store in physical comfort.

At least three days a week were set aside for delivery of designs and solicitations in the New York factories, where, more and more, he had become aware of the anti-German element surfacing. Hitler's attempted Nazi takeover of Austria had failed, but no one believed he would stop there. As hatred for Hitler grew, Emil found his own reputation pulverized along with it.

At times, the long train ride into the city produced little or no work at all, and he was obliged to return to Riverview empty-handed. Unlike in the old days when his designs were superior to most and therefore keenly desirable to the factory managers, the influx of European engravers and jewelry designers had changed that. He either had to return to New York and earnestly seek employment or tighten his belt once again and live on his savings until things settled down in Germany. He opted for the latter. It was familiar ground.

Riverview offered him full-time painting pleasure with its majestic Hudson and its riverboats, and its stone quarry with fascinating machinery cutting jagged holes in the mountainside. The village itself was a picture waiting to be painted. He gladly complied. When the snows came, he welcomed them as one might welcome a new coat of paint on a well-seasoned building, glorying in the freshness and brilliance it offered the simple street scenes. Giving little thought to the absence of a job, he worked with the vigor of Monhegan Island days. Early evenings moved swiftly, for he enjoyed the companionship of Rett and Newton, proprietor of the town's only hardware store. Too, Schliemann, a part-time Riverview resident, boosted his morale considerably. As his painting collection grew, he gladly accepted Rett's offer of storage space in the wine cellar of his private residence. "If you fill that up, you can use one of my houses," Rett told him. He owned houses throughout the village which were filled with junk and a few antiques.

Rett and his wife took Emil in as if he were family, allowing him special kitchen privileges in the restaurant. One day they were well into their second bottle of Rett's home-made brew when he confided to Emil his attachment to Hitler and his cause. "He's just what Germany needs."

"You're wrong, Rett. You're wrong. He'll destroy Germany. If you had only seen what happened after the last war. The German mark was useless, and the whole country was in ruins. Everyone was starving. What did it benefit them?" He stared at Rett as if he expected a retraction.

"Ah, but they prevailed. You've been away from Germany too long. You forget the superiority of the German race. They'll take over the world, mark my word. You should attend our meetings in the cellar. Where is your patriotism?"

There was a coldness in Rett's eyes that matched the one in his voice. Emil kept shaking his head. He couldn't identify with, or tolerate such talk. "Hitler is insane," he shot back. "If he continues as he has been, the United States will step in, just as they did in the first World War, and it'll be impossible for a German to walk the streets here." The vertical wrinkle on his forehead deepened, narrowing the space between his outraged eyes. He waited impatiently for what he hoped would be a reversal of opinion, perhaps an admission of error, on Rett's part, but it didn't come.

"Bah! Germany was humiliated by the Versailles Treaty. England and France should have borne the guilt. Hitler unified Germany's spirit. Those goddamn Jews need to be put in their places," he raved. "Sons-of-bitches buying property all over the world for nothing." He slapped his fist so hard against the countertop, it jostled his fat belly, stretching his belt to its limit. "Ah, hell, you needn't worry. Roosevelt won't fight," he moaned. "He said as much already."

It was a comforting thought and one Emil would rest his hopes on, though nothing short of Hitler's demise would bring him total comfort. Before saying good night, Rett mentioned the cellar meetings again. "Come on and join us. Just say hello to a few friends?" he pleaded.

Emil shook his head. The idea of meeting with a group of Germans while war waged overseas was the last thing he wanted. He was quite unnerved by the whole conversation.

With his funds dwindling and Germany still not under control, he had begun to worry about his future, fearful that the Camp Wah-na-gi position wouldn't be available for a German. As the time approached for leaving Riverview, Rett derided him for depending on the trains for his transportation. "Hell, you need a car."

"And who would drive it for me?" Emil laughed.

"I can teach you in thirty minutes," he bragged.

Emil gave the conversation no more thought, but the next morning, Rett had a jalopy waiting outside the restaurant. "Got it for ten dollars. Don't worry. You can pay me when you get a job." Emil knew nothing of automobiles or their value, but he was certain Rett had found a bargain, as his reputation had been built on his uncanny ability to do just that. If he wanted ten dollars, chances were good that he had paid five or less.

He wouldn't be dissuaded by Emil's protests or lamentations, He led him to the car and motioned him into the driver's seat, then bravely seated himself on the passenger's side. After a few instructions, and a little practice, Rett accompanied the would-be driver to city hall for a driver's test. Emil watched painfully while another candidate executed his skills of turning, stopping, starting, and parking, only to be instructed in proper driving techniques by the policeman in charge. The man had been refused a license and sent home.

"Please, let's leave," he begged. "I can't do nearly as well."

"Don't worry about it," said Rett, who approached the policeman and exchanged greetings well out of Emil's earshot. Reluctantly, Emil remained in the driver's seat, humming nervously. Returning with the policeman, Rett introduced them. The uniformed man climbed into the passenger's side.

"Okay, Mr. Holzhauer, let's see what Rett's taught you. Just drive around the block and return here."

Emil silently rejoiced. Apparently, he was not to be subjected to the same difficult turns and stops the preceding driver had been ordered to perform. With much jerking and jolting, he managed to make a short block and return with a sputter to the original spot. He knew that no police officer worth his weight in human intellect would issue him a license. He only wished the ordeal to end so that he might get on with the business of the day.

"Just relax now," the policeman said gently. "Start your engine, and pull up to the curb. Over here where you have lots of space with no other cars around." Without putting the car in neutral, Emil stepped on the starter. Again, the engine died. "Don't forget neutral this time," the officer gently reminded him.

Irritated and embarrassed, Emil started the engine again, slammed the accelerator down and headed for the curb. When the policeman's parked cruiser suddenly loomed up in front of him, Emil couldn't find the brake.

A tense moment followed while they all examined the cars, Rett and the officer exchanging comments, Emil spouting German curse words, all under his breath. Most of the damage was to Emil's car, both the men agreed, and that could be repaired by a friend of Rett's at a local shop.

"Hell, give him a license. He'll learn," said Rett. The officer quickly complied, making Emil an official New York state licensed driver.

Rett drove his own car to the garage and instructed Emil to follow him in his. Emil protested but he was overruled.

"Shouldn't take more than a couple of hours," the mechanic told them.

"That's wonderful," Emil said. "I can still make it to Lake George."

Rett scratched his head thoughtfully. "I don't know about such a long trip. You ran a red light on your way over here, and you damn near hit that old man crossing the street back there. You better practice a bit before taking a long trip."

"But the officer said I'm licensed to drive anywhere," he reminded Rett.

"I know," Rett groaned. "Well, go ahead. Hell, I'll stay off the road till you get there."

The car changed Emil's life. For the first time, he was able to cover areas he had only heard about in the past, drive to another area if one didn't inspire him, and carry extra painting materials, snacks, and water. Neither was he limited in the number of paintings he could carry back home.

It made for a delightful summer at Camp Wah-na-gi, but when it ended, he was faced with finding work again. It was to be a difficult task. It was September, 1939. Germany had just invaded Poland. Nobody in the city seemed interested in carrying on a conversation with a German, much less hiring one. Many Germans were employed in the factories, but they had been there for years, not flitting in and out as Emil had.

Even as bitter-cold weather began to make its entrance into the city, Emil remained jobless. As his savings dwindled, his options narrowed, and he began to feel trapped. He returned to Riverview to bide his time among friends until tensions in Europe eased.

He climbed the steep and narrow wooden steps to his apartment, glad for the early darkness that would shield him from prying eyes and probing friends who would ask the inevitable question: did he find a job? Sympathy was the last thing he wanted. He settled in for the night, comforted by the familiar odors of home and eager to meet the morning when he would have his choice of subject matter: the quarry and its workers, the icy Hudson's choppy waters; muddy streets with their bundled-up passers-by hunching against the bitter winds, falling snow, or pelting rain; the distant mountains, either barren and brown or covered in winter's white coat. And if all of that failed to inspire him, or if the weather was too severe for outdoor work, he could paint the shopkeepers. He could scarcely fall asleep for thinking of the possibilities.

When daylight finally came, he greeted it with prodigious energy and enthusiasm, a combination that had been in the making throughout the long night. It was not a hopeful day. Skies were dark and gloomy in the beginning hours, the sun stealing only an occasional glimpse of the frozen earth below. By afternoon, the sun finally broke through, but it never lingered long enough to melt the thick ribs of ice, or counteract the bite of frosty winds. It did act as a golden mediator, casting flaxen and plum-colored streaks onto the glimmering waters of the Hudson, and highlighting the snow-covered roofs and once-barren mountain-tops. Emil was still painting when the fiery ball made its descent, darkness its entry.

In spite of his German descent, he enjoyed the respect and admiration of the village folks, many of whom had foreign backgrounds. Not everyone knew his name, but all of them knew "the artist" who painted the river, the quarry, the main street, and the villagers themselves.

He painted during the day and spent early evenings dining with Rett or Newton or Schliemann, then engaged in lively chitchat with them and other villagers who frequented the popular German restaurant. He often "retired" to Rett's basement, where he agonized over which paintings, if any, he should exhibit, then matted and framed them. When the Balzac Gallery invited him to enter an exhibit, he was prepared. There was the pre-judging at the Whitney Museum Exhibition for which he chose a watercolor of the Riverview main street painted during the previous snow-covered winter. It was titled *Village Street, January*. He studied it carefully, wondering if it would survive the pre-judging. It was a traditional sort of snow scene, painted from one end of the street looking northward at a long line of buildings.

He had made use of heavy subtle lines, almost ephemeral, that gave the painting a feeling of depth. The painting featured sharp edges and clear delineation up close, but the most distant building was a mere blur. He liked the end result, not only when it was completed but much later, when it mattered.

Pondering the choice a while longer, he wondered if something else might come closer to surviving the pre-judging. With the human element of judging involved, one had to be lucky. Knowing that, and realizing the strain such an exhibition put on his declining savings account, he vacillated between exhibiting and not exhibiting. As time was running out, he settled on the entry, framed it himself in one of the bargain purchases from Rett, and shipped it.

The Balzac exhibition brought a great deal of critical acclaim. One writer referred to Emil as "one of America's first and foremost watercolorists."

In the midst of the Balzac exhibition, Emil received news that *Village Street, January* had survived the pre-judging. While it hung in the Whitney Museum Exhibition, the *Literary Digest* and several newspapers carried reproductions of it.

Eventually, it was selected, along with works by other artists, to be exhibited at the New York World's Fair. The Riverview press covered the honor, making Emil quite a celebrity.

Before the Balzac exhibition closed, critics declared he was "finally realizing his potential." They described his oils and his watercolors as "solid constructions," and they complimented him for his "balance, organization, and depth," and "excellence of design."

Still, there were no sales. He seemed destined for monetary disaster. At forty-seven, his savings had nearly bottomed out, and the factory employers continued to turn him away. There was only one option left open to him. Felix would hire him in a heartbeat, glad for an opportunity to lord it over him. With that in mind, he was about to return to the city when the Camp Wah-na-gi director contacted him. One of the regular art instructors at nearby Browder Junior College was gravely ill. The camp director had recommended Emil as a temporary replacement. The job was his.

Rett insisted it was a special occasion calling for a celebration, not in the restaurant but in the confines of the wine cellar. The party would begin promptly at eight that evening. Emil protested vigorously, bent on celebrating the event with one drink then and there, just the two of them. But Rett was adamant. Everyone had been notified, he declared. The party was on.

Reluctantly, Emil entered the dimly-lit basement that evening, where he was greeted by jovial voices, all speaking German. That he didn't like, not while the war was going strong. He decided on a quick drink after which he would make an equally quick exit.

"Emil," yelled Rett, "come, my friend, grab your glass. Even for professors, *in vino veritas*" he toasted as he held the glass high in the air.

"Come on, come on," he urged. "God, why do you tarry? Come on in and say hello to a friend of mine and yours." He could hardly restrain himself as he gestured toward a short, stocky man seated at the end of the bar. The man rose to greet Emil.

"Muller! I can't believe it! But what are you doing here?" Even in the poor lighting, Emil discerned something different about him. Physically, he was somewhat thinner, his round face more lined, but it was more than that. The once-eager eyes showed traces of fatigue, the kind that comes from lengthy anguish.

"Rett didn't tell you?" Muller asked.

"He can't blame me. I've invited him time and again," Rett declared. "He's always too busy to meet with his countrymen."

"I have been admiring your paintings," Muller said. "You have really come into your own." Coming from Muller, a man Emil had come to think of as a connoisseur in everything, the compliment was well received, but it wasn't enough to ease his tension. Rett had tricked him into coming. Rather than make a scene, he opened the conversation, focusing on the one thing they had in common. "Please, tell me about Marcy. You've seen her?" he asked Muller.

Muller scrunched his eyebrows together, causing a vertical wrinkle in his brow. "Bad news there. Schliemann didn't tell you about the cult?"

"Yes, of course. I heard she'd been working in the fields in Israel, all to cure her stage fright. Still listening to Sue? Nothing new? I had hoped—"

Muller tapped the table with nervous fingers. It was obviously a subject he didn't care to discuss. "I'm afraid she's drawn the shade over the window. Divorced herself from musicians in favor of the cult. You wouldn't recognize her I'm afraid. Painfully thin."

Emil detected a coldness, so unlike the Muller he once knew. "She never really recuperated from the loss of the baby. Or rather the ordeal she put her body through during pregnancy."

His voice sank as he rose from his seat, then sat down again. There was an unnerving calm about the atmosphere as if they were housed in a bomb shelter and were listening for the all-clear signal.

"Perhaps," Muller said with obvious disinterest. He often made eye contact with Rett while attempting to carry on a conversation with Emil. "I understand she was forced into heavy labor in Israel. Labor meant for a much stronger person. And she's going back there," he added with disgust.

"Really?" Emil's rising voice pleaded for details, but Muller seemed anxious to end the conversation.

Emil shook his head, silently recalling happier days for a very talented but tormented woman. With Muller's disinterest in the subject, Emil initiated talk of Hitler. "He's going to bring war right to our doorsteps again," he wailed. The comment captured the attention of everyone in the cellar, but none of the men responded to it, at least not seriously. They made a joke of the whole thing.

"Well, don't worry about that aspect of it, Emil. They won't call on you again," teased Muller. Everyone laughed, including Emil. That type of teasing he could handle.

"Anyway, we wouldn't want to take another chance on you defending us," laughed Rett. "Probably drives a tank like he rides a horse." The group broke out in uproarious laughter. Emil was irritated, not for the reference to his military stint, but for the lack of concern for Hitler's reckless moves.

Amid the uproar, Muller left the group's semicircle at the bar and began walking purposely around the room, stopping to view Emil's paintings. "I like this one," he said of *Morning on the Hudson*. "What price do you have on it?"

"For you, two hundred dollars." It did not occur to Emil that Muller would actually purchase the painting. As far as he knew, the man's only residence was a hotel room.

"Goddamn! I would have sold it for half that," joked Rett.

"I think it's a bargain," declared Muller. "I'll take it," he announced. Walking back in Emil's direction, he took a roll of bills from his pocket.

"You're serious," noted Emil. His shadow followed him across the poorly-lit underground as he marched determinedly toward Muller, humbled and embarrassed. He never thought his work good enough to hang on anyone's wall.

It was an unexpected thrill. Muller had been a lot of things, but never a buyer, at least not to Emil's knowledge.

"It's what I came here for. I've watched you grow—mature is a better word—beyond the early heavy-handedness and into restrained enthusiasm, I'd call it. I'm not an artist, but I know a keen eye when I see it.

You've captured the mood of this place," he concluded. Emil stood speechless, his expression one of gratitude.

Moments before, he had intended to excuse himself and dart out the door. He was not fooled into thinking the group had gathered to celebrate his new job, as Rett had suggested, for many of them were relative strangers. But Muller's gesture called for diplomacy, so he accepted Rett's offer of another drink. As there was no further mention of Hitler or the war, he relaxed a bit and took part in their bantering.

In a moment, Muller rose to go, and the others followed, one by one citing this or that excuse for their departure. As had Muller, each one congratulated Emil on his new teaching job and wished him well. The whole scene was most perplexing.

During the short walk home, a bevy of questions presented themselves. "Was the purchase an act of charity on Muller's part?" he questioned. His thoughts centered on Muller: always a broker, never a buyer. Before reaching his apartment, he was convinced the purchase had been out of pity. Apparently, Rett had shared Emil's financial plight. He pulled the bills from the depths of his pocket, then began a determined march toward the cellar. He would confront Rett and find out if he had been a party to the gesture, or if Muller had acted alone. In any case, the money had to be returned. Just before reaching his destination, he noticed several figures taking the back entrance to the cellar, the same ones who had marched out only minutes earlier, all except Muller.

Again, a host of questions crowded Emil's mind, none of which appealed to him. After a few agonizing moments, he was decisive. He didn't want to know. He returned to his apartment, dismissing the events of the evening, and began concentrating on Browder Junior College.

Anxiously, he reported the next day, certain that college would be beyond his realm of understanding. As there was no art instructor to consult, the dean sent him to Mrs. Dolores Thomas, the dance instructor. "She has the same students in her classes. Maybe she can advise you as to where to begin."

Dolores had been schooled in Madrid, where she had met and married an American playboy from whom she had long since been divorced. Judging from her firm body, she was barely thirty, but harsh lines and deep-set wrinkles about the face and neck suggested forty. Emil sensed immediately that life hadn't always been kind to her. It gave them common ground.

"You can begin at the beginning, believe me," she told him. "To you, their knowledge will be elementary. Most of them have had little instruction. Copying is about the only skill they've been trained in, if that. They'll be overcome by your demonstrations." He liked her immediately. With her European roots, she could identify with his woes in the unfriendly atmosphere of an adopted country. With a bitter divorce to share, they had the makings of a good friendship. She often dropped in on his classes and watched in awe and admiration as he taught enthusiastically.

In a matter of weeks, even the dullest students began to show an interest in drawing, and those with a natural talent in art often remained after class or joined him on field trips.

Dolores complimented him on his progress. "I'm not surprised by their enthusiasm. The poor kids never knew what a demonstration was before you came. If you only knew the incompetence of some of our faculty members," she moaned. "I wish you could stay."

"If you only knew how much I'd like to," he confessed. He had never imagined that teaching others would offer such fulfillment, or that it would lead him to a newer and deeper understanding in artistic expression.

"Why not apply elsewhere?" she asked.

He had felt at ease with the dance instructor from the beginning. She was honest, unpretentious, dedicated. She taught dancing with the same enthusiasm he taught art. He had no qualms about discussing his problems with her. It was a grand feeling.

"You don't understand. I was turned down in Westchester because I have no college background, and that was elementary school."

"Rot," she scoffed. "That was Westchester. Sure they have requirements everywhere, but they'll take someone with your credentials, believe me. Send your resume to the schools where there are vacancies. List all your experiences, your awards and honors in art. The dean's secretary will tell you where the vacancies are."

It was shortly after their conversation that Emil's painting, *Village Street, January* was chosen by the National Art Association as one of the most representative pictures exhibited at the World's Fair in New York.

Only sixteen pictures had been selected for the honor and reproduced for the society's portfolio.

Dolores was quick to praise him. "Add that to your resume, and send it proudly to any school that needs an art teacher," she told him. "If they have any sense, they'll fight over you." Her vast black eyes, moist and shimmering, spoke for the compassion she felt at the prospect of losing him.

He did as she advised.

As news of the latest honor spread, he was approached by a representative from the National Art Society. *Village Street, January* was to be the subject of a half-hour radio broadcast over WEAF and the National Broadcasting Company. The little village and its inhabitants would proudly share national attention with their artist, as his painting of Riverview's main street was featured along with a biographical sketch of his life.

In preparation for the event, the *New York Daily* headlined the show. It was the talk of the Browder campus as well as Riverview. Several of his friends planned to meet at Rett's for a listening party, along with Emil, the village's new radio star. Meanwhile, Emil was in a quandary, gloating in his renown one minute, sinking to the depths of uncertainty the next. The airing of his life's story was as painful as the showing of his work in public had once been. To preclude an argument with Rett and the others, he spent the day painting at the isolated quarry, then returned to the privacy of his abode after darkness had closed in on the area.

Alone and anxious, he waited for the radio show to begin. A glance around the shabby living quarters revealed the radio itself his only luxury. He could almost hear Henri's warning, 'Don't expect to make a living from your art. You'll be lucky to make expenses.'

Emil sat painfully upright when the drama began. He listened to the story of his youth in Germany as an apprentice and as a student in the arts and crafts school, all dramatized by two young boys named Emil and Karl. From the beginning, selections from Debussy could be heard in the background. Then a woman's voice was introduced.

"Listen, Emil, here is the way you paint," the voice said, as listeners heard jagged chords from Chopin. "But it is not the way of life. Listen," the woman's voice repeated, as a thin stream of Debussy melody could be heard in the background. “This is the way life is, nothing so definite, nothing so rugged, only aimless gatherings of color.”

Emil cringed to think what Marcy might think of it. The female voice on the radio gained volume again. `Anyone can draw the shape of a tree, but only you can find its color. That’s your genius, Emil.’

Without realizing it, he had finally admitted that until he met this influential woman, he had seen things in the wrong light. `All things have the same shape. Only their colors are different. Color is like breath, it is soon gone,’ the woman’s voice said.

Unable to remain seated, he began to pace the floor, the haunting relationship with Marcy forcing itself into his thoughts. He wished he had been more mature and more understanding. The truth was, Marcy had taught him to view life as a song, to look beyond the crude shapes of things and to see their colors.

At first, the size and vigor and noise of the new country had seemed to overwhelm him. Everything he had drawn and painted was huge and sprawling and crude, but Henri, and then Marcy, had made a difference. Gradually he had developed color perception and sensation, often to the extent of feeling the kinship of painting to music, of likening his aimless gatherings of color to her Debussy.

Henri had been a tremendous influence in his life and his art, but Marcy had given it breath. Instead of learning from her insight, he had pointed out her own shortcomings. He saw himself as an immature blockhead, a notion that sent him pacing back and forth in the confines of his small quarters.

At the end of the program, the celebrated artist beat on his chest as if he were a madman, then let out a stifled yell. Momentarily, and quite unconsciously, he retrieved from his knapsack a day-old sandwich. It was his evening meal.

Letters of congratulations from friends and acquaintances, especially in the art world, began to arrive soon after the NBC airing. Clarle was among those who called, but after five years of separation, she still made no mention of a divorce.

Most surprising was the letter from Marcy, not only as there had been no contact in years, but because he half-expected her to be somewhat deranged. It was with much anticipation, he read her letter:

> Congratulations! What a thrill it was
> listening to your story last Saturday
> evening on radio. What a fine tribute
> to you, and one you richly deserve.
> When I see your name on the art pages,
> I think of Emil, that indefatigable
> worker who has put himself through
> torturous stages of slow development,
> letting nothing stand in his way. And
> now you have awakened to find yourself
> fluent. Your friends here rightly refer
> to you as the "undoomed warrior". It's from
> *Beowulf* you know: 'Fate often saves an undoomed
> warrior when his courage endures.'
> Thank you for the credit given me. I
> wonder how we would feel about each
> other now...

He broke out in derisive laughter. Little did she realize he was still fighting the same problems of support. Work a while and quit, work full time and save, use his savings for a vacation, search for work on his return. Time had changed those things a bit, but only for the worse. Jobs weren't always available anymore.

Even so, life was exciting. He could scarcely wait for classes to begin each morning. Teaching was the most rewarding thing he had ever done. When the first response from a job application came, he agonized over its contents, fearful of being turned down, or worse, laughed at.

The dean of Ashton School for Boys in North Carolina would like to interview him for a teaching position, the letter said. The dean indicated his appointment to fill the vacancy was almost certain. For Emil, it was like arriving in America all over again, only this time he could speak the language. North Carolina seemed like a foreign country as he had seen only a small northeastern portion of the United States. A cursory glance at the map gave him reason to celebrate. The winters should be milder. He could expect to paint year round without suffering frozen extremities.

Rett was first to know. “Don’t say another word,” he told Emil as he reached underneath the counter and pulled out a bottle. “This calls for a toast.” Emil chuckled as he moved his beer aside, making room for a glass of Rett’s home concoction. In Rett’s house, everything called for a toast. He always accompanied the toast with a bite off the end of a new cigar, then struggled with bits of loose tobacco on his tongue. Friends waited, sometimes in good humor, but more often reluctantly, as he performed the irritating habit.

“Where is this new job, anyway?” he asked with one last spat.

“North Carolina. Ashly or Ashdown or something like that.”

Rett lowered his glass. “The hell you say,” he yelled.

“Oh, yes, now I remember. Ashton, that’s it. Ashton, North Carolina. Have you been there?” He could scarcely wait for Rett’s toast. Always a lengthy spiel and delivered in several languages, it was a source of laughter and entertainment for all in hearing distance. At the same time, something gnawed at Emil’s happiness. Leaving his Riverview friends wouldn’t be easy. Nobody in his adopted country had accepted him like they had.

Rett gulped his wine in one swallow. “No, I haven’t been there, and I’m not going. Why the hell don’t you get a job around here?” He rested his fat belly on the counter and left it there while waiting for an answer.

“My God, Rett, I take what I can get. I sent applications all over the country. Most of them want college degrees. You know I don’t have that. Don’t worry. I’ll be coming back for a visit.”

“You won’t like it there,” Rett said. “They won’t like your accent, for one thing. Better talk to Dolores. She’ll tell you.”

“Heaven’s sake, with Hitler still a threat, they don’t like my accent anywhere. But you’re wrong about Dolores. She’ll be happy about this, believe me.” He chuckled knowingly.

When Dolores heard the news, she congratulated him heartily. “Which school?” she asked.

“Ashton School for Boys in North Carolina,” he said. A broad grin monopolized his face, pushing his sun-browned cheeks into a puff before drawing attention to the sparkle in his anxious eyes.

Dolores’ shoulders slumped noticeably. Her smile faded, and her eyes narrowed. “But that’s in the South.” Emil was familiar with the expression for he had seen it when she shared her past with him. But he was confused.

"What's wrong?" he asked innocently. "I should be able to paint all year. No frozen fingers. Sometimes my hands get so numb here, I lose my feel."

Dolores' dark skin paled. "I don't like it."

"Not you too?"

"It'll be your death-knell as an artist," she said mournfully. "You're not serious?" he asked.

"Never more so." She paused, a sense of gravity consuming her. "One thing I didn't share with you was my stint in vaudeville. Everything about it was grand except the tour of the South. They're art-ignorant you know. If you think you're ostracized here for your German background, wait till your southern friends learn you're a Yankee! They're still fighting the Civil War for goodness' sakes." Again she paused. "Surely you realize New York is the heart of the art world. Everything cultural begins here. If you want to be a part of it, you must stay here."

"But even now, I have to ship my work out—Chicago, Philadelphia, New York. What would be the difference if I ship it from North Carolina?" he asked, hoping for some encouragement.

He didn't get it. Others echoed her sentiments, painting a colorless abyss of the South and its inhabitants. He listened, but heard nothing. His Riverview friends hadn't lived through the torture of nine-hour factory days, of insults from factory employees. Nobody was more prejudiced; nobody more art-ignorant.

If his friends were right, it would mean no more awards or radio shows, or other recognition. He saw it as a chance to paint during working hours, and an equal chance to associate with would-be artists instead of uninspired steel engravers.

He made arrangements to store his paintings and a few other incidentals in Rett's cellar and he headed for North Carolina.

Twenty

North Carolina's mountain country was a welcome sight to Emil. He resisted the urge to climb every accessible mountain along the way, but gave in to the call of a soaring fire tower atop Spivey Mountain and climbed to its pinnacle. From there, he gloried in the luscious panorama of valleys and mountain ranges below. In the distance he could see Ashton nestled in the valley and surrounded by green hills and dales much like his own Schwabisch-Gmund. He was feverish with excitement.

A narrow road circled the hillside and led him the last half mile to Ashton School for Boys. Flowering trees dotted the grounds and shaded the scattered buildings. A simple wooden chapel, its steeple pointing gingerly toward heaven, held a sacred spot in the center of everything. The last half-mile up the hillside had been exhilarating to Emil, bringing his steadily-increasing heart rate to a pounding climax by the time he arrived on campus. Once there, he was somewhat comforted by a panoramic view of the distant mountains and the green valleys below. The school was isolated atop one of the very hills he had admired from Spivey's fire tower. Again, he was reminded of Schwabisch-Gmund.

He was astonished to hear the position as art director was his, and yet, he expected it. His self-image was a mystery to him, for one moment he believed himself capable of reaching the ultimate in art, and the next was mortified by the mediocrity of his efforts. As a full-time staff member at a reputable private school, he became quite solidly rooted in the first notion, at least momentarily.

The students at Ashton, ranging in age from ten to eighteen, needed coaxing to express themselves in art just as the girls at Camp Wah-na-gi had. But it was his experience with student reticence that made Emil something of an expert at bringing their personalities to the forefront.

He was beginning to understand that many American teachers had at least one thing in common with their German counterparts. It was rare to find art teachers who would give a demonstration of their work. Emil was the exception.

All faculty members at the private school were given extracurricular activities in addition to their classroom duties. Fortunately, Emil's assignment was to hike in the mountainous countryside with eight to ten boys at a time. At fifty-three, he could hike up the steepest mountain near the school and reach the top minutes before any of his students. His enthusiasm and stamina amazed and delighted the impressionable boys, and eventually broke their timidity barriers that threatened creativity.

When a new student made the trip in thirty-eight minutes, beating Emil by a full forty-five seconds, the competition was on. From that day forward, it was the ambition of nearly every student at the school to beat Mr. Holzhauer to the top of the mountain.

To the boys' delight, classes often convened on the school grounds where Emil demonstrated the use of watercolor. He was surprised and delighted by the wholesome, natural approach most of them demonstrated. There was one exception: Sam Coakley. He was known among his classmates as "the rebel," a title he seemed bent on earning. He had rebelled against mountain climbing, but showed a keen interest in the magic of the pencil forming designs at his bidding. Emil saw in him an unusual talent, but an obstinate personality stood in the way of its development. While others experimented with color, Sam persisted in using a pencil, mostly drawing a traditional idea of a cowboy on horseback, or an Indian complete with feathered headgear and bow and arrow.

While monitoring study hall one day, Emil teased Sam. "Drawing cowboys and Indians again? How many cowboys and Indians have you seen around here lately? Why not draw from life?"

Sam's face reddened. He snatched the drawing off his desk and crumpled the paper, embarrassed by what he considered ridicule. "And what would that be, sir? Nigger shacks? Outhouses?" It was an obvious reference to Emil's own choice of subject matter.

"Perhaps when you learn to *see*, you'll appreciate the simple things. Maybe then you'll use color to give your thoughts voice."

"The newspapers don't agree with you." Sam glanced at some of his peers, looking for approval and a bit of admiration for his candor. While southern critics had bragged of Emil's "consummate artistry", they often complained of his "uninspiring subjects."

Emil laughed triumphantly. "I'm not shocked that newspaper reporters don't know that the very essence of life can be captured in the common things, but I am disappointed that you don't."

Sam was left to repair his image as his classmates took it all in. For a week or so, he was noticeably absent from Emil's painting treks across town, but he eventually became a regular. From the beginning, Emil had invited the boys to join him after school hours and on weekends. He took them to the potter's shack, the sawmill, the railway station, and Ashton's "colored" section. One rainy Saturday the group was obliged to paint indoors, where Emil arranged a still life.

Sam observed silently as his teacher began an outline. His buoyant black eyes darted from Emil's palette to the drawing paper, from Emil's face to his hands, apparently with great interest.

Emil noticed the boy's unusual behavior. He felt vindicated, certain Sam was finally contemplating the use of color. When the boy began a sketch with his pencil, Emil lost his patience. He grabbed Sam's pencil and tossed it angrily across the room. "If you won't use color, at least try charcoal."

Sam tried.

Emil was soon barking at him. "Everything you're doing is wrong. Look beyond the surface. Then when you see something, begin your sketch with an outline."

"But Mr. Holzhauer, an empty bottle and a piece of rotten fruit doesn't inspire me." The apple, a shriveled has-been, snuggled cozily against a cracked Vat bottle, its faded label still clinging tenaciously to its side.

"Look for the unusual," Emil advised. It was an oft-repeated phrase and one he had spent many classroom hours explaining and demonstrating. His voice reeked of irritation.

Sam reacted with silence. Finally, he began anew, but when his meager efforts brought more criticism, he slammed his sketchbook shut, retrieved his pencil from the floor, and left the room in a huff.

Emil was despondent. He hadn't the leisure for courting the boy as he was swamped by exhibition requests, speeches, and jury duty. Once a week, he addressed the Ashton Sketch Club which was composed of a fledgling but inspired group of would-be artists. Contrary to what his Riverview friends had intimated, local artists were imaginative and free of the artificial. They had taken a natural approach to art. Teaching them was a pleasure.

The Sketch Club responded with one-man exhibitions of his work as did the Ashton Artists' Guild. In an effort to educate those who showed an interest, he demonstrated his work at the show's opening. To the members' delight, he followed that with a discussion of his work or a lecture on American art or other subjects they had indicated an interest in.

While artists appreciated his talent, the general public echoed the sentiments of writers who continued to criticize his choice of subject. "Why does he paint outhouses and run-down sections of Ashton when the area abounds in mountain ranges, flowing streams, winding trails, and mountain flowers?" they asked. He laughed at their protests and continued to paint what he saw.

Early in the semester, he exhibited sixty watercolors in the school gymnasium. Most had been painted in Maine or New York, but some were recent paintings of Ashton. One painting came from the Art Institute in Chicago and would be shipped to the Metropolitan Museum following the Ashton exhibit.

In late fall, he entered the annual exhibition of North Carolina artists held at the George Vanderbilt Hotel in nearby Asheville. His entry, *Former Aristocrat*, a typical Holzhauer watercolor of a crumbling old southern home, placed first. His genius lay in his ability to create a solid mass, seemingly without detail, yet fill it with unobtrusive description. He was a master at drawing the viewer's attention to one area of the work without being obtrusive. As his genius unveiled, critics made less and less reference to his subject and concentrated on "his masterful interpretation of small town Americans."

Meanwhile, the National Art Society worked hand-in-hand with the Chicago Board of Education in paying tribute to him and his painting, *Village Street, January*, with another half-hour radio program on NBC.

Somehow, he managed to paint, canvassing the city and its surroundings. The potter at work in his shack became an obsession with him. Behind the shop was an old-fashioned well, something he craved to paint, but the excitement of painting the potter at work had always taken precedence.

On his agenda from the beginning had been a weekend trip to the university with Paul Bosch, the school's congenial music teacher. One morning during his regular bulletin board perusal, Paul insisted the time had come.

A young man in his twenties, Paul was a talented musician who sported an abundance of ebony hair, always lustrous and carefully groomed, and impetuous deep-brown eyes that dominated a youthful but enlightened face. His outgoing personality, and tall, carefully molded body brought him to the attention of more young women than he could easily entertain. Still, dating posed a problem as he had no vehicle. He implored Emil to furnish transportation, in exchange for which he would guarantee female companions for both of them. Emil had finally agreed, but only to occasional outings.

"Can't wait any longer, Emil. How about this weekend?" In spite of his popularity with the young women in Ashton, Paul's heart was set on a special girl at the University of Georgia.

"How am I to entertain myself while you're courting?"

"Paint of course. If I told you anything else, you wouldn't go. Say, you might enjoy visiting Henry Dunn, head of the art department. A real pioneer in the area. Instrumental in getting museums in Athens and Columbus off the ground."

"I'm familiar with Dunn's work," Emil told him. "One of his paintings was selected along with mine at the World's Fair."

A rare blush colored Paul's face. "Please forgive me. I quite forgot. Your show airs on Saturday. We can go another time."

Emil scoffed at his concern. "Don't worry. I only agreed because the school wanted the publicity. I detest the dramatics. The script calls for me to have twelve brothers and sisters." He cast his eyes upward in a sarcastic gesture. "I'd like to meet Dunn. I'll go with you."

It was agreed. The two arrived on campus around noon the next Saturday. At the university, Emil found himself something of a celebrity in the art department. Dunn pressed him anxiously to address the students about his days at the Henri School.

"I'm afraid I can't take 'no' for an answer," admitted Dunn. "When Paul told me you were coming, I called a special meeting of the art classes today. I'm certain the turnout will come near to a hundred per cent even though they're usually scattered on Saturdays. They've spent their morning listening to your story on the radio. Wonderful production. You must've missed it?" Emil winced. "I don't like hearing my story. They doctor it too much. As to lecturing, I don't do much, really. I teach with a brush in my hands." The thought of addressing the university students unnerved him. But, feeling obligated to Dunn, he agreed to share his experiences in the Henri school, the academy's objections, the Armory Show, the independents and their final liberalization of art.

"I suppose we must always have rebellion in the arts," he summarized. "Freshness of vision demands it. For some time artists have been abandoning subject matter, some completely and successfully, I might add. The idea excites me as do all ideas in art, but I can't abandon my own notions just to please the public. You shouldn't either. Don't be guilty of falling for the latest fad just to promote your work. Well, I'm afraid that's another subject," he finished.

Students questioned him as long as Dunn allowed it, then gave him a standing ovation and made him promise to return.

At home, divorce papers awaited him. The pain, he noted, had dissipated; regret had not. He ached for the companionship of a woman in the home.

Twenty-One

Emil made frequent trips to the university, much to Paul's delight. The university president, and father of Paul's lady friend, saw to it that Paul was kept busy during these visits. He was prevailed upon to lecture in the music department, lead university chorale groups, and play the piano for informal gatherings. It left little time for courtship, but the arrangement didn't discourage the smitten teacher from going.

Meanwhile, Emil and Dunn became good friends. Instead of lecturing to Dunn's classes, Emil insisted on leading them outside "where subject matter abounds." As the news spread of these activities in and around the campus, the president joked that they had more students on the weekend than they ever had during the week.

These occasional weekends, and the excitement of teaching, demonstrating, exhibiting, and painting at Ashton made for a lifestyle Emil treasured. He often worried that something would happen to change it all.

It did. Japan had attacked Pearl Harbor, and, in less than a week, the United States was at war with Germany. Tension and fear were made manifest in the anti-German element. Pointing fingers, and snide remarks came from the faculty members and bold students who mocked what they heard in their classrooms and homes.

When the Christmas vacation arrived, Emil was bent on canvassing the city and its surroundings, brush and palette in hand. His painting agenda was lengthy: scenes along the French Broad River and West Ashton's negro section and the railroad station and the potter's shack and street scenes and maybe a few outhouses. The biggest challenge facing him was choosing a scene. The potter's shack took precedence on his first free day, but when he arrived at the scene, the potter was gone, the shack boarded up. He saw it as a good omen, a forecast of fourteen exciting days to come, of everything at his disposal and no classes, no students, nothing to hold him back. It was a chance to paint the challenging old well behind the potter's shack, a scene he had dreamed of painting, but had never found the time.

There it stood in its age-old glory, a weathered-gray boarded frame supporting a slatted-wood bucket held together by metal rings. A frayed rope and rusty pulley completed the image. Hastily, he set up his trumpery old easel. He poured water from an old crazed jug into a paint-splotched bowl, both holdovers from Henri days. He opened a battered black paintbox containing a myriad of colors, then studied the scene with the same fervor as a thousand times before. He soon became lost in his work. Only the sounds of the country pierced his thoughts and entertained him, a cacophonous symphony that spoke for the awesome forces, allies and enemies, sharing the universe.

When sounds of a vehicle interrupted the spell, he felt intruded upon. Then he remembered the potter, and he was comforted. Sounds of a car engine, a door slamming, and a deep chest cough that drowned out everything else became apparent. He wondered if the potter had taken ill. Then a booming voice rang out.

"You better come with me," the intruder said. Almost immediately, Emil felt a slight pain in his side, as if he had jabbed himself with a sharp brush handle. The blow moved his arm, causing a wide swipe across the painting, one that would take some time, as well as expertise, to repair.

"Now see what you've done?" he yelled at the intruder.

"Listen, you German son-of-a-bitch, this here's a gun in your ribs. If I was you, and I'm glad I ain't, I wouldn't worry about a pretty picture."

Emil turned his head sideways, affording himself a glimpse of the intruder, a bull of a man with a deep, angry voice. The smirk on the man's sun-reddened face spoke for the joy he expected to receive for his efforts. He pushed a rifle barrel deeper into Emil's side, nearly knocking him off balance.

"Please tell me what I've done," Emil bellowed. The sparkle in his eyes, so brilliant just moments earlier, had faded into a memory, leaving only dull, lifeless sockets in their place. He had become accustomed to intrusions by the police as well as private citizens, but never in the countryside. He let out a low moan, a cry of frustration.

"I don't know yet, but I'm making it my business to find out."

"Please!" Emil pleaded, throwing something of a tantrum, "let me finish the painting." When his protests went unheeded, he reached in his pocket for identification, a move that brought another poke in his side.

"If you move another muscle, I'll shoot. Come on now. You and me are going to the police station." He motioned with a jerk of his head the direction Emil was to take.

The limit of Emil's tolerance was tested. "What harm can I possibly do out here in the wilderness? You'll be laughed at if you persist on taking me in." He picked up his brush and began to paint.

"You think we don't shoot German spies?" the man asked. His voice, though still threatening, had lost some of its bite. Except for a few grumbling comments about the damage done to his painting, Emil's answer was the squeaking sound of an unstable easel.

"All right then! We'll go when you finish. And we'll take the picture with us for proof," he added, as if to re-establish his authority.

At the police station, Emil was allowed to make a phone call, but he wondered who he might call. The school was closed for the holidays. It was hours before he was able to get in touch with the headmaster, who rushed to his aid.

"Arrested in the countryside? By an irate citizen? Painting the potter's well? What is this?" the headmaster raved to the police chief. "This man is a teacher at the boys' school. A better American citizen you'll never meet."

The chief was far from apologetic. "He was brought in by an officer of the law who was hunting nearby. They're all under orders to watch for anyone suspicious these days."

"Be reasonable," the headmaster urged. "The man would use a camera if he wanted a picture."

The chief seemed a bit embarrassed. "We're understandably a little edgy, especially about anyone with a German accent." Finally, he relented, apparently aware of their misguided haste in bringing in a teacher from the nearby boys' school. "Don't worry, it won't happen again," he promised.

Emil had little faith, recalling the times he had been accosted within sight of the school, when neither pleas nor credentials had induced the arresting officers to take a chance on his innocence. Nor was it unusual for him to be questioned for hours before being released.

He pleaded with the police chief to hang a photo of him in the station, one that would acquaint all police officers with his likeness. "I can't work for being carted off to the station," he moaned.

"You bring it on yourself," accused the arresting officer. "I agree," said the police chief. "Painting here and there in view of everyone, and with your German accent. It looks suspicious in a time of war. You should paint indoors till the war is over."

Emil exploded. "Heaven's sake! Think what you're asking me to do." His voice was a mix of pleas and frustration, his reddish-brown sun-painted face a contortion of self-imposed wrinkles.

"Well, I could ask the newspaper to carry a story on you."

Emil laughed at such a suggestion. "I've had stories. Exhibition write-ups and—"

"Everybody don't read the art pages, Mr. Holzhauer. But not many miss the front pages these days." The headmaster agreed. "Why not take a vacation for a few days, at least until the notice appears in the paper?"

Emil reluctantly agreed. He left the station, despair his unwanted companion, and his hope of spending two glorious weeks painting dissipated.

Where would he go? Who would allow a German artist the freedom to paint the cities, the countryside, the people at their tasks? The answer came to him almost instantly: Riverview.

It would be more than a painting trip. It would be a chance to visit his old friends and retrieve the paintings left in Rett's cellar. By early morning he was on his way, and not too unhappy with the change in plans.

Outside Rett's hotel and restaurant, passersby yelled and waved their greetings as he strolled into his old familiar haunt. Inside, diners and employees made a fuss over him as well.

He noticed, however, something unexplainable about Rett's behavior. True, he brought out the usual bottle of home concoction and smiled as he filled their glasses, but it was a forced smile, one that tugged at unwilling facial muscles, so unlike the happy-go-lucky Rett that Emil remembered.

"You see how they all miss you?" Rett asked rhetorically. "You put us on the map, then deserted us," he complained. "Ah, but you have come back to stay, haven't you?" He twisted his mouth in a playful grin, bringing to life a dimpled right cheek. Still not himself, he did exhibit something of the old sparkle he was noted for.

Emil was quite taken by the warm welcome, his ego cascading, flooding his whole body with euphoric madness. For one fleeting moment, he wished he had never left. At least there, he and his palette were welcomed on the streets, inside their businesses and their homes, along the riverfront, and in the quarry.

With all eyes upon him, he was forced to respond. "No, no," he declared, somewhat long-faced. "I have a contract to fulfill in North Carolina."

"Don't let Dolores or Newton or Schliemann or anybody hear you say that," Rett demanded. He had busied himself phoning all of them even as the group bantered on. "They'll all be here in a heartbeat," he promised.

Emil felt a penetrating warmth surging through his body as if coming in from the bitter cold and finding a warm fire awaiting him. One by one, his old friends began to arrive, Dolores first. She threw her arms around him in a passionate show of enthusiasm. "Emil! You've come back to us, and just in time," she announced. "I was about to contact you. The teacher you substituted for last year is retiring. The dean will be delighted to see you." Her eyes were saucers, her mouth parted as if anxious to continue but more anxious to hear his response.

Everyone waited, their eyes fixed on Emil.

"Your chance to return to civilization," said Rett. In a moment of excitement, he waved his glass of home brew in the air, spilling most of it near the cashier's desk. His earlier reticence seemed to have disappeared, a light-hearted mood of old having replaced it.

Emil decided the change had been a figment of his own imagination. "No," he laughed. "Really, I'll be going back right away."

"Has to be a woman," Newton shot back. Emil almost choked on a swallow of home brew. Once he regained control, he sat straight up in his hard-backed chair and let go with roaring laughter.

Schliemann stood in the doorway, watching and listening. "Is that a denial?" he grinned. Emil jumped up to greet him, and Schliemann returned the warmth. The two grasped each other's hands and held the pose for a long moment. "I'm sorry you won't be coming back to us. Guess we'll all move to North Carolina," he teased. Everyone happily agreed.

Looking around him, Emil was reminded that all of them were foreign-born. "If you do, be prepared to get arrested."

"Ah, yes, Dolores told us you've been bothered with frequent arrests," said Schliemann. "Too bad."

"Ah, what do you expect. He's a damn spy," railed Newton.

Everyone laughed heartily, everyone except Emil.

"Oh, if only you knew," he groaned. His face was still youthful except on these rare occasions when he allowed resentment to convert his sun-darkened skin into a harsh pallor. His body slumped in recognition of life's interruptions, but he quickly recovered, unwilling to mar the merriment of the gathering. "It's been a problem right along, but the war can't go on forever. Other than that, it's been a fulfillment of my dream. I've only come to paint and collect my paintings. I hope I can get most of them in my car." Against the objections of Rett, he insisted on "taking a look" at the work in the cellar that very evening.

"We have to talk first," said Rett.

"Talk? Of course, but I want to see the paintings you know. Get an idea of how many I can take with me this time."

When the party ended, Emil insisted on a trip to the cellar. With no hope of dissuading him, Rett finally confessed. "I'm afraid I don't have your paintings, *mein Freund*." His attempt at nonchalance failed, as witnessed by the hush pervading the small gathering.

"Not have them? But where are they?"

"Come, I'll show you," he motioned, lowering his voice in an effort to exclude the others.

When they were out of everyone's earshot, he explained that there had been a burglary and the paintings had been stolen.

"It's the price of recognition, Emil. Perhaps the radio shows? People heard the show and they knew your work would be valuable. If not now, certainly in the near future." He talked in spurts, rattling off one thing and following it with quite another.

Emil stood still a moment, trying to take it all in. "But why didn't you let me know? When did this happen? Even Dolores didn't mention it in her letters. Schliemann either. Why keep it from them?" he asked, suddenly realizing Rett had gone out of his way to exclude them from the conversation. "How is it they didn't know? My god, Rett, did they take every goddamn one of them?" His anger grew as the news began to penetrate.

Rett faltered in his story-telling at times, his gaze fixed elsewhere, never making eye contact with Emil. The short walk to Rett's home and the cellar seemed longer than usual, Emil milking Rett for information all the way, Rett stingy with answers or explanations. All the while, Emil felt confident that some of his work would still be there. The walls, however, were bare, and the boxes that contained perhaps fifty of his paintings, empty.

"All of my Hudson River scenes. Every goddamn one of them," he moaned. "Thank God Muller bought one," he remembered with a bit of satisfaction. "Where is Muller?"

Rett shrugged. "Don't know. Haven't seen him for a while. I can't tell you how bad I feel about this," he kept repeating. "I hoped we would find them before you returned." He cleared his throat endlessly, and coughed a shallow cough occasionally.

"The police? Do they know?" Hope faded with every question, but he was too shattered to keep quiet.

"Of course," Rett answered with a meaningless wave of his hand.

Emil left with Dolores shortly thereafter. She was as shocked by the news as Emil had been.

"Rett's not what you think," she said. "I don't know the whole story but I know enough not to trust him. The bastard sold your paintings and kept the money." Her dark eyes danced with anger.

"Rett? You're not serious? Rett doesn't need money, certainly not the paltry sum my work would bring. He owns everything in town."

"Believe me, it's true," she insisted, her eyes afire. "I saw one of your paintings in a friend's home. He told me he had bought it from Rett. I thought nothing of it at the time because I assumed he had your permission."

Emil's anger was uncontrolled. "I'll confront the son-of-a-bitch," he declared. He bade Dolores a hasty goodbye and headed for the restaurant.

By the time he arrived, the anger had risen within him like a raging river. He wasted no time on niceties, and it was with great effort he managed to keep his voice low enough that only Rett could hear. "You sold my paintings, didn't you?"

His eyes were fixed on Rett, his wide mouth grim, his body trembling with rage. Rett struggled for composure as a violent flush darkened his face. His dynamic voice had been weakened by the confrontation of a man who had trusted him with his life's work. Without a word, he took Emil by the arm, attempting to lead him into a private room, but Emil jerked free.

"I had no choice," Rett told him, attempting again to leave the public dining room. "You know I didn't need the money. They brought very little. The FBI came here and ransacked the place."

"FBI? But what would they want with my paintings? Do you think me stupid?" He flailed his arms in angry protest.

"You don't understand. They thought I was running a spy ring here. You know how edgy everybody is about Germans. You don't have to paint to attract suspicion these days, my friend."

"Oh," he mused. It made sense. He followed Rett into a private office at that point, but stopped short of taking the seat offered him. "Wait a minute. You sold my paintings. Dolores knows a man who bought one."

"If you'll let me, I'll explain. Don't you see? I had to convince them this was not a meeting place for German spies, but a place to store junk I buy and sell." His voice began to gain strength. "All because I had my friends meet there, all in fun of course, but those bastards tried to make something of it."

"Junk? My life's work? All my Hudson River series?"

"I'm sorry. I'll give you the money," he said as he pulled a wad of bills from his pocket.

"You insult me with money? Nobody prices my work but me. Nobody sells my work without my permission." Too frustrated to continue, he stomped out the door and headed for Dolores' apartment. When he arrived, Schliemann was there, anxious to hear the story.

"I'm afraid everything he told you was false," said Dolores. "Don't be as fooled by his outgoing personality as the business people are," she warned. "I can assure you there has been no robbery in Riverview. He's in cahoots with the police too."

The scene at the police station crept its way into Emil's thoughts. Without Rett's influence, he would have been sent home without a driver's license, perhaps even jailed for running into the police car. Another scene presented itself as well, that curious night in the cellar. "Where was Muller in all this?" he asked.

"I'm not acquainted with Muller," said Dolores, "but say what you will. Rett runs a house of ill repute, and I'm not referring to sexual favors. It's for people sympathetic to Hitler. You may as well know, people suspected you for a while," she added. "Somebody probably reported the activities there. Didn't you know about them?"

"No," he said, but quickly followed it with a "Yes." Schliemann and Dolores waited, their eyes focused on him. "I suppose so, but I always hoped it was harmless." He winced from embarrassment.

Schliemann had been taciturn throughout, his thoughts dredging up unpleasantries. "I've seen Muller now and then, and I've noticed a change in his personality, but I know nothing of its background. Nothing," he repeated, as if to dissuade further questioning.

In the confusion, Emil had forgotten to obtain a room at Rett's Hotel, the obvious, and previously perfect, lodging for a man who wished to come and go at odd hours, paint at leisure, and take his meals in the restaurant anytime he wished. Circumstances what they were, he gladly accepted Schliemann's offer to spend the night at his home. Like so many Riverview nights, it was a sleepless one. He spent the long, seemingly endless, night taking stock of himself. His Riverview friends had raised a question to which he had no answer: What was it that attracted him to the South?

A year before, he would have given his hearing for the job at Browder. That such a position was no longer appealing was as astonishing to him as to anyone.

Before the night ended, he knew the answer. At Ashton, he was free to paint, to express himself as he wished; not to please the art world, the critics, the gallery owners, or the so-called art patrons. He knew his work was good, perhaps great, and he needed no one to tell him so. If others recognized its worth, so much the better, but he wouldn't wait, nor depend, nor consciously seek approval. The satisfaction of expression was to him, an end in itself. He ached to develop this to its limit.

Teaching took second place in his heart, as well as his mind, but only to painting. It too was an opportunity for self expression, of sharing with others his passion. The two opportunities went hand in hand, each complementing the other.

When daylight approached, he headed south.

At the boys' school, Emil eyed the government forms on his desk, forms that everyone at the school, from janitors and maintenance men to instructors and assistants, were required to complete. How best can you contribute to the war effort, Uncle Sam was asking.

As the situation worsened overseas, everyone was moody and uncommunicative, at least with him. Even Paul's usual ebullience had waned, and he had become almost taciturn at times. One day, he shared his innermost thoughts with Emil.

"You may as well know. I plan to volunteer for the armed services. I've been thinking about it a great deal." Emil had never seen him so uncomfortable.

"God, what a mess," Emil said solemnly. "I hate to see you go." It was an understatement. Paul was the closest friend he had at the school. It was Paul who explained away the ugly remarks and the frequent arrests, and it was Paul who socialized with him on double-dates and other outings, and it was Paul who joined him for frequent meals at the German restaurant. Instead of the age difference alienating them, it had brought them together, Paul familiarizing Emil with southern culture, and by associating with him, taunted those who harbored prejudice. Paul welcomed an opportunity to enhance his own German background and feed at the same time on Emil's spirit, experience, and expertise.

"I'm no hero," Paul admitted, "but I know I'll be drafted soon, anyway."

"But what will we do for teachers?" Emil asked. He felt drained of his usual energy and zest, the more so as Paul's countenance was one of gloom.

"I'm afraid you'll be asked to fill the shoes of more than one teacher. War touches everyone." He grimaced, a gesture obviously designed to quell his own emotions.

A sense of intense loneliness came over Emil, his face bereft of color. It was almost as if Hitler knew and hated him personally, bent as he seemed to be on ruining Emil's life.

Soon thereafter Paul Bosch and several other young teachers were called to military service. At fifty-five, Emil was too old for the draft, but not too old for double duty at the school. Library monitoring took the place of his free period, and evenings were spent in the boys' dormitory, as he was given the added duty of chaperon, or disciplinarian as it turned out. His freedom had been taken away.

With the students' first exhibition scheduled for early spring, Emil made a concerted effort to assist the boys, who had begun to agonize over their exhibits. He drove them to outlying villages and sections of Ashton overlooking the French Broad River, then invited them to join him on campus or in his dormitory room where they painted still life or turned to each other for portrait work. Sam was a regular attendee at all of these, but he was still using his pencil.

With the exhibition only two weeks away, several boys joined Emil for a painting excursion through the black section of Ashton. Street after street featured row after row of unpainted wooden dwellings huddled in close proximity to each other. On a hillside behind the houses stood a similar building, but there was one difference: a tiny white steeple stood proudly on its rooftop, keeping a vigilant eye toward heaven.

As always, Emil began with a demonstration. "Study the scene until you see something you want to say about it. Then start with an outline." He reminded them often to "save your lights" (leave some paper unpainted) and "don't be afraid to try something new." In silence, the boys began their own interpretations. Without warning, one of the boys cried out, piercing the silence like a peal of thunder. "Ahhh!" he screamed. "Look at the rebel!"

At the expense of losing his macho reputation, Sam had resorted to using color. He kept pushing his mop of black hair off his forehead only to feel it creeping back to its original position. It was a habit Emil had come to recognize as therapeutic, an effort on Sam's part to temper his emotions.

Emil waited longer than usual to peruse Sam's work. When he did, he was disillusioned. "You've gone from drawing cowboys and Indians to painting them?" he asked.

"This is a cowboy?" Sam asked. His ungainly body stiffened and his thin boyish face worked itself into a disappointed grimace.

"Same as. Did you begin with an outline, or did you dive right into a conventional sketch of what you think others perceive as a row of houses with a church behind them?"

"It is a row of houses with a church behind them," Sam reminded him.

"If that's all you see, you may as well use your pencil," Emil said pointedly. "Look beyond the houses and the church. Learn to see what others don't."

Sam looked around him. As his classmates seemed lost in their own studies, he hadn't lost face. He studied the scene at length, then began anew.

It was almost supper time before Emil made his rounds. When he reached Sam, he was pleasantly surprised. "Well, well," he mused. "Now you're onto something. You finally heard the sun crackle."

Sam was spellbound by the comment. "The sun crackle?"

"Yes, and it obviously assisted you in your interpretation," he said without reservation. "What about the steeple?" he asked. "A leaning steeple? Shouldn't you point it heavenward? Show the purpose of the building is to worship God?"

The comment evoked a giggle from Sam who assumed it was made in jest. Seeing his error, he sought to redeem himself. "But sir, you don't believe in God."

The other boys mumbled to one another. Some glanced up from their drawing boards while others peeked in whatever fashion they could without being detected. All were anxious to catch Emil's expression.

The response was quick, but tempered. "Why do you say that? Because you never see me in church? I'm afraid that doesn't inspire me, but God's creation does. Look around you. His presence is everywhere. I feel it every time I paint."

"Sorry, sir." He shuddered with self-disgust. Instead of running away as he had done in the past, he remained rooted to the spot. Finally, he smiled knowingly, then turned to address his teacher.

"Mr. Holzhauer, you're the first show-me teacher I've ever had. All the others have been tell-me teachers." He spoke with an air of enlightenment.

Emil chuckled. "Show-me teacher?"

"Yes sir. Must take a lot of confidence to draw while you're teaching 'cause you never know what the finished product will look like. Exhibiting would be easier. At least then you've already finished the work before anyone sees it."

"Exhibiting would be easier?" Emil repeated, directing the question more to himself than to his student. *If only it were true*, he thought.

From then on, Emil watched Sam grow in mind and spirit. It was especially rewarding for the teacher as he was experiencing a deepening of his own insight, a growing power of vision. But the new and unwanted lifestyle, the constant companionship with unruly youth, of dealing with shenanigans all hours of the night, prompted him to contact Henry Dunn and inquire about a possible vacancy at the University of Georgia. If the war had brought about a shortage of teachers at Ashton, there had to be a shortage everywhere, he surmised.

Dunn wrote immediately to say the university had no opening but that he knew of a vacancy at Sudduth College in Mallon, Georgia. Dunn had already recommended Emil for the position. He had only to apply. "It's a Methodist school, but I'm certain they won't hold you to their faith," wrote Dunn. He implored Emil to "paint the copper smeltery in Tennessee. It's on your way. But be certain to obtain permission first," he warned.

Before leaving Ashton, he asked the dean for directions to the smeltery.

"I'll tell you how to get there, but be careful. That's mountain country, and mountain folks are suspicious of foreigners even when there's no war. Get permission from the officials first," the dean warned.

"Don't worry," Emil promised.

As he neared the smeltery, the awesome sight of black smoke belching into the oppressive sky sent the artist's emotions racing long before he could read the signs directing him there. The closer he came to the awesome structure, the more he was aware of impending rain. He drove as fast as he dared, sometimes unconsciously flooring the accelerator, anxious with every turn to catch a view of the complex. Finally he saw it, a massive array of structures silhouetted grimly against the darkened sky. The black smoke he had seen billowing from the towering smokestacks devoured the sugary white steam rising from another source.

Rather than chance a lost opportunity, he finally brought the car to a halt and hurriedly pulled out his sketchbook, still a good distance from the complex. He could do a sketch from the highway, a nonthreatening distance away from the sight. Later, he could use color if the rain held off.

In no time it seemed, he heard a fierce voice, apparently addressing him. "What are you doing?"

He had long since grown weary of curious passers-by and had learned to discourage them with impatient, and sometimes insulting, comments. "What does it look like?" he asked, without looking up.

"You better come with me," the stern voice demanded. When Emil turned around, he came face to face with a uniformed guard, his hand resting on a holstered pistol.

Realizing his mistake, he began an apology, but the guard was in no listening mood.

"Don't talk. Just drive," ordered the guard as he motioned Emil in his own car. It was with some difficulty the large man settled himself on the passenger's seat he had to share with Emil's belongings, most of which were paintings. "No tricks," he warned, eyeing Emil one moment, then perusing the suspicious stack of paintings the next.

Emil cursed himself in German, an act that didn't enhance his situation in the least. Once he reached the depths of frustration, he still found it difficult to think in English. He knew his situation was serious. The smeltery was engaged in war work, he had a German accent, and there was no one he could call on for help.

At the office, the guard motioned Emil inside. "Got a German spy here, Mr. Buie," he told his supervisor. "Caught him red-handed drawing the plant." He spoke with the authority of a man in charge of the situation, thrusting his jaw forward in a defiant gesture once his duty had been completed.

Unable to make anything of the sketch handed him, Mr. Buie grunted knowingly. "Probably in code. Or might be invisible ink. These goddamn Germans are sneaky all right. Better call the FBI."

"Be careful," warned the guard. "He understands English."

"Of course I understand English!" Emil snapped, eying the guard with disgust. "I'm an American. And the drawing is just that, a drawing. I'm an art teacher, for Christ's sake."

The guard sneered as he stepped forward, a gesture suggesting he would protect Mr. Buie if the need arose. Ignoring both of them, the supervisor riffled through some papers, then picked up the phone. Anger overcame Emil's concern for his safety.

"If you would only listen to me. I have been an American citizen for over thirty years, and I served in the American Army during World War I." His rage only heightened their suspicions. Realizing that, he lowered his voice, and continued his spiel in German mumblings.

Soon, a few people, apparently employees, had gathered outside the superintendent's office. "Good God," Emil moaned, "am I to be lynched?

The FBI official was on the phone. He spoke at length with Mr. Buie, and even with the guard who had brought Emil in. Both of them spoke with certainty of having caught a spy "in the act."

"Here," the guard said gruffly, handing Emil the phone. "He wants to talk to you."

Given a chance to speak for himself, Emil began with an apology, then poured out his soul, ending with a plaintive cry. "If you could have seen the smeltery as I did against that threatening sky. It was truly inspiring."

"Yes, it's a marvel, that smeltery," agreed the FBI agent. He soon asked to speak with the superintendent again. The guard latched onto Emil in the interim.

The phone conversation ended, Mr. Buie announced that they had to wait while the FBI did a background search.

The wait seemed endless to Emil, bringing to mind a full day at the engraving bench. When the phone finally rang, he jumped to attention, as did everyone else.

Mr. Buie grasped the phone while the guard's squinty eyes darted back and forth from Emil to Mr. Buie. Without comment, he handed the phone to Emil.

"Mr. Holzhauer?" asked the caller. "This is Roger Smoltz. You know, Mr. Holzhauer, I'm familiar with your art work."

Emil grinned broadly. "You are?"

"Yes, I had an opportunity to become acquainted with it in Riverview not so long ago."

"Oh, really?"

"I'm sorry we had to destroy your paintings, but this is war you know. We kept tabs on you for a while, but we satisfied ourselves that you are just an artist. You may paint the smeltery anytime you wish. If you'll give the phone to Mr. Buie, I'll let him know. But be careful. Everyone is nervous these days."

"Yes, yes, of course," he agreed "Thank you Mr. Smoltz." The feeling of relief was instantaneous but he realized, perhaps for the first time, the depth of hatred Americans felt for Germans. All of his paintings destroyed, all because of hatred. He wondered if it would ever change.

"Let him go?" asked the superintendent incredulously. "Yes sir."

Given only a small opening as his exit through the dozen or so people who had gathered, and no space at all past the guard whose ego had been mutilated, Emil moved cautiously, aware of their disapproval at allowing him to go free.

Twenty-Two

The episode at the smeltery had its impact on Emil's thinking. He had attributed previous encounters with the Ashton police to their arrogance and ignorance. But the FBI was another story. His record was clean, but what if someone should frame him, he worried. *I would be easy prey*, he moaned. It was a sobering thought, but one that dissipated once he arrived in Mallon. Just as Dunn had promised, the job at Sudduth was his. Almost immediately, everyone referred to him as "Professor," a title that had always been awesome and intimidating to him.

Sudduth, a four year college for women, was the only college in the South that could boast of a fine art department that included many other disciplines in addition to drawing and painting. It was obvious to Emil that the students themselves might be more advanced than he, perhaps with more training, and he was certain to be eclipsed by faculty members who could boast of having multiple college degrees.

Encouraged by the school's publicity department, the newspaper flaunted his background:

> ...nationally known watercolor and design artist, master craftsman in engraving, designing, and modeling...featured in radio shows...Logan Medal winner...painter of murals for public buildings...*Fortune* magazine artist...permanent collections in museums in New York, Los Angeles, Denver, Rochester, Albany, Syracuse...teacher, speaker and juror...Henri student...

Conspicuously missing from the laudatory description was mention of any college degrees to his credit. All of the other faculty members could boast of masters' degrees, and many held doctorates. The thought of mingling with such learned superiors put him in a state of panic.

As much as he liked the praise, he disliked it more. His only consolation was the hope that newspaper coverage would introduce him to the general public and to the local police department. The episode at the smeltery had unnerved him, even though he had known the sweet feeling of revenge in the end.

He began his portrait classes with demonstrations, using one of the students as a model. He then directed them to make three to five minute sketches of each other. "Don't worry," he told them. "We'll use paint right along, but first, I need to know your weaknesses and your strengths. How else can I help you?"

All of the students showed keen interests in his demonstrations, but only a few responded with pencil or charcoal drawings of their own. Their lack of interest prompted him to wonder if they had entered college to learn or to find husbands. The college had a reputation for refining students, for training them in social graces and domestic skills, as well as in academic competence and fine arts.

In class after class, only a handful showed an interest in self-expression, and even those showed little promise. Emil was painfully aware of the gulf between them.

He tried a new tactic with the third and fourth year students. "Paint," he urged them. "If the classroom doesn't inspire you, then we'll go outside. But for heaven's sakes, show me your work." Most of the girls smiled as if in approval of everything he said, but none of them wielded a brush. He was confused and irritated.

When one of his first year students asked if he ever gave assignments, he threw up his hands in despair.

"Assignments?" he asked, then repeated the question with a disconsolate moan. "My dear girl," he admonished playfully. "I have been giving you the same assignment day after day after day. Your assignment is to sketch! To draw! To paint! What else would you do in an art class?"

Silence reigned. The girl who questioned him sank into her seat, her eyes fixed on an unopened book. Others in the class followed suit.

"What's wrong with you people? Students in my other classes don't want to paint and you don't want to sketch. Why did you enroll in art classes?" he asked. His playful guttural voice, while welcomed by all the girls, brought only a few uneasy smiles.

Determined to bring them out, he tried a different tactic on a class of juniors. "I have an idea," he told them. "Since I can't interest you in painting in the classroom, we're going outside today. I wish we could go to the Farmers' Market or the brick yard or one of the city's crumbling old streets, but I'm afraid we don't have permission to leave the campus just yet. However, you might like to join me on my field trips on Saturdays or in the afternoons. I can tell you where you can find me each day." With little encouragement, he began listing his itinerary on the blackboard. "Farmers' Market, Saturday morning," he wrote, adding that he would be there by ten in the morning, shortly after dismissing his last class. He laughed at himself before adding that he seldom left the spot before darkness fell. "Oh, yes," he remembered, nearly dancing with delight. "What about all those run-down sections of town? You know, with the unpainted shacks and dirt streets and black wash pots. Absolutely tantalizing subject matter." The comment was met with blank stares and a few suppressed giggles, neither of which made sense to him. He continued his discourse. "They're all over town, but I particularly like the one with that old store building at the entrance. Do you know the one?" He pointed in the general direction he had in mind.

The girls began to giggle freely, each encouraging the other to join in. "You mean nigger town," one finally snickered. She looked to her classmates for recognition of her bravery. They duly responded with more giggles, a sure sign of support.

Their immaturity agitated Emil, but he was grateful the topic moved them beyond silence. "I see you have a lot to learn. Believe me, nobody epitomizes the essence of man and his emotions like the common folk at their daily tasks. Or their leisure, for that matter. You can never exhaust the possibilities there."

Emil realized they had been sheltered from the very things an artist needed to be aware of. Introducing them to the real world would be a challenge, and one he relished. On their first outdoor painting excursion, he led them to the campus grounds, certain the colorful Victorian conservatory would inspire them. With blank faces, they stared at the building where many of them had lived and attended classes for over two years. None seemed moved by its irregular rooftops, rambling porches, round columns, decorative white railings, and colorful bricks, all shaded and framed by magnolias, oaks, and dogwood trees. Emil could scarcely wait to get started with a demonstration and make his rounds to watch them in action. Unfortunately, things didn't go as he had imagined. Timidly, they dipped their brushes, but none of them did more than stain the surface of their papers. Dismayed, he snatched the brush from Tassie, the most graphic of the group, and began working on her paper. He dipped his brush but it came up bare.

"Where's your paint?" he shouted. "You can't expect to paint without materials." Squeezing greedily on a tube of blue acrylic paint, he continued his discourse. "Don't concentrate on one little area as you did here," he told her, his tone somewhat subdued. "You'll only get piecemeal. You must unify, bring it together. You must have your lines, your colors, everything interact with each other in order to make a statement. You can't have a piece here and another there." He spoke harshly, his voice sullied by disappointment and frustration.

Tassie wept in silence as she tried to do his bidding. In a moment, he grabbed her brush and began working on her painting, then tossed the brush aside, grabbing another and then another. Totally frustrated, he broke all three brush handles, one by one, across his upraised knee and sent them sailing through the air.

"Get a brush, for goodness' sake." Snatching a larger brush from her supplies, he continued with her painting. "Pull your colors together. When your drawing is too apparent, soften it. Then build up in whichever form you want. How do you expect to give your painting life?"

Tassie watched in anguish at first, then as the painting began to come to life, she wiped her face with the sleeve of her cotton dress and took notice.

"I'm afraid you have a Holzhauer," he admitted. "You should start another."

Others watched in anxious silence, afraid to paint, but afraid not to. With growing timidity, they feigned efforts to paint.

Emil approached Mary Helen, a wisp of a girl whose delicacy pointed to a sheltered life. Unlike Tassie, she was dressed with precision, her long blond hair in a stylish page-boy, her slim body housed in a polished cotton peplumed top and slightly below-the-knee skirt. While Tassie appeared to have been thrown together in a moment of carelessness, Mary Helen rolled off the pages of the latest style magazine. And yet, the two were close friends, both bent on a career in art, though neither showed much promise as far as Emil could tell.

"No, no, no!" he bristled. "Listen, all of you. Look at this," he said, pointing at her errors. "She has shown no relationship here. Remember, one thing derives from another. You must strive for life in your painting. You'll never get it in pieces. You must unify."

The students watched in awe as their professor imposed, superimposed, juxtaposed color. He softened contours with cool green, gradually working into other areas until he had covered the entire scene with shades of green. He built up color, warm against cool, just as he had done earlier, seeming to repeat himself. To their amazement, he outlined again, and softened it later with the same cool green. With each build-up, he probed a little deeper, giving the objects unity, and tying the composition together. As he painted, he talked.

"Another Holzhauer, I'm afraid," he admitted sheepishly, his show of embarrassment somewhat easing the class' tension. A glance at the others' less than inspiring efforts prompted him to ask what they had been doing in their previous art classes.

Meanwhile, Tassie had gotten hold of her emotions. "We've never seen a demonstration before," she explained timidly. The comment encouraged others to speak up as well, except for Mary Helen whose tear-stained face had muddled her makeup, a fact she found most distressing. Even so, she stood there quietly, her interest piqued by it all.

Emil soon understood that his demonstrations had constituted their first art lesson. Their only classwork had been history of art studies. Memorized information about artists, technique, periods, and dates described their "training". As for him, he would instruct the students at the next class periods to put their paints away, for they were to concentrate on learning the fundamentals of drawing. He then proceeded to the office of Mrs. Poole, the department head, with a complaint, certain she would be as shocked as he had been.

"It's a disgrace," he declared. "Their studies have been limited to the history of art. No background whatsoever in drawing or painting. It's unfair to the students and to their parents who send them here for an education." Once the message was delivered, he relaxed a bit, realizing for the first time that he had worked himself into a sweat. With the back of his hand, he wiped the perspiration from his high forehead, satisfied at last that something would be done about the abominable situation.

He was amazed at the lack of emotion the department head showed. She was a plain woman with short-sighted eyes too squinty to reveal their color, and thin graying hair that appeared never to have been combed. Although taken aback by her apparent disinterest, he couldn't help thinking what a grand subject she would make for his canvas.

"Mr. Holzhauer, surely you realize the value of having the students study the history of art?" She peered over tiny, round reading classes that clung to the bridge of her bulby nose.

"That's fine," he agreed. "But is that all we're going to teach them? His once-eager eyes narrowed, almost as if he were mocking her.

She seemed shocked that he dared question her integrity. She began walking back and forth in front of him, her hands clasped loosely behind her impoverished body. Her gaze was planted first on the floor, then the walls, purposely avoiding Emil's own gaze. "Now we know how fortunate we are to have you in our department." She spoke appeasingly, suggesting to him that his notions were to be humored, but otherwise ignored. "And I wish to congratulate you on the progress you're making with the students."

"Progress?" He laughed mockingly. "There's been no progress, believe me. How could there be?"

Ignoring the comment, she continued in the same detached vein. "As to the problem you mention, I think you surely exaggerate and I—"

"Exaggerate?" he interrupted angrily. "I invite you to visit my classes and see for yourself." He surprised himself with the outburst for he had always respected those in authority. He apologized immediately for the interruption and waited for Mrs. Poole to finish. Unfortunately, she had.

The problem was minimized, and he was told to "do as you see fit." Before he left the office, she asked him to arrange an exhibition of his work in the school conservatory as soon as possible. The request only magnified his disgust. The college seemed more interested in publicly displaying the talents of its faculty than educating its students.

Within weeks, he managed to frame eighteen oils and mat and frame fifteen watercolor paintings for the show. Many were North Carolina or

New York scenes, but he hoped to include local scenes if time permitted him to paint them.

Mallon publicized the exhibition as a one-man show by a "nationally known artist," a real plus for the little city that still carried scars from Civil War days. Antebellum homes that had survived the torture stood at a dignified distance from the grand old streets, and sprawled lazily behind huge oaks and magnolias. The massive arms of the trees lined wide pathways and shaded luscious green lawns. Emil had chosen several of these "old aristocrats" for his canvases, but mostly the ones that had not been renovated. He included one in the exhibition.

Within an hour of its opening, the exhibition hall was filled. Dr. Greenlee, the college president, was the first to congratulate Emil on the show. "I can't tell you how proud we are," he said. "Art groups from several states are represented here." In stark contrast to some faculty members Emil had come to know, there was a degree of innate civility about Dr. Greenlee, a man who never seemed to slump in his character or duty, thus characterizing the image Emil carried of a headmaster.

Most of Emil's students were present, even though they had attended the preview. Several art associations from nearby cities asked that he address their groups and allow them to sponsor exhibits as well. Other colleges requested exhibits and accompanying lectures for their art students. He was prevailed upon to exhibit at the High Museum in Atlanta, where he would be guest of honor at a Sudduth Alumnae Association tea. Midway through the evening, he realized he had agreed to accomplishing more things than time would permit, but the excitement of being sought after and of being totally respected for his accomplishments gave him the confidence to reach out to the community as a whole and respond to its embrace. Inching to the surface was a welcome sense of confidence as well, one he attributed to Sam Coakley.

Sam had inadvertently pointed out a blatant flaw in Emil's thinking, if not his character. He had never had difficulty demonstrating an idea, giving it life on canvas right before a viewer's eyes, and yet, he was reluctant to hang it, the finished product, for that same viewer's perusal.

Quite pleased with himself, he walked from painting to painting, taking the opportunity to speak with those who hadn't the courage to approach him. It was a new and welcome feeling.

One woman in particular caught his eye. Dressed smartly in a chocolate-brown gabardine dress with a sleeveless jacket in luscious brushed orange, she stood out from the others who wore drab wartime attire. In her forties, she was not particularly pretty, with a sharp pointed nose and an air of arrogance her trademark. All of this might have gone unnoticed if she hadn't shown an unusual interest in several of his paintings. When she caught his eye, she brazenly motioned him in her direction. With renewed confidence, he approached her.

"What do you think?" he asked, an expectant smile parting his moist lips.

"I'm confused," she said. "Are you laughing at us here in Mallon? Painting negro huts and brickyards? Have you no eye for beauty?"

Emil was too shocked to interrupt.

"And when you did choose one of our old Mallon houses, you chose the ugliest one in the city, an eyesore in disrepair. And this one," she pointed, "don't think I ever saw a purple mountain." There was a measure of certainty in her sprawling drawl.

A crowd had gathered around them as gasps of outrage competed with mixed mumblings of shock and anxiety. The muscles around Emil's mouth began to tighten, a precursor to less subtle reactions.

"My dear woman," he began. It was an overused expression on his part, and one friends and acquaintances soon learned he used only when angered. "I've spent a lifetime sharpening my thinking and learning to see the unusual. We've already fought the academy," he gloated, "and I might add, we won." She hadn't the vaguest notion of what he meant, but he couldn't identify with art ignorance, so he continued his oration. "Look at this," he demanded, pointing to the last painting she criticized. "Look how the colors dance together. I've made light of shadow, and you don't mind. Why should you object to purple from black? I don't copy nature. I'm an artist, not a camera. An artist interprets. He creates. I can see beauty where others can't. When you learn to *see*, perhaps you'll qualify as an art critic. People who know nothing of art shouldn't presume to be experts," he added.

The stunned circle of onlookers gasped at his outburst as did the young woman in brown and orange. To his own amazement, he didn't care. He was an artist, and a damn good one, and his work could speak for him, he concluded silently.

Not everyone agreed, but at least one art critic did:

> ...his work is solid...has
> harmony of color...demonstrates unusual
> technique with curves and shadows...sees
> beauty in the most common scenes and paints
> them with colorful and glowing
> sympathy...has great understanding of the
> American scene...

Others noted that "Holzhauer's work has taken on a softness, a subtler way of viewing things" since moving south. His recent exhibits in New York had prompted the same comment from new York critics. He didn't disagree with them.

The exhibition apparently encourged Mrs. Poole to join his night class, though not in any conventional manner. Instead of sitting in the classroom, she secluded herself from the group by setting up her materials in a dark hallway. Periodically, she appeared in the classroom doorway, signaling for help, strands of thin, unruly hair clinging mercilessly to her damp forehead. "Please come inside," Emil begged. "We're getting a cool breeze through the windows. And the lighting," he grimaced. "It's horrible in here. Quite impossible to paint under these conditions."

"Oh, no. I'll be fine here," she insisted. "Just tell me what you think my problem is and I'll work it out." She motioned him to a darkened corner of the hallway, well-hidden underneath the staircase.

Even in the poorly-lit area, one glance was sufficient, for she had done nothing more than stain the surface of a sheet of drawing paper. Emil's gaze met hers, he in astonishment, she in hopes of encouragement. He saw in her face the hint of a smile, an expression she seldom used, but one that pushed her narrow eyelids even tighter together.

Her problem was easily identified. She couldn't draw. No wonder he had failed to get her attention about the plight of the students.

"Please, I must insist you come inside with the others. You may get some ideas from them. Later, I'll give a demonstration which may help you also." He was clearly agitated.

She refused. As he became engrossed with the classwork inside, he forgot about his hallway student, but her constant appearances in the doorway kept him running from the hallway to the classroom while the students snickered.

After the class had been dismissed, he invited Mrs. Poole to join him and the other students at the Farmer's Market on Saturday.

"The Farmer's Market? With the students?" Apparently insulted by the remark, she opened her dim-sighted eyes as wide as her overhanging eyelids would allow, giving Emil his first view of their color, a spent green that might once have brightened an otherwise colorless face.

"Of course," he emphasized. "You can learn from them. Believe me, some of my best lessons have come from students." But Mrs. Poole scoffed at the whole idea, pausing to push the thin hair strands away from her wrinkled brow.

For Emil's part, the market was the next best thing to the smeltery, a beehive with its bustle of activity around an open shed, one where farmers brought in their fresh goods, where townspeople gathered to barter for the best produce and price, and where shuffling feet constantly rearranged the sawdust floor. The shelter had character of its own, with its intervaled, rough-hewn posts supporting a large, tapered roof. There were bean shellers, corn shuckers, hand-made signs, and traders. The sight of it always sent him scampering for a spot in the crowd.

When Saturday came, four of his students had arrived in advance of him. It wasn't long before the outing attracted eight to fifteen students, mostly the same ones, always Tassie, and usually Mary Helen.

One of his most devoted students, Tassie was often caught up in the emotions and prejudices of the times. Although she had no Italian accent, as she had been brought up in Georgia since she was a small child, there was no mistaking her Italian ancestry with her dark hair and matching skin, fiery eyes, and dominant nose. Then, too, she was a devout Catholic, an unforgivable affiliation for some of the staunch Methodists at the school, particularly within the faculty.

The more they ostracized her, the more it endeared her to Emil. As their relationship grew, each confided in the other the problems they bore as foreigners. The common ground led to a mutual trust in each other. For the first time since arriving in Mallon, Emil shared his innermost thoughts with someone, including the problem he had been experiencing with Mrs. Poole.

"I'm not in the least surprised," announced Tassie. "She doesn't have a clue about art."

"Then why is she heading the art department? Isn't it insult enough that she teaches it?"

"Believe me, it's a source of entertainment for the students. Always has been." Tassie's drooping eyelids were misleading, suggesting a constant downcast state, one her sparkling black eyes always denied as did her zest for life.

"Wouldn't you think she would be embarrassed?"

"Of course she's embarrassed," Tassie laughed. "Spends all her time trying to keep the students from knowing she can't draw when only a moron wouldn't know it."

A feeling of powerlessness came over Emil, a feeling made manifest by his vacant expression.

"Why not talk with Mrs. Moore?" suggested Tassie. "She's the only one who knows what's going on."

"Oh, really? Tassie, how do you know all these things?"

"Everybody knows. Besides it's my business to know. My family has limited funds for sending me to college," she said with decided fervor. "I can't waste my time as it wouldn't be fair to them or to me. So if the instructor has nothing to offer, I don't enroll in the class, at least not a second time."

He stared at Tassie, reflectively.

"Did I say something?" she asked.

"No, Shotsy," he assured her. It was a title he often used when pleased with someone, especially students. "I was just admiring your spunk. Too bad your professors have no such principles."

The twosome became involved with their work at that point and left to chance any ideas that might have surfaced for solving the problem both were keenly aware existed. As the morning grew, so did the activity at the busy market where the farmers gathered with their families and goods, not just for survival but as a social event. Black and white children raced around the vegetable bins playing hide and seek, while their mommas kept the trays filled with shelled beans, shucked corn, and scrubbed potatoes. More often than not, it was daddy who peddled and bartered, weighed and bagged the goods, then took in the money and made the change. The constant chatter, the squeals, the sighs of boredom, relief, and joy; the changing facial expressions of buyer and seller, of child and mother, of worker and shopper, kept the artist reaching beyond himself, as new ideas filled his spirit.

Curious passersby often investigated the artists and their canvases, sometimes commenting to each other, but seldom disturbing them. When a man asked Emil what he planned to do with his painting, he responded with little forethought.

"Oh, exhibit it, maybe." It was a common inquiry for which he had a common response, one he could deliver without losing his concentration. The answer usually discouraged further conversation.

"Where?" the man demanded.

"Where?" Emil repeated haughtily. "What difference does it make?" Laymen never seemed to understand how devastating an interruption could be to an artist. Without looking up, he tried to answer the inquisitor without ruining his concentration. "Atlanta, or Gainesville, maybe."

"New York?" the man asked.

"Possibly." Why not, he thought. His work in Ashton had been well received in the Eastern galleries, and in Mallon he had been even more inspired.

"I thought so. You better come with me to the office."

"Heaven's sakes," growled Emil. "Let me finish the painting first."

"What office?" asked Tassie. "What's the problem?"

"Don't tell me I'm to be arrested?" he groaned.

"Arrested!" screamed Tassie. "Whatever for? Sir, we've painted here for months now." Mary Helen led a group with groans and admonitions, but none of them went beyond that.

"Young woman, this doesn't concern you," he said sternly. "I don't think the manager's going to like it. Better bring your painting along," he directed Emil.

Tassie attempted to tag along, but the man made it clear she was not invited. She cringed when her professor snatched at his painting in anger, causing a ragged tear in the canvas. "Half a day's work," he grumbled.

Tassie touched him on the arm, gently. "I think I know what the problem is. Remember the lady who criticized you for painting the mountain purple? You know, at your exhibition?"

"Oh, yes. Why?"

"High society," she whispered. "Her husband's the market superintendent. The manager's probably smarter than she is. Go ahead. Show him your painting. He'll probably appreciate it."

The other students chanted agreement and Mary Helen and Tassie assisted him in removing the canvas from the easel without further damage.

He made a clumsy entrance through the narrow door with the large canvas. While waiting for the market manager, Emil's thoughts wandered. *Was Tassie right*?, he questioned. *Or was it the business with the FBI again*? He had informed Dolores and Schliemann of the smeltery incident, but there had been no word from either of them.

Just then, a warm, friendly voice greeted them. "Oh, my, you've painted the market, I see."

"He's gonna show that up north," Emil's companion noted sarcastically. Obviously unmoved by the comment, at least until the angry man whispered something in his ear, the manager seemed dumbfounded by it all.

Politely, and seemingly with some embarrassment, he begged Emil's pardon. At the accuser's urging, the manager followed him into an adjoining room, but not before politely asking Emil to excuse them a moment.

Emil ventured outside, where he could take in fresh air and survey the activity being captured on his students' canvases, though mostly their easels remained idle while they gathered together in support of whatever catastrophe awaited their professor.

In a few minutes, the manager emerged from his office, alone. He apologized to Emil for the disturbance, then told him to go ahead and paint the market. "For now," he added. Emil was too elated with the good news to notice the change in the man's countenance, the warmth with which he had spoken a few minutes earlier having cooled considerably.

The morning after the market episode, Emil was in Ethel Moore's office. If, indeed, she had a handle on things in the department as Tassie had suggested, he realized it was time they became better acquainted.

Ethel was a woman with a retiring disposition, a quality Emil admired, but it did make conversation with her difficult as he was always obliged to initiate it. It was not one of his strong points.

Ethel bore a strong physical resemblance to Marcy, a fact that hadn't escaped Emil for a moment. Her knowledge and appreciation of the arts brought Clarle to mind as well, but the similarities ended there.

Her lustrous black hair glistened with lighter shades of black and brown, her full bangs bringing attention to dark wide-set eyes. Hers was a natural beauty requiring little or no prompting, her short hair hugging her face in a neat and casual embrace, her flawless white skin free of makeup. Full, but pouty Shirley Temple lips completed a picture many might have envied except for one flaw. There was a dormancy about her, an unknown, a constraint. One had to watch closely for subtle changes in her countenance and demeanor to have any notion at all of her mental state. She never seemed to laugh when others did, and yet a smile often emanated from her lips when no one else saw humor. Most had written her off as an eccentric. Then too, she was a "foreigner" herself, having come to the college from Boston, or "somewhere up east" as locals explained it. None of that was of any consequence to Emil, but it apparently weighed heavily on the minds of some southern-born faculty members, and parents who sent their daughters to Sudduth for a "good" southern education.

Emil had formed no opinion about her at all. It was Tassie's comment that brought him to her office. He began, as always, in the middle. "How is it that the department chairman has no background in art?" he began.

Patience was not one of Emil's strong points. When Ethel didn't respond, he tried explaining the comment. "What I mean is, an art teacher, and head of the art department, and she can't draw?" Ethel was silent and expressionless.

"Surely Dean Perkins will be outraged and demand an apology," he continued. Realizing he had followed one blunder with another, he was beset with embarrassment and irritation. "Forgive me, I should explain. You see, I've brought up two subjects, both of which have caused me a great deal of stress. Yesterday, I was approached by a man who was incensed that I was painting the market." With Ethel expressionless, and apparently confused and bored as well, he wished ever so much he hadn't come and that he could erase the whole conversation from both their minds.

"The Farmers' Market?" she asked. Small lines formed around her tightened mouth. "Did your class disrupt their business?"

"On the contrary. The customers seem to enjoy the whole thing, always watching the students and asking questions. If anything, we've brought them more business."

Ethel was clearly shocked. She fixed her eyes on Emil, but said nothing. It was as if she expected an explanation. When none came, the slightest color appeared in her cheeks and tiny lines of derision circled her mouth. "I can't imagine their motive."

"They?"

"The people who run things," she said knowingly. "Self-appointed leaders. You'll find lots of them here, usually people with the least to offer in leadership qualities." It was obviously a touchy subject with her and one she had given a great deal of thought to. "Of course Mrs. Poole is a different thing altogether."

"Should I talk to the ceramics teacher about her?" he asked.

"Catledge? Why?"

"Well, I thought he might talk to her."

"She would probably tell him to mind his own business, and rightly so. How could he cast a stone? The man has never thrown a pot."

Emil was shocked by the unfair accusation. "You must be mistaken. He has spoken to me about it on many occasions."

"Oh, he has a wonderful speaking knowledge on the subject. He makes designs, but never executes them. The man has never thrown a pot," she repeated. She had a way of bringing a conversation to an end without emotional outbursts. Emil made no further comment. He was, however, in a state of shock.

Twenty-Three

Emil was confused and frustrated by the conversation with Ethel. It was weeks later when a letter arrived from Schliemann that his thoughts turned to other things. The letter was well-received as he was anxious to learn what had transpired since his last visit to Riverview. Enclosed with the letter were newspaper clippings that covered Emil's latest exhibition. Schliemann issued a firm reprimand:

> …can't believe you didn't let us know about your exhibit at the Barbizon in New York. We saw it in spite of your reticence, *mein Freund*! Guess we shall all eat crow as all of your efforts have come to fruition, your work solidified in the South. Teaching has meant enhancement rather than deterioration. Admire you for thumbing your nose at everyone else's notions of what you should do or where you should go. You have ignored us all, and you have proven to be the victor…
>
> Saw your Mallon brickyard scene in the International Watercolor Exhibition in Chicago this week. Appreciate the tests a work must survive in order to reach that distinction…

Good old Schliemann. Emil had particularly cherished their friendship. While others of social standing were instrumental in getting Emil's name and his work in the forefront, Schliemann's interest in his paintings seemed rooted in genuine appreciation.

He urged Emil to return to Riverview often. As to news about Rett, Schliemann apologized:

> ...about your paintings. I'm afraid that
> all my efforts have been in vain. I have been
> able to locate a few in area homes, but I have been
> unable to determine the whereabouts of most of them.
> Perhaps I will have a better report for you
> during your next visit here. We all look
> forward to seeing you this summer.

One bit of news had been saved for the last paragraph:

> Marcy is dead. She died in Israel. It was
> inevitable as the poor girl was not strong
> enough to keep up the self imposed pace....

The news evoked a multitude of emotions, all of which he was reluctant to give in to. Instead, he found himself laughing. It was a nervous sort of laugh that irritated him, but one he couldn't stifle. It was not Marcy's death that most disturbed him; it was her failure to cure her stagefright, and most of all, his own failure to make their marriage work. *A good marriage might have been given her the confidence she needed*, he mourned.

As to Rett, he would let the matter rest until he could return to Riverview. Meanwhile, he painted. He savored Saturdays when he could paint at the exciting market, a handful of students beside him. Then one Saturday, the friendly manager approached him.

"How long will it take you to finish your painting, Mr. Holzhauer?"

"Finish? I never finish," Emil laughed. "I just quit, usually at dark. Why do you ask?"

"I'm sorry, but I must ask you to leave."

Emil protested vehemently, finally accusing the manager of misleading them. "You told us it was okay."

"The students can stay. I'm sorry. It was my mistake." The man himself appeared to be distraught so Emil left without further comment. Incensed by it all, his students followed.

On Monday morning, he was in Ethel's office, repeating the episode at the Farmers' Market. "Can you explain to me what harm there is in painting the market?"

Ethel regarded him closely as dark color oozed into her creamy-white face.

When she didn't respond immediately, he raved on. "I'm certain Dean Perkins will be outraged." His words sounded like an echo from days past when he had first discussed the incident with Ethel.

"Don't waste your time with Perkins," she said. "He's a puppet." A moment of silence followed. "I never thought they'd go this far."

"Who? Please! Can't you be more specific?" Emil studied her large wide-set eyes for signs of anger or indignation or animosity, but as usual, they were expressionless.

Ignoring Ethel's warning, he proceeded to Perkins' office and demanded intervention.

Like Catledge, Perkins ached for attention from the female students. At five feet, ten inches, he was taller than Emil, but he appeared shorter because his legs were disproportionate to his long body. His pudgy build cut an ugly figure, a fact he seemed all too aware of. He attempted to hide his receding hairline by combing his straight hair at an angle across one side of his forehead, thus creating a likeness to Adolf Hitler. With the war going on, it was an image that didn't enhance his own in the least. He often made comments about Germans and their bushy heads, comments meant to be degrading, but with nearly everyone lavishing attention on Emil's "frosted white crop," it fell short of its mark and made Perkins the laughing-stock of students and faculty members alike.

Though earthshaking to Emil, the market dilemma was of little consequence to Perkins. "I agree it's unusual, but we don't want trouble with the authorities," he said with disinterest. "Perhaps the college will be better served if you stick to some of Mallon's prettier scenes?" With that, he was content to dismiss the topic.

Emil was incensed. Before he had a chance to vent his anger, Perkins began praising him. "The college is receiving a great deal of publicity from your exhibitions. All of us here are quite amazed by your enthusiasm and your energy. Full teaching schedule, speaking engagements, exhibits across the country. And you still find time to paint. I understand you do your own framing as well? How do you manage all that?"

Emil was not appeased. Remembering the label Ethel attached to the dean, it occurred to him that the "puppet" was merely echoing the words of his superiors, whoever they were. Too, he was still seething over the dean's reference to "prettier scenes".

"I'm content doing what I do. That's your answer to how I manage all these things. But if I'm to check with you before choosing my subjects—" He raised his voice, signaling the remark was a question he wanted an answer to.

Ruffled, Perkins pushed an unruly stack of papers across his neglected desk. The breeze created by the ceiling fan scattered the papers across the room. Irritated, he snapped at Emil. "I don't care what you paint, Emil, but if the market manager told you to leave, you'll have to leave." He grabbed a handful of flying papers and crammed them in the wastebasket, then quickly straightened up and smoothed his hair across his forehead.

Emil said nothing, but he made no effort to leave.

"Something else?" Perkins asked.

"Yes. What about Catledge? I know for certain there's nothing wrong with the potter's wheel. Maybe a bit dusty from lack of use."

Perkins turned his head aside, avoiding Emil's gaze. "You know, Emil, I'm reluctant to tell Catledge anything. The man has an impressive background in his field. Perhaps you didn't know Northeastern has asked him to teach this summer?"

If true, Emil was certain of one thing: Northeastern had been misled. He wondered what embellishments had been added to the man's resume. What exaggerations? Rather than waste any more time, he left the dean's office and headed across town to the main campus and the office of the president. He felt certain Greenlee would see the immediacy of the situation.

Greenlee listened without interruption. Emil knew immediately he had done the right thing in revealing the problem at the market as well as the intolerable behavior in Catledge's classroom. He could scarcely wait for the president's reply. Greenlee seemed shocked by the news, but he was quick to point out there were no options if the market officials asked him to leave.

"But they have ostracized me I tell you. The students are free to paint there anytime." He jumped up from his chair, the only protest he dared use to a superior.

"Even so, it's their choice, whatever their reason."

"How can you pass it off so easily? Surely, the college president could…"

Greenlee shook his head vigorously. "I'm afraid it's quite impossible for the college to intervene in such matters." Although issued with feeling, his message was clear. There was to be no further discussion of the matter. "However, I think I may have a solution for the ceramics department."

"Oh, really?" It was enough to set Emil's tanned cheeks aglow. "Well, I'm glad someone finally recognizes the problem."

"With Mrs. Poole resigning, I was about to ask you to take over the department chair. That way, you could see to the shortcomings in the department yourself."

Emil bristled. "Mrs. Poole resigning? But why? No!" he said emphatically. "I don't want it. I have too little time for painting and for my students as it is."

"In that case, I'll have to call on Mr. Catledge."

"Catledge! But you don't understand. I'm constantly exhibiting in New York and Chicago. Even locally at the city hall, the library. So many lectures expected of me outside the college. I hardly have time to paint anymore," he grumbled.

"I fully understand," said Greenlee. "You're teaching whether in the classroom or on the streets or at the exhibitions. I appreciate everything you're doing, but if you don't assume the position left vacant by Mrs. Poole, I shall have to call on Catledge."

"What about Miss Moore?"

"Good teacher. Perhaps one of the best the college has, but not a leader. Too intolerant."

The president certainly knew how to make his point. To keep it out of the hands of Catledge, Emil agreed to take the added responsibility of department head.

He left the president's office more depressed than ever. As the end of his first year at the college approached, he felt like throwing a childish tantrum until he realized that he had been doing that for months, and nobody cared.

Twenty-Four

Emil's new assignment as department head only widened the communication gap between him and Catledge. He found conversation with Catledge difficult at best, and always nonproductive, but he was determined to do whatever it took to improve the ceramics classes.

It wouldn't be easy. Catledge lacked stamina for anything but endless talk. This he did mostly with his students and an occasional colleague who had nothing better to do. Dean Perkins, who delighted in the tomfoolery Catledge staged with his students in the privacy of his office or classroom, was often one of them. Emil tried dropping in Catledge's office for a one-on-one discussion, but it was always jammed with poorly motivated students whiling away their time in lively chitchat with their animated professor. He was obliged to settle for a formal meeting immediately following a general faculty meeting.

Catledge entered Emil's office brushing his jacket. Without a word to Emil, he made a few swipes across his shoes, straightened his tie, and tucked his shirttail in. When he took a handkerchief from his pocket to smooth his greasy hair, Emil couldn't resist comparing his unorthodox behavior with that of his teaching ability. Both needed fixing.

While others often laughed, Catledge prided himself on his appearance. The truth was he was saddled with a dull-black mop of hair that nature had apparently abandoned. To control it, he had resorted to saturating it with a greasy substance, giving it the appearance of having been lacquered right along with the finest furniture. He combed it straight back more in the style of a movie gangster than a college professor and was often seen admiring himself in his office mirror. He walked with his shoulders thrust back and his head held high, giving him the appearance of being even taller than his six foot frame and enhancing a self imposed aura of superiority. At thirty-five, he was twenty-three years Emil's junior but he had already developed a small paunch below the waistline, one he attempted to hide by wearing jackets a size too large.

By contrast, neither time nor Emil's persistence had tamed his shock of bristling white hair, but a stylish crew cut kept it out of his face. Clinging sideburns framed his bronze face, heightening the glow in his lively blue eyes, and softening the plumb-bob path his steely strands cut across a high forehead. Women admired his white-thatched top and men envied it. Instead of aging him, it gave him a look of youthful dignity.

While waiting for Catledge to complete his self improvement, Emil pondered his best approach to the ceramics dilemma. It was useless, however, as diplomacy was not one of Emil's assets. If he had something to say, he began with the heart of the matter, foregoing all niceties and pleasant introductions. "Don't you think the potter's wheel has been idle long enough?" he began. "The students—"

Instead of sitting, Catledge walked about the room with a lofty attitude, his manner one of resentment. He had come prepared for the confrontation. He interrupted Emil. "Ah, yes, the potter's wheel. I've been anxious to get started with it."

"Oh?"

"Certainly. It's just that the students are only now beginning to reach that stage. I expect we'll be calling on the old wheel in a matter of weeks now." The whole thing was minimized.

"Weeks? But I should think—don't undersell the students. I'm afraid they're smarter than we give them credit for. Most of them are here to learn, and they resent it when we waste their time."

"I quite agree. Always on their toes. They know who's qualified and who isn't. They're always in my office, you know, seeking information." He threw his head back and thrust his chin forward in an obvious show of triumph.

Emil ignored the reference to teacher qualification though he knew it was directed at him for not having a college degree. He also knew Catledge was playing games with him, trying to avoid the inevitable. Emil was in no mood for his lofty talk. "I asked the department secretary to research the possibility of pottery classes being available in Atlanta.

Fortunately, she discovered at least one offered on the weekend," he said pointedly.

Catledge was outraged. Just moments earlier he had taken a seat, but Emil's remark put him on his feet again, this time in a rage. "I think you'll find my credentials superior to most in this college." He steered clear of names, but Emil knew his own was first on Catledge's list.

"We're not talking credentials here," Emil said. "If the students have no training, how are they to train their own students? Don't you see the responsibility we have? We must do more than tell them what they could learn if they stayed home and read a book." His voice tightened as he addressed the back of his reluctant listener.

Catledge merely pooh-poohed the idea with typical arrogance. "No problem at all. Perhaps you're not informed. Northeastern has asked me to teach there this summer. Famous for its ceramics classes," he added haughtily. He said a huffy goodbye even though the meeting had scarcely begun. In spite of the self-praise, Emil noticed less bounce than usual in Catledge's step. Emil wondered why.

He also wondered if anything he could say would make a difference and what action was available to him, if it didn't. While pondering his next move, he became aware of a hard pang in his stomach, a reminder that he hadn't eaten since breakfast more than twelve hours earlier. At home, he treated himself to a beer and cold cuts, adding a few moments of private thought to a typical German supper.

The next day Emil accompanied several of his classes to nearby Lake Legend. The lake was just awakening from a quiet evening when the students, their chaperon, and their instructor began to gather on its shores just outside Mallon's city limits. It was a grand day for picnicking, swimming, boating, horse-shoe pitching, and of course, sketching and painting. The girls would do all of those things, and before the day ended, they would have persuaded their instructor and chaperon, Emil and Ethel Moore, to join them.

The excited girls gathered around their instructor for they knew he would begin the outing, as he always did, with a demonstration. Ethel stood by, quietly taking it all in. It was a first for the young teacher, who had finally been persuaded by the students to join them on one of their Saturday outings. Though not a verbal person, she was well-liked and respected by the students for her expertise and fairness, and her dedication to seeing them educated.

"Ahhh," Emil hummed. "What a day. The sun is talking to us. Catch her message, as she sneaks through the trees and casts her magic wand on the rippling water." He pranced about, waving his arms toward the clear sunlit sky one moment, and the glittering tree-lined lake the next. The girls joined him in a Maypole dance around Mrs. Moore, who gave no sign of disapproval.

"Okay, okay," he said by way of ending the initiation of the day's activities. "Oh, save your lights, oh save your lights," he sang. "Don't get caught without light areas in your work," he explained, then broke into song again. "Oh save your lights, oh save your lights," he sang, and the girls sang with him. It wasn't unusual for him to begin their classes by singing the phrase.

When he finished with the demonstration, he invited the girls to scatter about the lake area in search of a scene that inspired them. Eagerly, they began their studies. It was with much anticipation, as well as anxiety that they waited for their teacher's critical input.

With the students settled about the area, Emil realized for the first time that Ethel had nothing to do.

"Well, I hope you won't be too bored," he said. "There are some row boats at the edge of the lake, if you care to take a short ride. Perhaps a swim?" Just then, he noticed the book in her hand. "Oh, good, you've brought your own entertainment. I should have known," he said approvingly.

"How did your meeting go?" she asked. The question took him by surprise.

"My meeting?"

"With Catledge." Her huge dark eyes sparkled, apparently peaked by her interest in the subject. It was the most telling expression he had ever witnessed on Ethel.

He liked the art history teacher immensely for she was the lone faculty member he could pour his heart out to. For some time, he had toyed with the idea of inviting her to dinner, but had always stopped short of doing so. "The man is despicable. No regard whatsoever for anybody but himself," he told her. "It was a wasted effort on my part. I can't understand why Greenlee doesn't fire him."

She didn't respond immediately, but Emil knew he had a silent ally. "Greenlee's only a figurehead," she finally offered.

The comment failed to register with Emil. He continued his rage. "But surely the man detests incompetence just as we do. You've heard him at faculty meetings encouraging all of us to arrange public exhibits of our students' work: painting, ceramics, dressmaking, cooking, everything. Why doesn't he exercise his authority?" The shimmering light in his eyes turned to a cold glare as he took in the truth of his own words.

"Why tolerate Catledge and some of the others who make a mockery of everything he advocates? It's an insult to the entire college." The thought of it always sent him bouncing with anger.

"Greenlee is only a figurehead," Ethel repeated, without raising her eyes from her book. "He should wear khaki," she added.

"Khaki? What's that?" he asked.

"His silk ties and gold cufflinks. He should wear khaki," she repeated.

Thinking it a joke, Emil laughed, but as Ethel failed to follow suit, he wished he hadn't. "What does that matter? He doesn't impose the same dress code on us."

Ethel actually raised her head and met Emil's gaze. "It's his only weapon. Thinks it makes him presidential, as if he's in charge of things. It's all a farce." Except for a slight drop in her voice, she showed no emotion. She depended entirely on words to get her message across. For those who could fill in the blanks, she offered enlightenment, but few could. She remained an enigma, this woman whose vision appeared to penetrate the mindless and the intellects alike. She was a crystal ball, delving into the future, and keenly aware of the influence of the past. She clearly did not like the situation any more than Emil did.

"You must know Catledge and some other faculty members have been campaigning for student enrollment in their classes."

"What?" he yelped. "What do you mean 'campaigning'?"

"Haven't you noticed the size of their classes? They don't draw enough students to keep their jobs." She paused, assuming he understood, but his startled gaze indicated otherwise.

"Most of the art students are enrolling in your classes. The others are afraid for their jobs. They've become the butt of the serious students' jokes."

"Surely you exaggerate," Emil insisted.

"You're possibly the only one who didn't know."

Emil felt like a fool. *How is it I never seem to know what's obvious to everyone else*? He remained silent for a long moment, unaware of the idle brush in his hand or the unfinished sketch in front of him. Turning to face Ethel, he admitted knowing some of the faculty had called him an atheist. "I should have known it was their way of dissuading students from enrolling in my classes." He shook his head in disbelief. "But I tell you, I'm amazed that any intelligent adult would stoop to such measures."

"Yes," was Ethel's only response. She moved her eyes across a page of her book. Emil wasn't certain if she was reading or if she simply wished to end the conversation.

"Maybe Catledge," he mused. "But the others?" Had anyone else delivered the message, he might have been skeptical, but Ethel had no interest in idle gossip. A full ten minutes passed before she broke the silence.

"You didn't need to know all that," she said. Emil recognized it as an apology. "Some of your most devoted students persuaded me otherwise. Tassie, of course." Her voice fell sharply: no trailing off, no indication she intended to elaborate.

Is this a guessing game? he wondered. "Tassie?" he queried anxiously.

"'It takes a foreigner to put those dodos in their places,'" she quoted. "Tassie's exact words," she explained. She tightened her grip on the open book with such pressure, her fingertips turned white. It was obvious to Emil she had agreed reluctantly to do the students' bidding.

He felt responsible for her discomfort, but as there was no means of rectifying the situation, he settled on kind thoughts of her. While many faculty members regarded her as sullen and insensitive, he saw her as vehemently passionate about her responsibility as a teacher. He had a deep respect for her.

He tried laughing the whole thing off, but it was a thin laugh, one that spoke for his deep humiliation.

Two years had passed since that outing at Lake Legend, though there had been many others. All the while, Emil had continued his fight for students' rights to learn, but nothing had changed.

The time he spent away from the campus painting, often with the students, sustained him. Too, he enjoyed light workloads and long weekends during the summer sessions at Sudduth. He made the most of the opportunity for painting excursions to Gainesville, Macon, Sara Beach, Palm Beach, and Ashton. When at home, he used his time wisely, really acquainting himself with Mallon and its outskirts.

As another summer approached, Emil eagerly accepted an offer from Jim Seligman to teach summer classes at the Institute of Art in Chicago. Dean Perkins would be going there as well, presumably to revise a textbook.

Teaching at the Institute would be like having a paid vacation in New York, with its art and artists, and its guest instructors, all professionals who truly had something to offer. Mostly, it was a golden chance for Emil to free himself from the hostile climate in the Sudduth art department. College officials knew the prestige the college had taken on as a result of his joining the faculty. He had put Mallon on the cultural map, as witnessed by the Mallon Art Association, the most active in the South, and there was no question of his popularity with the students. Catledge and a few of his cronies still resented what they saw as a formally uneducated and cocky German who was seemingly bent on putting the students first, but they had been unable to wrest more than a few uninspired students away from his classes and into their own.

After two years as department head, he felt his battle for an improved ceramics department had gained him nothing except promises. As to the Farmers' Market, Ethel had researched the situation endlessly. She had stooped to asking questions of town officials, and finally obtained an audience with the market superintendent. She reported her findings in her usual emotionless candor.

"You won't be allowed to paint at the market, not now, or ever," she said.

"Did anyone give a reason?" Emil asked. "What's the mystery?"

Instead of answering the question, Ethel offered advice. "Just give the mountains color, but don't try to move them." She did seem beset by an undefined misery, one she refused to identify. The advice would go unheeded, as Emil didn't understand it.

For some time, he had harbored thoughts of a relationship with Ethel, one he felt certain she desired. He wished for the comfort of marriage and the settling effect a good one could have. The preliminaries were too time-consuming in any relationship, and Ethel, by all accounts a newcomer to the game, would require a lengthy courting period and perhaps as lengthy an engagement. It would require much more time than he was willing to relinquish. He had cast the notion aside and continued to wallow in loneliness each time he entered his empty apartment.

The assignment in Chicago would take his mind off all the trauma and the might-have-beens, a fact he looked forward to. Before leaving the Sudduth campus, he confronted Perkins again.

"The ceramics department? Any plans for improvement?"

Perkins was seated behind the desk, almost as if he intended to work. Emil soon realized the change was all for the sake of his hair. As long as he remained behind the desk, the breeze from the ceiling fan didn't disturb his half-bangs and uncover a deep receding hairline. Too, it left his hands free to thump on the desk while Emil aired his problem.

"Apparently you didn't see the exhibition put on by Catledge's students."

"Please," Emil scoffed. "If you saw it, you know a first grader could have done the work. No more than half a dozen pieces, none of which showed any insight."

"It's hard to argue with a man who's so popular with the students."

"Popular?" Emil rolled his eyes disparagingly. "Perhaps with a few poorly motivated students. They like the jam sessions he's noted for." He stopped short of mentioning that Perkins was often an attendee at the sessions, but the thought of it increased his anger. "Catledge's lack of training has made him the laughing stock of the better students. The whole thing threatens the credibility of the department. And every year we turn out graduates, it threatens the credibility of the entire college."

"I suggest you talk to Catledge yourself."

"Ahhh," he belittled. "I've tried, believe me, but his only response is to remind me of his college degrees. All the while, the potter's wheel continues to gather dust." Perkins' lackadaisical attitude incensed Emil, and he realized, for the first time, that nobody intended to do anything about Catledge. He was moved to act in whatever capacity was available to him. Rising to leave, he announced in no uncertain tone that "either Catledge learns to throw a pot before the fall semester begins, or I quit." The dean sat upright, a move that sent his bangs flying in the breeze. Emil left him in the lurch, battling shock and runaway bangs, both at once.

Emil was well aware now that Ethel had not exaggerated the situation with Catledge and his followers, who continued to openly solicit students for their classes. Nor had they given up on convincing a handful of devoted Methodist faculty members and students that Emil was not only poorly qualified for his position, but was an atheist as well. It might have been unnerving if his class enrollments hadn't continued to break records while many teachers in the department went begging for sufficient numbers to prevent cancellation of their classes.

Meanwhile, at the Chicago Institute, Seligman prepared the students for a treat, the pending arrival of a "lecturing demonstrator and demonstrating lecturer". Due to conflicting schedules at Sudduth. Emil was unable to arrive in time for the first class meeting, so Seligman took the opportunity to introduce the visiting professor prior to his arrival.

"Holzhauer is one of the few inspired artists who is also an inspired teacher, a rare combination," he began. "If you've studied his exhibit, you know Holzhauer is a realist, though not in the general sense of the word. He paints so spontaneously and smoothly and vaguely that all his forms are related, and yet, all vary. His mountains and his clouds, et cetera, are identifiable, for example, but the shapes take over and the colors take over until his work is almost abstract.

"Don't assume, however, that this talented man is incapable of detail. He has the steady hand of a steel engraver, the kinds of things we see on fine pieces of silver and jewelry, candlesticks, and arbors. Although you might think steel engraving would be detrimental to him, it hasn't been. Instead, it taught him how tight things could be, and he could get spontaneous even in those tight patterns because of his incredible control.

"As a designer he created beautiful compact arrangements that were pleasant to the eye, but he disliked the lack of freedom afforded him by the consumer and by his employers. In other words, he had to please the average person, and the average person is not an artist."

The already motivated students listened intently, more anxious than ever to meet this German-born artist who traded the heart of the art world for a classroom in a small southern college.

Seligman paused for a moment and surveyed the room. "I hope you realize what an experience you have ahead of you."

When Emil entered the classroom the following day, he was overwhelmed and humbled by the students' standing ovation.

"You're too kind," he began. "I understand Mr. Seligman has been telling you things about me. I hope he hasn't overdone it." The response was hushed laughter, one that signified graciousness as well as expectation.

"I never teach painting without painting materials," he began. The formality of the classroom dissipated immediately as he cluttered the area with his materials.

"Do you mind if I ask a question while you're doing that?" asked one student.

"Not at all."

"Some of us are surprised that you left New York for a teaching position in the South, especially in light of the recognition your work received in New York."

"Why teach?" He laughed mockingly. "I'm often asked that question, and frankly I didn't always know the answer. You might say I got lost on the way to my dream, but found a better one along the way—teaching!" The aspiring artists were startled by his comment. They waited in silence for an explanation.

"It's impossible to teach without demonstrating your ideas. Anybody can tell you, but few can show you. Great for the student and even greater for the teacher. Every teacher should do it no matter the subject they teach. Far from stifling me, teaching has strengthened me. In sharing my insight, I have deepened it. In helping others grow, I have grown. Teaching has made me more sensitive to art, as well as to life. For those who take it seriously, teaching is an uplifting and lofty profession. Of course, for those who don't, it's a farce." With Catledge coming to mind, his thoughts trailed off, but he quickly checked himself.

"Why leave New York? Freedom. In the South, I can paint year round. No frozen fingers and toes, no frozen paint." He paused to chuckle. "Frankly, I didn't find recognition and rewards satisfying. I won't say I didn't appreciate being singled out by others, but in New York, the tendency was to measure success by others' standards, by what others think is good. It stifles your creativity. You can't follow the trend and still remain true to yourself. If you can't paint what you see and what you feel, what's the point in painting?

"Every artist has rules, or should have, that he has established early on. What's right for him, and what's wrong as well, and he should never sacrifice what he believes in. Subject matter has been my rule, for example. I may get abstract to a point, but I never lose touch of who I am. Certainly I have seen the modern art shows with no subject matter at all, and I can tell you it excites me. I have tremendous appreciation for these artists, but it's not me. Nonobjective art was inevitable, but its not a totally new idea.

"Look at Rembrandt and other great Renaissance painters. They never painted everything that was there. They created shapes and colors to balance their work. It was what they left out, even in a very descriptive painting, that was important.

"Look at the impressionists. Didn't they almost lose form altogether? They chose just to use color and the reflection of color off forms and objects and nature. They didn't care about the objects themselves. They stood on the scene until they got the right mix of atmospheric color being reflected off objects.

"But, subject matter or not, you must learn the art of choosing a subject. You must look at a scene and decide what part of it to paint, then eliminate all those cluttered details that will detract from the best design and best arrangement. Think essence." At that point, he noted *The Cribbage Champion* had been placed on an easel along the wall behind him.

"Well, well," he grinned, "what have we here?"

One student answered with a suggestion. "Why not tell us about this painting? You know, how you happened to choose this subject, what details you left out, and—."

"Ah, 1929?" he said as he noticed the date on the canvas. Then, assuming his playful guttural voice, he asked rhetorically, "Could it have been that long ago?" The class was amused by his mischief, the more so as it seemed mixed with memories. "The fishermen…" he said, his voice trailing off. "Great subjects. It was on Monhegan Island off the coast of

Maine. You must go there if you haven't already," he insisted. The atmosphere of the room was electrifying, the students quite anxious to hear him discuss his own work.

"It was very dark in the little shack where the fishermen played cribbage," he began. "The only way I could get out of that little dark box was to open it up. As soon as I put in the window, I let the light in and opened up the painting. Then I used the light and broke the light planes across the fisherman's head and hand. Without the window, there would have been a dark wall in back and the huge man would have been too much of a presence. No balance. Why the fisherman? Character. Honesty. No pretense. But really I shouldn't try to analyze my own work. No artist should. When the artist is truly inspired, he loses consciousness. How can he explain the result?"

The students objected vociferously, begging for more, throwing out question after question, but Emil was adamant. "Get someone else to analyze my work. I'm afraid you'll find an artist really doesn't know why he does what he does. But I shall do the next best thing. Demonstrate. It's the one thing I never had enough of when I was an art student." He picked up his brush and spread a few colors on his palette, inviting the students to crowd around him.

"Of course, I detest working inside when the whole world poses for us outside in the sunshine. Bring your materials tomorrow, and I'll show you." It was a popular assignment for the instructor, as well as the students who responded day after day in full force. The students' maturity and enthusiasm made teaching them a pleasure. Their work inspired Emil just as his inspired them. Classes never seemed to end as he worked with them throughout the day and often into the evening hours.

When Emil returned from a class outing one day, Seligman told him there was a gentleman, a Mr. Schliemann, to see him.

"Schliemann!" he cried. The prospect of seeing his old friend again sent him racing through the normal clean-up procedures so as not to waste a moment. God, how he hoped they would have an opportunity to talk at length. So much to say.

He made his way swiftly to the office and flung open the door. "Schliemann!" he yelled. He matched his friend's broad smile with one of his own. The two shook hands, both unwilling to let go their warm grasp. "What a wonderful surprise."

"Ah, Emil, we've missed you in Riverview. Everyone was looking forward to your visit this summer. When you wrote that you couldn't come after all, I arranged a business trip to coincide with your stay here."

He couldn't ignore Schliemann's stylish attire. While Emil still nursed his pre-war clothes, succumbing to alterations to fit the times and his body changes, and wearing them to a threadbare stage, Schliemann's stylish suit featured a lower double-breasted closure, longer lapels and the return of cuffed trousers. Emil felt quite tacky in the man's presence. In reality, Emil's muscular, well-proportioned body, neatly groomed hair, and sun-tanned features cut a handsome figure no matter what he wore. Women still admired him, and men, including Schliemann, envied him his good looks.

"Your New York friends are jealous of your love for the South," Schliemann teased. He studied Emil a moment. "You really have found your niche, haven't you? New York art critics often speak of a softness in your work since you moved south. Surely it can't all be attributed to the warmer climate?"

Emil laughed at the man's subtleties. His Riverview friends had clung to the notion of Emil returning to New York, and Schliemann had always been their spokesman.

"It's been great, really." The glow in his face spoke for his sincerity.

"No more arrests?"

"No arrests."

"And the problems you mentioned in your letters?" Reference was to the market and Catledge.

"Disgraceful," he admitted. "I've agonized over what to do about it." Just thinking about it dulled his spirit, but he didn't want to spoil their time together. "But you know, it doesn't affect my work or my lifestyle for that matter. I can't explain it."

"I can," offered Schliemann. "Your discipline. You've never allowed anything to stand in the way of self-expression, the one thing you want most to do."

Tiny lines around Emil's eyes softened as he gazed in wonder at a man who seemed to know him better than he knew himself.

They left the institute together, both anxious to catch up with all the news. During a leisurely dinner, the subject of Rett and the Hudson River paintings surfaced. "It's one reason I wanted to see you in person. I really didn't want to discuss it by phone or letter. Apparently, your paintings were indeed destroyed by the FBI," said Schliemann.

"But why?"

"Remember the painting Muller purchased?"

"Yes, yes, of course. I was glad at least that one was saved. It's the only one left of my Hudson River series."

"I'm afraid it too is gone. Muller left the country with it but was detained somewhere overseas. The painting was confiscated."

Emil was so confused, he could scarcely listen. His constant interruptions made telling the story nearly impossible for Schliemann.

"Apparently, your paintings were being used to carry secrets—"

"My god, Schliemann," he interrupted. "Secrets?" His eyes widened, lifting his eyebrows to the point of forming deep creases in his forehead. "But how?"

"It was in code, of course. My information is patchy because anything associated with cipher-systems is still hush-hush. Your paintings had letters and numbers written on them, perhaps microscopic, I'm not certain, all of which meant something to the enemy. Americans were far behind Europe in cryptographic expertise, that is, in deciphering the messages, so Muller had a field day for a while. Apparently, Americans learned to decode the latest German cipher system around 1940 or so, and when they did, Muller was doomed."

Emil tried to take it all in, as scenes of the past flitted in and out of his thoughts. "But how—"

"I've told you all I know," said Schliemann. "Muller was an enigma, really. Most people in that position have an obvious occupation as a coverup. Maybe Muller had the right idea. Who would suspect a man who did nothing but accommodate folks?"

"Yes," Emil agreed. "But where was Rett in all this?"

"I'm not certain. I'm guessing he was merely a go-between, perhaps aware of the messenger but not the message? They never detained him, at least not for long. But the whole episode took its toll on him. He's never been the same. Closed the business. Stays to himself. I hear he isn't well."

"No," Emil insisted, almost in argument. "Rett?"

"Yes, some say he just gradually lost interest in life."

"Poor devil," Emil said. In spite of the past, Emil had fond memories of Rett, who had seemed to personify Riverview's charm. The two exhausted every subject they could think of, often returning to mull over the codes and messages, each attempting to understand it.

Before saying goodbye, they promised to stay in touch. As shocking as the news had been, at least the episode had closure for Emil, and the all night camaraderie with Schliemann made the loss of his paintings almost worth it.

Soon after that, Seligman offered Emil a full-time position at the institute.

"It isn't often we find an artist who has your enthusiasm and your maturity for painting and for teaching," Seligman told him. "It's usually one or the other. Surely I don't have to tell you how you have inspired the students, energized them, actually. The positive feedback from all directions has been tremendous. We can certainly offer you a raise from your Sudduth salary, but we need your answer right away."

"I'll let you know before the end of the week," Emil promised. The truth was, he hated to leave the four year college where returning students, year after year, offered him an opportunity to maximize their progress, as well as his. If only Catledge would seek training and the dean could promise Emil an assistant, the decision would be easy.

He approached Perkins and was taken aback by the dean's new hair style. His Hitler-style bangs had been cut short, leaving his receding hairline in plain view. It was a vast improvement to his appearance. Perhaps a Chicago barber had convinced him of that. It freed Perkins considerably, giving him a chance to move about as he pleased, to sit where he liked without worry. "I know what's on your mind and I can assure you Catledge has been attending ceramics classes this summer at Northeastern." He grinned broadly, apparently quite pleased with his efforts, however belated they might have been.

"Oh, that's wonderful. I can't believe it." The teaching position Catledge had boasted of was obviously a cover-up. Emil raised his bushy eyebrows, revealing a pair of shimmering blue eyes. A broad smile parted his full mouth, baring two rows of straight, white teeth. The deeper his tan, the whiter his teeth, or so it seemed. "Well now, just when I've come to discuss the possibility of not returning to Mallon. I have been offered a full time position here at the institute."

Obviously shocked, Perkins jumped to his feet. "No, you mustn't even consider it," he raved. "We can offer you the same salary, whatever it is, beginning immediately. Colleges and art associations all over are asking for your exhibitions and your lectures—Agnes Scott College, Athens, Miami High Museum, even St. Petersburg." He glanced at Emil, but saw nothing in his demeanor to indicate a change of heart.

Emil had never heard the dean talk so fast or so positive. He smiled inwardly as Perkins' hands flew up to hold his bangs in place before he remembered they no longer existed.

Recalling Emil's passion for the students, Perkins suddenly bristled with delight. "You can't desert the students. They're depending on you to take them all the way to state with their exhibits, and maybe national."

"I'm afraid you don't understand. It isn't a question of money," Emil told him as he unconsciously ran his hand through his own full head of hair. "I have been doing the work of two at Sudduth. It takes away from the time I like to spend with the students outside class."

"Don't worry. You'll have an assistant by the second term. You have my word."

It was exactly what Emil wanted to hear. He gladly returned to Sudduth.

Twenty-Five

It was 1947, two years after Emil's summer in Chicago. Tassie and Mary Helen had long since graduated, but they had kept in touch with their old professor. Mary Helen had opened an art gallery in one of Mallon's old aristocratic homes, where she featured fine art, antiques and other items of interest she had collected from the southern countryside. She delighted in featuring Holzhauer exhibitions, which she and Tassie managed with Emil's assistance, and often without it. The gallery became quite popular as a market place for Holzhauer's work, as well as the work of many of his students.

Meanwhile, Tassie was a sought-after private drawing teacher. She was a regular on Emil's field trips and class outings, and she had become an unofficial, as well as unpaid, assistant to him. They often joked, though neither of them laughed, that she might be the only one he would ever have.

The salary increase Perkins had promised more than two years earlier had never materialized, nor had it been mentioned except on occasion by Emil. He might have pushed the issue, except that Catledge had finally wiped the dust off the potter's wheel. The elementary course he enrolled in at Northeastern had created an interest in him for learning more. Too proud to attend a public class in Atlanta, he had begun to observe an old potter who worked on the outskirts of Mallon. According to Catledge, the two were "exchanging ideas". His newly acquired skills were comically elementary but at least the students had been introduced to the potter's wheel.

As to the promised assistant, Emil was always told "soon". When he mentioned it to Greenlee one day, the president was shocked. "An assistant? A raise?" He regarded Emil with a stern and questioning glance, almost as if he thought it a joke.

"Perkins had no authority to promise you these things. The simple truth is that the college has no funds available for this." Sympathy for Emil's situation took precedence over his own annoyance. "I'm truly sorry for this misunderstanding. However, I may have a solution for the problem with Catledge." He smiled uneasily, a clear indication it was a "maybe" at best. "I have received applications for the faculty to apply for Carnegie grants for study in Mexico. Think what this could mean for your department, especially if Catledge receives one."

Funded by the Carnegie Foundation for the advancement of teaching, the purpose of the grants was to improve and revitalize university instruction by stimulating creative activity among select faculty members, Greenlee explained.

Emil brightened a little. "If only the Carnegie Corporation committee knew that no art department is in need of revitalization more than ours—" He thought a moment, then added, "And no department in need of it more than ceramics."

"I suggest you see that they find out. You might also encourage everyone in your department to fill out an application. Need I remind you that Catledge's forte is words?" He grinned facetiously.

"True," Emil mused. They broke out in laughter.

"I regret the other matter you came about. Perhaps—"

"Perhaps," Emil interrupted, "we could hire just one person to fill the job of two." The idea had come to him in a flash. "We have a jewel in Miss Tassie, an honor graduate of our very own. I understand the college needs an assistant in dressmaking? This young woman could fill both vacancies for the price of one."

Greenlee liked the idea. He called the committee together, attended the meeting himself, and spoke for Tassie, listing her qualifications for the position, her talents and enthusiasm just as Emil had presented them to him.

Every vote was "nay" except for two, that of Emil and Ethel Moore. A lengthy silence followed the voting, nobody offering a reason for their objection to Tassie. Perkins tapped his fingers on his knee while Catledge managed a distorted smile, both confirming their lack of interest in the matter. Ethel sat forward, the creaking of her chair breaking the deadly silence and causing everyone in the room to look in her direction. She answered their stares with a deep and troubling grimace, an unusual show of emotion on her part, and an obvious feeling of contempt for their actions. Suddenly, Emil rose as if her support had lifted him.

"Not one of you admitted as much, but I'm afraid you have rejected this talented young woman because of her Italian background and her religious preference. If you allow these prejudices to stand in the way of giving the department a much needed boost, I refuse to be associated with you, or the college any longer." He could feel the flush in his face, the nervous twitch in his facial muscles. It never occurred to him they might tell him to pack his bags. While waiting for a response, he brazenly met the gaze of everyone who had the courage to look his way. Few did.

There was an anxious stirring in the room, of paper-shuffling and throat-clearing, some eyes facing the floor, others staring at the wall. Finally, Greenlee asked the committee to reconsider, and return for a second meeting the following day.

"What do you think?" Emil put the question to Ethel later.

"They'll vote her in, but they'll make life miserable for her," she promised knowingly.

"At least Greenlee's on our side," he reminded her.

"No consequence," she assured him. "You have more influence than he does. Him and his diamond cufflinks. Will that change the minds of anyone on that committee?" she asked rhetorically.

Emil lightened the conversation with a joke. "Well, maybe. Did you notice Catledge and Perkins have been making supreme efforts of late to compete with Greenlee's attire?"

"I'm afraid neither man's physique does much to enhance his looks regardless of the cloth he wears," she quickly responded.

Emil's hearty laughter brought a rare smile to Ethel's usual singleness of expression.

The next day, the committee reluctantly agreed to take Tassie on a trial basis, but only if she could maintain the work of two teachers and do so for the price of one. Ethel had read the tea leaves once again, and Emil knew that with one false move, or perhaps without it, Tassie might be ousted.

Emil exulted in his newfound freedom. Tassie relieved him of several classes in drawing and painting, and some of the ceramics students were learning to use the wheel in spite of Catledge, thus breathing a hint of new life into the art department. The results were apparent by the students' new enthusiasm, and by Catledge's own admission that he had become an expert in the field.

As the Farmer's Market remained off limits to Emil, Tassie excluded it from her agenda as well. The twosome often led their students to "nigger" town, a section both of them loved.

Entrance to the section led them past the old corner store run by the area's inhabitants, its weathered gray planks of the same caliber as the residences and plastered with signs advertising snuff, tobacco, and RC Cola. The proprietors lived upstairs in a screenless abode that overlooked street after street of shotgun houses, one room following the other with no hallway separating them, and all housing more inhabitants than could easily find standing room.

Emil marvelled at the women's easy manner, commenting to Tassie that they went about their daily chores with less energy than a New Yorker would expend in a stroll through Central Park. A blaze of red fire under a black iron pot demanded both artists' attention and sent them scrambling to investigate.

Habitually, Emil hurried, his white hair spilling over his printing press visor as if as eager for self-expression as its master. Though his haste delayed him, he never changed. In an effort to preclude a time-consuming second trip, he tried to carry everything at once. He experienced occasional successes, but mostly, a second trip was necessary for retrieving objects dropped during the first. Tassie was nearly as bad.

They set up within a few feet of two black women humped over a washtub, rubbing clothes lazily across a metal board. When one of the women punched the clothes in the black iron pot with a broom handle, Emil strained to capture the moment. Looking up from his work, he met the woman's gaze, and he realized for the first time he had invaded her privacy. Embarrassed, he tried to make conversation. "I guess the children keep you busy washing their clothes?" Little ones nibbled on cold biscuits and leftover corn bread while chasing each other around the grassless yard.

"These is white folks' clothes," the woman explained.

"Oh," he said, clearing his throat unnecessarily.

"Why you paint us?"

"Why? You intrigue me," he said, smiling uneasily. Conversation was distracting, but he felt a need to be civil. "Do you mind?"

Shrugging her shoulders, she pointed toward a young man in the distance. "George Washington's always paintin' us. He over yonder," she added, pointing toward a young black boy who appeared to be sketching. "Hey, George," she yelled.

"Oh, no," Emil groaned. He wanted to stop her, to protest the intrusion, but it was too late. The young man was already kicking up dust as he crossed the dirt street in his bare feet. He looked to be twelve or so, his long arms and legs out of proportion with the rest of his thin body. His crusty feet appeared never to have been shoed, their skin toughened from a lifetime of walking the rugged streets and alleys. In spite of the dusty atmosphere and his charcoal-smudged hands, his pants were clean, his time-worn shirt tucked neatly inside. His cropped hair was cut straight across the neckline, obviously the work of a straight-edged razor. He stood before the intimidating white folks, his dark eyes dancing with spirit, but held reluctantly at bay, the full lips eager for expression but obedient to the protocol of his race, the strong chin resolute.

Out of kindness, Tassie looked at his drawings. "Oh, my, look at this, would you? Where did you learn to do this?" she asked.

Her excitement prompted Emil to steal a glance, one that lingered. "Who is your teacher?" he asked.

Embarrassed by such a notion, George shrugged his shoulders gently.

"You've had no training? I can't believe it," said Tassie.

"These are really good studies, my boy," Emil told the stunned youngster. The washerwomen put all their chores on hold and gave the matter their undivided attention. Even the smallest child stopped chewing, though her mouth was filled with bread.

"Just imagine if he had someone to help him," said Tassie.

"Do you mind if I take some of your drawings along to show the college dean?" Emil asked. The two black women's eyes darted from George to Emil to Tassie, then poised with a final glance at each other.

Too overwhelmed to respond, George allowed his facial expression to speak for his consent, as well as his gratefulness.

The next day, Emil asked the dean's permission to allow George in the night class. "Is there any rule against accepting a boy in a girls' school? Just look at these sketches." He almost squealed with delight as he spread George's work in front of them.

"I see no reason why he can't take part in your night class since the participants don't earn credits. All anyone needs for that is your permission," the dean said. "How did you happen to find this boy?"

Emil answered with a laugh. "You'd never guess. He was in that run-down section of Mallon, you know, where the shacks have holes big enough to push my easel through? Lots of children and big iron wash pots and, oh, its's a marvelous place." Describing the section was nearly as exciting as painting it.

The dean raised his eyebrows in a moment of disbelief. "You mean nigger town?"

"Yes, that's it. Marvelous spot. The boy lives there."

The dean made a short, convulsive utterance. "The idea!" he shouted. "You know very well we can't have a nigger in the school."

The contempt with which he spoke left no doubt in Emil's mind the subject was closed.

Twenty-Six

The experience with George had been a revelation to Emil. He realized for the first time the depth of hatred and prejudice that existed in his adopted country. In spite of that, he had been giving George private lessons on the streets of the boy's neighborhood for well over a year.

At fifteen, George's body had finally caught up with his extremities, forming a towering physique that was enhanced considerably by the muscles he had developed from hard labor. White families liked him for the intensity with which he performed a task, no matter how menial, and for completing the job in record time. They usually paid him for the hours he claimed instead of arguing for half as much as was often the case with others his color. None of them knew it was not entirely a sense of duty, but the call of the palette, that spurred him to a speedy finish.

In the beginning, the teaching arrangement Emil worked out for George was haphazard at best, for more and more, he was inundated by time-consuming framing for one-man exhibits in Atlanta, Savannah, Athens, and numerous local exhibits where he lectured and demonstrated his work at the show's opening. He matted and framed and shipped his work to Memphis, Jackson, New Orleans, Palm Beach, Milwaukee, New York, and as far west as Santa Barbara. While most exhibitors, including students, had their paintings professionally framed, Emil used discarded pieces of wood to create his own. Having spent a lifetime pinching pennies to survive, he found it too painful to spend money needlessly.

Meanwhile, George's maturing talent continued to show promise beyond anything Emil had imagined. Only Tassie had shown as much fervor or as much energy, Karl as much talent for drawing from memory, or Lamberty for expressing with one line what others needed a dozen for. His enthusiasm equaling that of Emil's, he could never get his fill of painting. He often cursed the darkness, rainy days, and other acts of nature that stole a moment of his painting time. To compensate, he called upon one of his siblings or his mother to act as a model, and painted or sketched them well into the evening hours. Mostly, he was satisfied with his efforts, but one day, he arrived for class despondent. He placed one of his night studies conspicuously on Emil's easel.

"You did this?" Emil asked, eying the drawing curiously. "Do you like it?"

"No sir, I don't."

"Why not?"

"It's dead, sir. No life."

"If you know that, why do you seek my opinion?"

George shook his head. "I don't know. I just couldn't seem to give it life," he brooded.

"You obviously had nothing to say about the subject, no emotions, no sensations. Remember that whatever you sense in the subject will be revealed in your work," Emil reminded him. He noticed a difference in George, and it wasn't just the canvas. A heaviness, perhaps. "Something weighing on your mind?"

"Yes sir. I've been thinking about what you told me. You know, about not being able to make a living with art." He rubbed his cropped hair nervously, then pulled his visor halfway over his forehead.

"Ah, it's a curse," Emil admitted. "But don't despair. It's just as well. If you were salaried for your work, you'd have to please someone else, or worse, the art-ignorant public. Wouldn't be worth the sacrifice. Train yourself in a trade or a profession, then paint to please yourself. You're right to be thinking about your future."

"I'm afraid you'd only laugh if I told you what I have in mind."

"Tell me anyway."

"I want to be a doctor. I'd like to take care of my own people, you know." He fell short of saying no white man would accept him in that capacity anyway. He discussed the possibility with enthusiasm at first, but was soon hit with a spurt of reality. "Of course it's impossible."

He felt the boy's despair. In an effort to raise his spirit, Emil began toying again with the idea of entering George's work in one of the student exhibitions. George had balked when Emil mentioned it in the past, citing discontent in the white sector, but Emil had discounted those concerns. With the Gainesville exhibit coming up, the timing was right. He entered one of George's paintings, certain the outcome would be in the boy's favor. With the winning exhibits going to the national exhibition in Syracuse, the jury would be more selective than usual, a point in George's favor.

Unfortunately, Emil had less and less time to give the boy, having spread himself too thin, often giving in to pressures coming from the college to serve on art juries and address art associations throughout the South. Summers were filled with teaching vacations in Chicago, an assignment he loved, or the Norton Gallery in Palm Beach, or painting vacations on Monhegan Island, Ashton, Macon, or Riverview. And when in Mallon, he couldn't confine himself to George's section of town, as he relished every opportunity to paint the brickyard and the crumbling alleys in the city's downtown section as well.

Still, George's plight stayed with him, and brought back memories of the war and the hatred Americans had displayed for him only months earlier. Since then, they had treated him with respect and apparently thought kindly of the ubiquitous little man with his "visored white head and deeply tanned face and arms, his nubby paint brushes, grimy paint rags, topless water jug and tarnished paint box, a common sight on Gladys Road, Clover Street, Stalwart and Mossy Lane". It was a common description in newspaper articles or word of mouth. For reporters who didn't know him, he was "that feisty little man with his bandy-legged easel and beggar-like knapsack". It was a scene that demanded attention from passersby, many of whom were inquiring newshounds.

Only the more daring reporters insisted on an interview once the artist issued vehement objections to being disturbed, but for those who persisted through his lengthy painting ventures, there was the shock of finding a congenial and compassionate man inside the crafty exterior.

Crushed by his harsh demeanor at the outset, Tassie had been the first to understand him, and she was instrumental in acquainting others with the professor's driving force.

When a freshman reported to Tassie's class in tears one day, she called her aside. "You just came from Mr. Holzhauer's class, didn't you?"

"Yes ma'am," she wailed.

"What did he do? Break your brush? Toss your paint in the trash? Reprimand you for painting piecemeal? Castigate you for not having the right materials? Tell me, which one was it?" She cupped the girl's devastated face with warm, gentle hands, and smiled knowingly.

An understanding voice, coming from an authority figure, appeased the girl. "How did you know?" she wondered.

"Because I've been there," said Tassie. "He's not angry with you when he yells or breaks a brush. His anger is directed at himself for not being able to help you. Don't worry if he tries too hard to convey his messages. He has so much to offer, he can't control it. And if he singled you out for criticism, consider it an honor. He knows you have talent and he wants to help you develop it."

"You were his student?" the girl asked.

"Yes, my dear, and it was the best thing that ever happened to me," Tassie declared. "I never paint a picture but what he's in me," she said. "Join him on his painting excursions. Watch him grab for a tenth of orange or an eighth of blue without a glance at his palette. Watch him use a chain of details, yet speak in monotones."

The girl was as mesmerized as her teacher.

"It's because of him that I can express the feeling of the earth beneath me and the sun burning down on me. I owe him everything."

The two bonded as they shared the knocks suffered under Emil's tutelage and then laughed about it.

Only George escaped the teacher's wrath, the boy usually able to "let your eye caress form," and "put your feelings into concrete form," much as his teacher demanded, and he often went beyond all expectations.

He and Emil had agreed upon GWE as the proper signature for the Gainesville exhibit. Once the exhibits were hung, Emil knew that any jury who overlooked the superiority of George's work would call attention to its ignorance. He needn't have worried. The drawing signed GWE was chosen best of show and would be sent to Syracuse for the national exhibit. Emil was left to identify the artist. It was with some satisfaction he announced to the jury that they had chosen the work of a private student from across the Mallon tracks, a black boy.

Every single member of the five person jury was appalled and angry that they had been duped into choosing the work of a "nigger".

In Mallon, Emil was quickly called to Greenlee's office. From the desk of the president's secretary, he could see Greenlee and Perkins pacing back and forth, both eying the floor as they strode. When Greenlee caught a glimpse of Emil in the outer office, he motioned him inside.

Both men pounced on him like angry parents on a wayward child. "How could you do such a thing? You have embarrassed the jury, our own students, the art association, the faculty, the whole damn college—" Perkins seemed somewhat vindicated by the length of his list, but irritated at the same time that he had run out of names.

Greenlee shook his head in agreement, adding an invective here and there. Having vented their anger and exhausted their objections, both of them stared angrily at Emil, startled by his uncharacteristic silence.

Instead of lashing out at them in anger, Emil's reaction was tempered by disgust. "Sorry. I thought the best was the best, no matter who did it."

The comment infuriated the two men. "The boy is not even a student in your night class," the dean reminded him.

"And whose fault is that?" Emil pointed out, jumping to his feet to better vent his anger. The determination in both men's faces told Emil that no amount of arguing would change their minds. George was doomed to be ostracized. "I had no idea it was this serious. I'll have the painting withdrawn," he said, his tone subdued, his demeanor unchanged.

"I'm afraid that won't be sufficient," announced Greenlee. "Jury members and the art association, the college board, all will expect an apology."

"Apology?" he asked. "For what? That the jury recognized his talent and singled his work out?" As neither of the men interrupted him, he continued. "I have entered private students' work in the past and you didn't object. Your only objection is the boy's color, not his ability. As if race had anything at all to do with his talent. I shall not apologize."

It occurred to Emil that he had embarrassed the two men, neither of whom seemed willing to respond to the accusation. Greenlee finally broke the awkward silence. "I'm afraid if you don't apologize, I shall have to report as much to the board. I'm rather certain they'll have to let you go."

"Do as you must," he told the president. "I shall not apologize." He walked out the door, leaving two stunned educators behind.

Descending the steps of the administration building, his ears still in tune with the vibration of the steel door closing behind him, and painfully aware of the gulf between him and the college officials, he hastened, covering two and three of the wide stone steps at once. He was more than halfway across the campus before his steps slowed, nearly coming to a halt, for he suddenly realized he had nowhere to go.

The moment he emerged from the shadows of the campus buildings, something magical touched him, beckoning him to follow its lead. The brilliance of the sun, tickling the earth with its sunbeams and enhancing everything in sight with glistening color, called to him, and calmed him. He was determined to answer the call as he had done so many times in the past, but not before taking care of some unpleasant business.

He headed for George's section of town, anxious to break the news gently before someone else had a chance to shatter him with it. Public school buses were already unloading their cargo along his route, a reminder time was of the essence. The trip took him through the rutted streets of the downtown section, eventually bringing the Farmers' Market into view. He lifted his foot from the accelerator, and took a long look. He ached to stop, to capture a thousand images, but reluctantly moved along instead.

Dark clouds had begun to gather in the distance. Even as he rounded the last corner of the trip, the clouds had moved closer, but the sun was still in her glory, painting everything in her path and his. He gasped at the sight of the entrance to the black section, its landmark a sign-laden store building, paintless but not without color, for the patched roofing came in several hues, and the metal signs, though rusty in spots and laden with nail holes, still maintained much of their original color. On the corner across the street from the store stood a lone figure before a crude handmade easel. He was engrossed in painting that very building, a scene that had beckoned to Emil many times in the past. It was George.

Emil pulled off the dirt road and abandoned the car on a weed-infested knoll, then called on all his strength to see him through a dilemma he blamed himself for.

Once in speaking distance, he found his voice had failed him. He gestured hopelessly, and needlessly as well, for his arrival on the scene brought only a cursory glance from George, and even that was staged as a courtesy.

"I must tell you something before someone else does," he finally began. "You see, I—" He bit his lip so hard he winced in pain. He wondered if it wouldn't be easier if George were facing him, but then quickly decided it wouldn't.

"I heard, sir," George said. "Look," he said. "Watch the RC Cola sign."

Emil hushed, for hadn't he known the feeling a thousand times before, of forces responding to the artist's appeal? A sudden wind had loosened the sign, causing a rhythmic wave, a motion that transcended the corroded metal and deteriorating edges, and led the young artist beyond the usual. George hastened to capture the moment.

Energized, Emil retrieved his materials from the car and began his own painting, pushing everything else to the background. Oblivious to the passing of time or other realities, they painted side by side until the wind picked up and the once-distant clouds began to gather overhead, bringing an immediate threat of rain.

As reality set in, Emil remembered his mission. "What do you mean you knew? I only found out myself a few hours ago."

"I always knew, sir."

He recognized the comment as George's subtle way of telling him, "I told you so." It occurred to him the young man was grieving inside, too proud and too hurt to talk about it.

"I'm sorry," Emil said.

"You shouldn't be," said George. He gazed into Emil's tormented face, his warm brown eyes smiling. "They thought my painting was the best, didn't they?"

Emil was astonished by his maturity, wondering at the same time what options he had. It occurred to him that George had had the last laugh, the joke being on the jury and all the other would-be superiors.

Before they could load their things in Emil's car, the sky was pelting down big drops of rain and the strong wind made walking difficult. Suddenly there was a rumbling noise of metal against metal. They watched with interest as the RC Cola sign was torn from the building. It scraped along the exterior of the building, finally landing in a weed-infested vacant lot.

"Ah, a scene for tomorrow," George announced, grinning.

Emil touched him gently on the arm. "Let's not forget about medical school. If you can make the grades and get accepted, I'll help you."

As he spoke, he realized the gravity of such a promise. After all, he had apparently been fired only hours earlier.

For want of knowing what else to do, Emil reported to work the next morning. As he walked down the hallway, he noticed a party-like atmosphere coming from Catledge's office. It wasn't unusual for Catledge to hold jam sessions with the students, but never early in the morning. When he passed the doorway, he saw professors, not students, most from other departments. One of them called to him.

"Have you heard the news, Emil? All four of Catledge's student entries have been chosen and will be shown at the nationals at Syracuse University."

"No! I can't believe it," he said.

"Just imagine," she beamed. "Four of them."

Emil joined the others in Catledge's room and extended his hand in congratulations. "Tell me all about it," he begged. "Oh, my, this is wonderful. Just the needed boost for the department." He fell into their merrymaking, forgetting again that he had been relieved of his duties.

Catledge, accustomed to self-praise, seemed to enjoy it even more coming from others. "I'm really not surprised. You'll call the newspaper right away?" he directed the department secretary. "Tell them I'll be in my office between one and two today for an interview."

Anxiously, Emil asked who the students were, but didn't wait for an answer. "What a story. Maybe a picture of all of them with their winning entries?"

"No, no, they wouldn't know what to say. I'll take care of it."

Catledge's ego shattered the excitement of the moment, a fact that other faculty members took notice of as well, but at least the ceramics genius was too enthralled by himself to dwell on Emil's struggle with George.

In his office, Emil began sifting through the past week's mail. As head of the art department, he would have received official notice of such an honor. A procrastinator of the worst kind when it came to paperwork, he realized the notice might well have gone in the wastebasket, or was still hidden among the debris facing him on his littered desk. Another notion struck him. *Catledge's students would have to win locally in order to qualify for the national show. How did I miss knowing about it?* He pillaged through the mass of announcements, letters, and notices on his desk, searching for an announcement of the honor, but found none. A recent request from Sara Beach Women's Club did catch his eye. The fledgling art group would "be deeply grateful and highly honored if the renowned Mr. Holzhauer would judge our first exhibition," the invitation read. He was reminded that Perkins had hand-delivered the invitation from the ladies' club in Sara Beach, his home town, and had candidly admitted to promising them Holzhauer would be there. Perkins had apparently scrounged an invitation for himself as well. He thought of it, no doubt, as an opportunity to show his influence.

Once the futile search ended, Emil began to mull over the idea of addressing the women's group. A trip to the little city might be just the thing he needed. Without a word to Perkins, he agreed in writing to judge their show and address them. Then he gathered his materials and proceeded to his first scheduled class.

Tassie was waiting for him. "You've heard, then?" he asked her.

"Yes. What are you planning to do?"

"Teach my art class," he said. "What else should I do?"

"I agree. They won't let you go in a million years. They know you've made the art department what it is." She hesitated a moment. "You may need to give them a bit of slack, though."

"What do you mean?"

She was a bit hesitant, an anomaly for Tassie. "Well, you might go easy. Southerners don't cotton to having their faults pointed out." She watched him closely before adding, "Especially by a foreigner." Only Tassie could have made the remark without raising his ire.

"I'll stay away from the Farmer's Market, but not from George."

"Exactly what I expected you'd say. We need to talk. Meet you for lunch at the *Roost and Bubble*?"

"Let you know. Say, did you hear about Catledge's students? All four of his student entries were chosen for national exhibition."

"Exactly what we need to talk about," she said. "Who's he kidding? You saw that junk his students entered."

Emil answered with a deep guttural laugh. Nobody could describe Catledge like she could. Emil had tried to dismiss the same thought. "Even Catledge couldn't pull off such a ruse. Could he? Tassie, what do you know?"

"It's here in my gut. Unfortunately, I have no proof." She grimaced. "What will he do next?"

The more Emil thought about it, the more he was convinced. After completing his classes for the day, he headed for the main campus and the president's office, totally forgetting the man had essentially fired him the previous day.

Greenlee seemed especially glad to see him. "I was just on my way to your office. I've been reading about your latest honor in Atlanta." Emil's entry in Atlanta's High Museum exhibition had placed first, an honor that had brought a great deal of publicity. One critic spoke of a "third dimension" in his latest work while another noticed a more abstract approach. A third critic deemed him "strong and forceful as an artist, a reflection of his powerful personality".

"I can hardly keep track of all your honors," Greenlee continued. "I appreciate how busy you must be. As to the business we discussed yesterday, well, sometimes we allow our tempers to flare. But certainly we're all too big to hold grudges. Of course, you understand that we can't open the college doors to just anyone."

Emil received no satisfaction from Greenlee's shallow explanation. The only reason he didn't fire him was that the college needed him. For that, he did receive some satisfaction. "I didn't come about my own fate or that of George," he said. "I'm afraid Catledge has falsely claimed national recognition for his students. Or rather for himself. He doesn't seem concerned about the students."

Evidently relieved that Emil was not resigning, Greenlee listened to the accusation, expressing more interest than usual. "Of course we must prove the allegation before any action can be taken. Certainly, the college would frown on such action."

"Frown on such action?" Emil mimicked. He had placed the president above the others from the start, though he never understood his tolerance of Catledge, who was allowed to thumb his nose at the rules and regulations, trample the students in the mire, and generally do as he pleased. In spite of Ethel's warnings, Emil had clung to the notion that somehow, Greenlee would see that Mallon's students received the education they deserved. He was beginning to have second thoughts. Like Emil, Greenlee was apparently at the mercy of unknown powers, but there was one big difference. He knew the unwritten and unspoken rules; Emil didn't. He was left to flounder in distress.

Twenty-Seven

To get away from the campus and the ordeal involving Catledge, Emil agreed to address the women's club at Sara Beach. The club was the nearest thing the old historical city had to an art association. It was an exclusive club composed of socially prominent women who either claimed kinship to the city's founders or could boast of friendship with someone who did.

It occurred to Emil that he might not find one single inspired artist among the group, but at least the trip to their enchanting city wouldn't be a waste. He canvassed the city's perfectly coiffed parks and statued squares its founders had gloried in creating, parks and squares that now stood within yelling distance of crumbling neighborhoods. Ragged black children played in dirty streets, their mommas whiling away the hours in apathetic languor. He was enchanted by the grand old port and marshy Sara Beach riverfront, the ballast rock streets and the old store buildings with their rusted tin roofs and grey-weathered wood. He had painted all of it in the past, but he wanted to do so again and again. He savored speaking and judging assignments that included dinner, as they enabled him to paint through the lunch hour and into early darkness.

At the women's club that evening, he was greeted by the group's president, then somewhat mauled by its members, each one clamoring to make herself known to the celebrated artist. It was through great effort the president was able to rescue him from their grasp and call the meeting to order. There were more comments about his hair than about his art work, a fact that troubled him considerably. It was, however, difficult to ignore. The hair on top of his head stood up like new sprigs of grass in a healthy lawn, epitomizing the zeal with which he met each dawn, while neat-clinging sideburns spoke for the awesome discipline he lived by.

They had barely taken their seats when Emil noticed a man entering the room. It was Perkins! Spotting Emil, he marched determinedly across the room and greeted him with a vigorous handshake, almost as if they were old friends who hadn't seen each other for a very long time. Quite shocked by his presence, Emil was speechless.

"Sorry we couldn't ride together. I'm just now arriving. It's been hectic at the college, you know." The scene was dramatized in the presence of the club's president and a few of her obsequious followers who had managed to claim a seat at the head table.

Both men were treated as celebrities, but Emil enjoyed special attention as the would-be artists wined, dined, and pampered him prior to his ribbon-pinning assignment. Some mentioned their husbands' status in the community before pointing to their masterpieces on the gallery walls. With everyone's attention diverted by the serving of dinner, the president managed to place a photo of her own entry near Emil's plate.

When the time came, he was whisked into the gallery, the president and Perkins on either side of him, all others following close behind. As he viewed each entry, all eyes were on him, and many smiled nervously when his grunts and groans became audible. His commission didn't take long. Instead of attaching ribbons to the best work, he went directly to the speaker's platform.

"Ladies," he began, then hesitated. The group was hushed. "I cannot in good conscience pin a ribbon on any of your work." The deadly silence that followed was different to the hush of anxiety that had preceded it. Their startled glances spoke for the awesome shock dealt them. Following a lengthy pause, he continued.

"Now that I have seen your work and I have heard some of your comments on art, I must say you have about reached the stage the rest of the art world reached before the Armory Show of 1913. I frankly don't know what to say to you, except to suggest you get yourselves a good teacher."

Silence reigned at the head table, where Perkins was seated as close to the president as protocol would allow. Both were ashen-faced in the beginning, but Perkins soon turned beet-red, aware that a roomful of eyes had focused on him, the accused whose verdict was guilty. Whispers grew into audible mumbles throughout the room before the president finally made her way to the speaker's platform. By that time, many in attendance had already begun to file out the door. Perkins' short legs couldn't move fast enough to catch up with most of them, and those he did reach either admonished or ignored him. When nearly everyone had left, he attacked Emil while a few remaining ladies huddled together across the room in pretense of straightening up the place.

"Did you have to insult them? Why not simply decline to judge their work?" He paced back and forth in front of Emil.

"I did decline to judge it."

"You know what I mean."

"I told them the truth. Their work is atrocious, and without help, it won't improve."

"Oh, you do have a high opinion of yourself, don't you? What did you expect? A bunch of van Goghs here?" He threw his hands up in despair and exited, slamming the door behind him and leaving Emil to fend for himself with a handful of unhappy women. Emil expressed regret to those who would listen, and announced again, this time with a bit of diplomacy, that they should find themselves a good teacher. The atmosphere having cooled considerably from the warm greeting of some ninety minutes earlier, he soon made a hasty exit.

As Perkins had a conference to attend in Atlanta that week, the two men's paths didn't cross for several days. By the end of the following week, Perkins called on Emil in his studio, unannounced and totally unexpected. "The Sara Beach ladies want you to teach them," he said without ceremony.

Emil was engrossed by the portrait he had been doing of one of the students. A few other students were involved with their own rendition of the girl as well.

Perkins made his way into the group's semicircle, but nobody appeared to notice, not even the model who was absorbed by the book she was reading. "The women in Sara Beach discussed the situation and wondered if you would give them lessons. They would be willing to drive to Mallon on the weekend or on weeknights for evening classes." He tried to sound indifferent, an all-out effort to conceal his anxiety as well as his embarrassment. When Emil didn't respond, he continued. "Think you could work them into your schedule?"

His nervous gestures spoke for his discomfort, brought on no doubt by his promise to the ladies they would have their lessons, then finding himself faced with delivering that promise. His fallen countenance hinted he was all too aware that the last time he had seen Emil, he had slammed a door in his face.

"We'll see," was the nearest thing to a promise Perkins would get. "Right now I have to concentrate on the Syracuse request."

"Syracuse? Ah," he belittled. "Let me worry about that." Clearly, he thought the reference was to Catledge and the questions raised by his claim to fame. "The school would probably receive a great deal of publicity from your Sara Beach group."

For the first time since Perkins' arrival, Emil took his eyes off his work and met the dean's anxious gaze. He couldn't totally suppress a grin.

"I have better things to do than worry about Catledge's vanity. I have received a formal request from Syracuse University for a permanent collection of my work." He wasn't accustomed to high-mindedness, but the occasion seemed to call for it.

Perkins was delighted by the news, though clearly shocked as well. "Syracuse University? In New York?" he asked incredulously.

"Is there another Syracuse?" Emil quipped.

For a moment at least, Perkins forgot about the Sara Beach women and lavished Emil with praise and adulation before insisting on knowing the entire story.

Emil had received the request from Syracuse for a collection to include his "working sketches, clippings, exhibition catalogs and the like so that students and art historians for generations to come will be able to gain a better understanding and fresh appreciation of your career".

Reporters as far away as Atlanta had interviewed him, but the articles would not appear in print until the following Sunday. The campus and much of Mallon was abuzz with the news, but Perkins had talked to no one on his return as he was preoccupied with the Sara Beach women. Emil's studio had been his first stop. The Syracuse request was well received by Emil, not only for the honor, but for the answer to a pressing problem: what to do about the mass of paintings he had accumulated over the years. They lay in stacks of fifty or more in his tiny apartment, in his pigeonhole office, and in the conservatory studio. The walls of every building on the Sudduth campus were papered with them. Everybody was running out of space.

Ethel had been first to congratulate him, nearly letting go her usual reserve. "You might find this honor will further empower you on the campus," she announced smugly.

"Further empower me?" he laughed.

A trickle of dark color became apparent in Ethel's otherwise colorless face. "You have more than you realize. Who else could have survived the episode with George?"

By the weekend, local newspapers boasted of Mallon's noted artist, while the college officials flaunted the opportunity to enhance public relations. None of them mentioned his "ugly" subjects. "All his lines and tones act in unison to create a perfect whole," wrote an Atlanta critic. In New York, the *Evening Post* spoke of "less rigidity, less absorption in the intricacies of design, and more freedom and warmth," and the *New York American* saw him as "expressing his forms with greater subtlety and conviction than ever before."

All the publicity soon brought Emil to the attention of Charlie Whitfield, a United States senator who made a special trip to the college to see Emil's work. He had focused at length on one particular painting, discussing its background with Emil for some time. Emil was surprised and disappointed when the senator left the campus without purchasing the painting he seemed enchanted with.

Several weeks later, Whitfield wrote to say he would like very much to have that particular painting hang in his Washington office, citing all the attention it would receive nationally and internationally. Money was not mentioned.

News that Mr. Holzhauer had received an official letter from a popular Georgia congressman made the college rounds and brought Perkins to Emil's door again. "Which one does he want? Does he want us to ship it? God, what publicity this will bring us."

Emil was amused. "Seems he likes a particular brickyard scene, but he sent no money."

"You're not serious? You should gladly give him the painting," he said. "Think of the publicity the department will receive if he hangs your painting in his office. What an honor it would be for you, as well as the college." The dean was clearly agitated.

"The best publicity the college can get is from its graduates," Emil said with a glare, his forehead a mass of angry wrinkles. "If we persist in turning out untrained graduates as we have been doing, we can't expect to fool anybody with glorious newspaper headlines, false ones at that, about the faculty. If Whitfield wants the painting, he can have it for two hundred and fifty dollars. Believe me, it's a bargain. Such a price would hardly pay for the materials, much less my time."

"Two hundred and fifty?" he ridiculed. "Bah! It's the same price you offered the general public."

"Isn't he part of the general public? I agree he should pay more because he can afford it, but when I put a price on a painting, it's everyone's price."

"Don't you understand? He'll be paying you with advertisement, for Christ's sake."

Emil was not swayed. "Politicians are like preachers, always expecting something for nothing."

Emil's earlier reference to Catledge's false acclaim had not escaped the dean, but he had ignored it in an effort to keep the conversation friendly. The time had come, however, when he could no longer quell his temper. He was still seething over Emil's treatment of the Sara Beach women, an act that damaged his position with the elite in his own hometown. "Where did you ever learn about preachers?"

Instead of raising Emil's ire as Perkins hoped, he laughed. It was a revealing laugh, one filled with confidence. "A reference to my churchgoing?"

"You're so quick to point a finger at Mr. Catledge. Well, he does attend church services," he bragged. "This is a Methodist college you know." He appeared quite pleased with himself for airing a subject he had held at bay far longer than he cared to.

"I'm afraid I'd put his church attendance right up there with his awards. A big show." His mood was light-hearted, made manifest by his joyful humming of *Barcarolle*.

"We each have our own way of communicating with God. If you only knew the spiritual harmony I feel when I'm painting. It feeds my spirit much as others may be fed by attending church services."

Regretting the comment, Perkins tried to interrupt, to change the subject, but Emil wouldn't be stopped. "I see beauty in everything— and not just conventional beauty—," he quickly explained, painfully aware that Perkins had no notion of such beauty's existence. "I feel compelled to paint what I see and share it with others, whether on Sunday or Monday. If you have found something real in your life, you should let others know about it. I believe the Christian faith is based on that premise."

Recognizing that any gains he hoped to make had been cancelled, Perkins left, a deflated ego his companion, and headed for Catledge's office. It occurred to Emil that the poor man was comfortless except for the attention bestowed upon him by Catledge's bevy of sycophants.

Emil had begun to tire of the low-level conversations with Perkins and Catledge, and even Greenlee, but with his days filled to capacity, he had little time for planning his activities, much less for dwelling on their rhetoric and tomfoolery.

It was only by virtue of lyng awake nights that he was able to take stock of his accomplisments or lack of them. During one of these nightly sessions, he made up his mind to fulfill a need in the community, one he had been proposing for some time, a visit to the "colored" school.

The superintendent was shocked, but clearly delighted, by Emil's visit. He extended a warm and gracious welcome. "To what do we owe this honor, Mr. Holzhauer?"

"I've been remiss in not coming sooner," Emil began. "You have at least one outstanding art student in your school. Who knows how many others there are? I would like to offer a class here in the evening for anyone interested. There would be no charge, of course."

The superintendent, obviously stunned by the offer, shook his head. "A generous offer, Mr. Holzhauer, but the truth is, we have our own art teacher."

"Really?" He was startled. "I wonder why George never mentioned it?"

"As a matter of fact, if you have the time, you could visit the class. It begins as soon as school's dismissed. And I might add the students are quite inspired. They can hardly wait for the last bell to ring." He glanced at his watch. "Be about twenty-five minutes' wait, though."

"Well, I don't know. I suppose if you have a teacher—"

"I think you'll be very glad if you stay. In fact, I can promise it."

With Emil's interest peaked, he readily agreed. When classes for the day had been dismissed, and things quieted down, the superintendent led Emil to the open school grounds where several students had formed a semicircle around a young man in the midst of a demonstration. His subject was a withered blackberry vine that clung to an old dry-rotted fence, its stubborn thorns refusing to give in to life's end.

"An artist must learn to see the unusual," the teacher was saying. "Look beyond the ordinary, the usual. When you do, interpret it. Say what you want to say about it." Although the group had barely begun their session, they were focused, and most were unaware of the intruders.

The teacher was George.

A visored hat Emil had given him shaded his eyes and soaked up the sweat. He wore a shabby apron of sorts that covered only a small portion of his tall frame, but one that would enable him to keep his only pair of school pants clean.

The superintendent motioned Emil to approach the group, but he declined. "No, I'd rather not," he said. "I know how frustrating disruptions can be." He insisted they return to the superintendent's office.

As the two walked back together, the superintendent sensed the emotions Emil was going through. "George says he never paints a picture that you're not in him. I think your influence on him has gone beyond artistic expression. In a sense, Mr. Holzhauer, you are teaching here. I might add, it's the only way we could accept your services."

"What do you mean?"

"If you taught at our school, you would surely lose your position at the college." The two had arrived at the office and Emil had taken the chair offered him.

He started to object, but the superintendent stopped him.

Leaning as close to the white man as he dared, he spoke just above a whisper. "Remember the Farmer's Market, Mr. Holzhauer?"

"Yes? You know about that?"

"Everyone knows, sir. Do you know why you aren't allowed to paint there?"

Speechless, Emil's eyes pierced the face of a man whose enlightenment clearly transcended his. A dozen thoughts coursed through his mind, none of which made any sense.

"There's always a chance your paintings will be shown up north. When you painted the Farmers' Market, you showed white folks mingling with black folks. They don't want folks up north to get the wrong impression about the South."

Emil drove back to the college in something of a daze. His mind was a whirl of things, all mixed with anger and frustration. With no conscious plan for doing so, he walked into Ethel's office, but she wasn't there. He waited, not knowing when, or if, she would return that day. It was a first for a man who never tarried, always running to complete a dozen tasks while contemplating yet another.

When Ethel arrived, Tassie was with her. Both were startled to see him sitting there, idle. "Emil, what's wrong?" asked Tassie.

"I know now what you meant," he said. His eyes pierced Ethel's. "How did you put it? You can paint the mountains the way you see them, but don't try to move them?" His demeanor was one of uncharacteristic gloom, tinged with hopelessness.

Both women were startled, but Ethel understood.

"You knew all along, didn't you? Why not tell me?" he asked Ethel. Tassie was too confused to interrupt.

"Why? Because nothing could be done," she explained.

"Should I leave?" asked Tassie. "Is this a personal matter?"

"Not at all," Ethel told her. "Tell me, how did you find out?" she asked Emil.

Emil related the episode with the superintendent. It was all Tassie needed to vent her own anger and dismay. "Ah, don't let them see you like this!" she warned. "I mean none of them, not the faculty, the students, the city fathers—nobody. You've denuded them. Pointed out their shortcomings. Naturally, they don't like it."

"So what? It doesn't change anything," he complained weakly.

"Yes it does," piped Ethel. "They've used color as a source of discrimination. You used it to interpret beauty in everything."

"Why can't they admit their objections?"

"People who discriminate are insecure," Ethel explained. "They don't have the courage. Cowards!" she added with unusual emphasis.

As Emil agonized, Tassie sought to reassure him. "It's beautiful, Emil. They don't quite know how to handle you." She was animated by the whole thing.

"I paint what I see," he protested weakly.

"So much the better. You did it unconsciously, totally without malice. What can they accuse you of?"

"But I had no intention—"

"You needn't explain," Ethel said. "You've painted everything with warmth and sympathy, the blacks and the whites, the laborers and their bosses, the shacks and the mansions—" She stopped to laugh, a vindictive smirk, an emotional outburst unlike anything he had ever witnessed in her. Emil wondered how long she had been a silent but seething rebel. He had a new respect for her.

He stood up for the first time since the women arrived. His large mouth tightened, pulling the muscles of his cheeks taut, and thrusting his strong chin forward. "Maybe I'll paint there anyway."

Ethel and Tassie exchanged anxious glances.

Twenty-Eight

Emil saw the episode at the "colored" school as one more incidence of the Deep South's prejudice, and one more disappointment for him who could do nothing to change it.

News that began circling the campus helped relieve the stess. Sudduth was buzzing with news about Carnegie Grants for study in Mexico being bestowed upon several of its professors, Emil and Catledge among them.

Tassie had been first to congratulate Emil. "Think Catledge will learn anything?" she asked facetiously.

"Has to," he insisted. "It's the best thing that ever happened to this college. He has to be a better teacher, once he travels and studies in a country where the pottery is sublime." He hummed *Barcarolle*, the tune that always came to mind when things went well. Tassie joined him. "Just think about it. A whole month in Mexico where I can paint seven days a week, all without interruption."

"And it'll give Catledge a chance to learn what he claims to know already." The two engaged in robust laughter before turning to a more serious topic. "Have you heard from Syracuse?"

"Yes, the curator promised to be here by the middle of October."

It was late September when he learned the date had been changed. "Probably be February before I can make it to Georgia," the curator had admitted.

Emil objected vociferously. "Please," he had begged. "No more delays. I shall be leaving for Mexico in the summer."

"That should pose no problem," the curator had promised. Meanwhile, Emil had agreed to teach the Sara Beach ladies' group. With his full daytime schedule, his night classes, and weekend painting excursions with the students, he could offer the women only one Saturday a month.

Apparently, they had given up on Perkins and his claim to clout, and opted to appeal their own case. The club president had called Emil personally. "We have come to realize you were right, Mr. Holzhauer," she told him. "We need a good teacher."

Perkins was last to know, a fact that agitated him considerably. Most of the society ladies had never frequented the black sections of their cities or surveyed old, rundown store buildings, or noticed the beauty of the marshy riverfront. For their first lesson, they arrived in heels and hose and silk dresses. By the end of their first day of painting, they had tied their skirts in knots to protect them from weeds and brush their new teacher led them through, fought the wind and merciless sun that burned their skin and tousled their hairdos, and emerged from it all carrying their shoes and hose in their hands. Emil wondered if any of them would return the next month. The few who did came in slacks and low heels, their hair tied securely in buns or protected with large-brimmed hats. They arrived early and stayed late. What they lacked in talent, they made up for in dogged determination. It was yet another challenge and one Emil delighted in.

The heavy schedule enabled him to move the Syracuse curator to an inactive corner of his mind, but when the time came, he was ready. Mr. Hill arrived in late February.

Emil's excitement was unbridled as he presented volumes of drawings, designs, engravings, sketches, and paintings dating from 1892 to the present, 1949.

Hill was visibly shocked by the size of the collection. He began perusing it, but after spending the day trying to choose paintings, he threw his hands up in dismay. "I have given myself only two days here. It's not nearly enough. I'll have to reschedule."

"When?" asked Emil. "I'm going to Mexico in August. It's such a hazardous situation I have here. Insurance won't help because money can't replace my work."

"I understand your concern, but you should know it isn't uncommon for us to spend three or more years collecting work we've contracted for," the curator explained wearily.

Emil didn't like it. He had already waited longer than he intended to. The more he thought about it, the angrier he became. He took the Syracuse contract to a lawyer to see what could be done.

"I could talk to them," his lawyer suggested.

"No! I've tried that," Emil said wearily.

The lawyer shook his head. "Well then, I'm afraid your only option is to break the contract."

Twenty-Nine

When August came, there had been no word from the Syracuse curator. Emil accepted the fact that nothing could be done to secure the safety of his work. He discounted its importance, and headed for Mexico. In San Miguel, he was a man possessed, beginning his quest at Belles Artes Institution, where Siqueros, the Mexican master, had painted a mural as a demonstration to the students. The fiery Siqueros had instituted a boycott by all prominent Mexican artists and the majority of American students, naming misuse of funds by the director of the institute. Siqueros had something to say, and just as Emil suspected, he had no equal in the United States in hurling his revolutionary challenges in the face of the world through his overpowering canvases.

One morning, he was off before daylight to Mexico City and the retrospective exhibition of Diego Rivera, an artist whose craftsmanship and fertile imagination brought Emil back to the galleries time and again. Canvassing the galleries day and night, and sandwiching in some valuable painting excursions of his own, left time for little else.

From Mexico City, he traveled to the ruins of Mitla, and the jewelry of Taxco, then back to San Miguel. All day, every day, in the merciless summer sun, he painted, rarely stopping for anything except an occasional swig of warm water which he carried in his faithful old jug. Darkness was his only deterrent.

In the evenings, he watched happy couples being serenaded by guitarists, singers, and violinists, and he realized how much he missed the companionship of a woman. An occasional fling in Mallon had led to nothing of lasting interest to him. His round-the-clock schedule had precluded any serious courting anyway. Aside from that longing, he thoroughly enjoyed the evenings in Mexico, dining and chatting with interesting visitors at the hotel and restaurants, or anyone who spoke one of his languages. He gloried in retiring in the evening, not for sleeping so much as to plan for the following day's activities. He reveled in knowing Catledge was having similar experiences that would eventually breathe new life into Sudduth's ceramics department. It was all a glorious feeling.

When the time came to return to Sudduth, he drove day and night in order to visit a tiny fishing village in Northwest Florida, an artist's paradise, according to Ed Weins. Now working for the Red Cross, Ed had been temporarily stationed at an Air Force base in Florida's panhandle. He had contacted Emil and invited him to visit. Ed had long since been transferred, but his praise of the area lingered with Emil. With it practically on his way home, he took a detour at Mobile, Alabama and headed east to Niceville, arriving early one morning.

The tiny village was situated on a bayou, dotted with fishermen's shacks that hung tenaciously over the water's edge. There were shrimp boats dry-docked for repairs, and others apparently abandoned by their owners, all dotting the shoreline near a cluttered boatyard. Along the waterfront, fishermen advertised their catch for sale or repaired their boats for the next outing while their women hung dingy clothes out to dry on makeshift lines stretched between the trees or fastened to a poorly constructed outdoor toilet. The narrow winding dirt road that led Emil around the bayou was a thing of beauty as it snaked through patches of blackberry bushes. Spanish moss clung to huge live oak trees, swaying in the hot summer breeze.

The narrow beach road took him past four wooden structures that comprised the entire town. There was a two-story building that housed a tiny post office downstairs, its proprietor upstairs; and an old wooden movie theatre that obviously offered the residents their only exposure to the outside world. On the corner was a concrete-block bar and lounge. Its dirty green paint had abandoned the building for the most part. Littered ground abounded in winos and other interesting citizens, some of whom slumped against the posts that supported the undulating porch or lay prone on the ground in a deep sleep. The main place of business stood in the center of all this, a two-story hardware store that advertised its merchandise by displaying it in the sandy yard. There were black iron cooking pots hanging over cane-bottomed chair arms, home-honed butcher knives, tin cups, and sugar cane adorning the entrance in front of the building. The proprietor lived upstairs and only ventured down when a customer beat on the wall.

In the midst of it all was a fashion shop for women. Judging from the attractive window display, the little village had a society section. Emil was mesmerized by it all and itching to paint a thousand scenes at once, but he knew there was no time. He must be on his way for orientation at Sudduth. Before leaving Niceville, he made himself a solemn promise. He would return.

The five hour trip from Niceville left Emil little time for sleeping or eating, but he arrived on the campus invigorated.

He had reason to be.

All the publicity about the Sudduth faculty receiving grants for study in Mexico had brought about increased enrollment. Catledge, though still not an accomplished potter, had learned enough from the old Mallon potter and the training he had received in Mexico to improve his skills considerably. Greenlee, Tassie, and Emil agreed he would probably apply his new knowledge, for he thrived on the praise and publicity he was receiving for his travels and studies south of the border. The three noted with some amusement that he had added a new prance to his walk, and that a king-size mirror had been hung in his office just a few days into the new semester.

As Catledge's students began to show a genuine interest in pottery, Emil opted to forget about Catledge's false claim to glory and look to the future. It freed his mind to prepare his work for the Syracuse curator, who would soon arrive to collect five hundred pieces of his work, thus making room for all he intended to paint in the future. He was determined to paint many of them in a remote little village called Niceville.

He shared the find with Tassie one day, describing it in detail. "Truly unspoiled country," he told her. "Natural beach front with tall cane and heavy grass growing wild in the waters' edge. Big shrimp boats," he gestured, "with high-strung nets protruding from their sides. Fishermen scaling and weighing and hawking— ah," he reminisced, "it's a whole new way of life there." With a meaningful wave of his hand, he discouraged Tassie's interruptions even during his frequent, and thoughtful pauses. "Apparently the people know little else. They live in everything from scrappy old boats to tin-roofed shacks. And all kinds of little boats," he gestured excitedly. "You can't believe it. Tiny rowboats, motorboats, sailboats with hand-made sails and makeshift rudders."

Tassie was under his spell. "Sounds like Innisfree," she said, evoking the passion of someone who had been there.

"Innisfree?"

"William Butler Yeats," she explained. "My favorite poet." She broke into verse:

> I will arise and go now, and go to
> Innisfree,
> And a small cabin build there, of
> clay and wattles made...
> And I shall have some peace there,
> for peace comes dropping slow...
> Dropping from the veils of the morning
> to where the cricket sings...

"Niceville must be 'where the cricket sings,'" she added passionately.

Visibly moved by her emotional outpouring, Emil studied his spirited friend. Tassie's depth had always astounded him. With little thought she could give an idea credence or denude it, whichever she thought it deserved. He was still dwelling on her poetry when the secretary called him to the phone. "Syracuse," she told him.

Tassie clenched her hands together in a hopeful gesture. "This is it." Her dark eyes sparkled as Emil thrust his thumb in the air for victory. Finally, he thought, a date would be set and he could relax.

Again, he listened to excuses. "I'm afraid we must postpone the trip to Sudduth. The curator has been delayed..."

It was the last straw. Emil instructed his lawyer to break the contract.

It was soon the talk of the campus. Greenlee didn't wait for a formal meeting at the main campus, but surprised Emil with a visit to his studio, bringing with him Ethel, Tassie, and Dean Perkins.

"Forgive us for interrupting your work," Greenlee began. "Frankly, we're all here on a mission: to dissuade you from breaking the contract."

"Please," Emil begged. "I've made up my mind."

Except for a backless cane-bottom chair the students used for modeling, and an old sofa-bed cluttered with fresh paintings, there was no place to sit. Perkins walked nervously about, pausing now and then to toss bits of trash in the bin, or stack charcoal and pencils in a pile. It was obviously a nervous gesture, as he was noted for having the most unkempt office on the campus.

Greenlee's attire, though not unusual for him, was especially noticeable in the informal atmosphere of the studio. Dressed meticulously in a dark grey double-breasted suit, a stiff collared, long sleeved white shirt complete with French cuffs, he appeared ready for a formal gathering at the governor's mansion. Completing his outfit was a colorful, but conservative silk tie, with a matching handkerchief in the pocket of his suit coat.

As always, Emil wore loose slacks and short-sleeved shirts, clothes that enabled him to paint in comfort and stay relatively clean doing it. He kept a coat and tie in his office for faculty meetings, speech-making, exhibitions, and other occasions. All in all, he was pleased with his skimpy, colorless wardrobe, at least until he found himself in the company of Greenlee. On this occasion, however, among turpentine cans, paint-splotched furnishings, and other artists' clutter, Greenlee was the sore thumb.

Emil had finally come to realize the college president was a politician, a man who sought to please everyone. Ethel had been right all along.

Both women stood silently by, an anomaly for Tassie, staring at Emil.

"What is this?" he asked, somewhat discomforted. "A lynching?"

Greenlee smiled though it was obviously a nervous gesture signaling his own discomfort with the whole thing. Unknowingly, he fingered the diamond on one of his cufflinks, apparently contemplating an appropriate comment. "I deeply regret the matter has come to this," he said. "I have no right to ask anything of you." He glanced at the others. "In fact, none of us do. But we all wish you would reconsider your plans to break the Syracuse contract. Perhaps you would feel better about your paintings if you had them distributed. At least then, no disaster would destroy all of them. I can offer some storage in my home. I truly hate to see you pass up this opportunity."

"That goes for me too," Tassie added warmly. "I understand you want your work in a safe place. So what if it's next year? Isn't it a matter of later versus a matter of never? I want to see your work in New York where it belongs."

Emil couldn't help noticing her long black tresses needed a good combing, her face a bit of powder and rouge, a common look for a young woman whose work and concern for her friends, took precedence over her appearance.

As for Greenlee, Emil wasn't certain if he meant what he was saying, or if he was simply using diplomacy in hopes of changing Emil's mind. In any case, it didn't work. He was amused by Perkins, who had resorted to twiddling the pencils in his fingers, landing them here and there, cluttering the place far worse than he had found it.

When Perkins caught Emil's gaze, he burst forth with his own input. "Why not swallow your pride? You of all people should know how understaffed all the colleges are."

Greenlee paled, obviously shaken by the remark, and confident it had cancelled any progress they might have made thus far. When Perkins avoided Tassie's angry glare, she purposely picked up a heavy wooden bowl the students used for arranging still life, and slammed it noisily against the bare floor.

Rather than allow a fracas, Greenlee was about to offer more of his diplomatic jargon, but gladly acquiesced when Ethel purposely cleared her throat. Everyone turned to face her, some anxiously, all with anticipation.

"In the past, I've seen this as a loss for you, Mr. Holzhauer," she began. Her voice was tight, its ruffled mistress having cast aside her usual reserve. She had finally given in to calling Emil by his given name, but she apparently thought this occasion called for a deeper show of respect. "I've come to realize it's the colleges' loss, Syracuse as well as Sudduth. One hopes it'll teach them both a lesson in competency." Her icy glare riveted first on Perkins, then settled on Greenlee. It was a daring gesture on her part, a silent signal sent purposely to both men, neither of whom was capable of interpreting it, but one that spoke for the outrage she felt by the whole college system.

The comment soothed Emil, sending his thoughts inward. He was able to rise above the Sudduth campus, and Mallon, and Syracuse, and everyone associated with prejudice, and jealousy, and academic shortcomings. In the past, when things began to close in on him, whether it was factory work, or marital difficulties, or monetary problems, or joblessness, he solved the problem with his palette. He could do it again, especially now with retirement nearing. At sixty-three, he had begun to look forward to retiring from the work force. Unlike many retirees, he would have no problem deciding what to do with his leisure hours. In the past, however, one problem had presented itself: where would be go? Now he knew the answer: Niceville, his "Innisfree". He wanted to hear the sun touching the waters of the Gulf, the bayous and the bays, to witness the sunrise and sunset on those same waters, to catch the fishermen at their work and their leisure.

He wanted to hear the crickets sing.

Epilogue

While completing his last two years at Mallon, Emil made many trips to Niceville. It was during one of these trips, he met, and eventually married Marion Scofield, the granddaughter of a former Wisconsin governor. Marion was a Wellesley graduate who had traded the upper social circles she was brought up in for a simple life on northwest Florida's isolated coast. It was her first marriage. She was fifty-one, Emil sixty-five.

When Marion built her simple abode on Boggy Bayou, a wide body of water that meandered its way into the Gulf of Mexico, there was only limited access to the area, mostly by boat.

Emil's first glimpse of her led him to believe she was one of the area's fishheads. It was a term attached to people who lived along the water's edge and made their living fishing. It was not a complimentary label. Dressed in loose-fitting slacks, pinned-together khaki shirt and raveling straw hat that appeared to have been plucked from a garbage bin, Marion looked the part. When she attached a two-and-a-half horsepower motor to a tiny fishing boat, loaded her fishing gear and motored up the bayou, Emil was in a frenzy as he tried to capture it all on canvas.

In all his years of painting boats, boatmen, fishing gear and the like, he had never seen a fisherwoman! Once she disappeared around the bend, he focused on other interesting waterfront subjects, but cast them all aside the minute she came into view again. When she returned to the boatdock, he watched with renewed interest when she removed her floppy hat and revealed a mop of sensuously tousled, warm brown hair. He had scarcely begun to rework the face in his outline when something else caught his eye. Marion had tied her cumbersome shirt in a knot at her small waist, and had rolled up her trouser legs to keep them dry. Hidden beneath the bulky clothing was a slim and shapely body. He was in a trance.

From then on, whenever he visited the area, he made a nuisance of himself, "accidentally" arriving at the dock the same time Marion did. As soon as an opportunity presented itself, he introduced himself to his subject. Just as he had hoped, their informal chats eventually led to more intimate contacts.

Emil was soon smitten by this passionate woman who appreciated the simple life. He admired her compassion for the less fortunate, as witnessed by her willingness to share her time and talents with them. Instead of lolling in the comfort she had been born into, she had volunteered to serve with the American Red Cross on the European battlefield during World War II. When the war ended, she found "Innisfree". She agreed to fill a vacancy in Niceville High School's history department and remained in service even after learning officials had made no attempt to replace her. When the women's coach resigned, she volunteered to coach the girls' basketball team. It meant working with a motley crew who depended on Marion for their training, as well as their transportation to and from the games.

From the beginning, Emil liked her immensely. Within six weeks of their relationship, he knew he wanted her for his wife. For once, he had no qualms about marriage. While he took much of the blame for the breakup of his previous marriages, he had never really felt Marcy or Clarle was meant for him. He often sought comfort in knowing he had not proposed to either of them, perhaps for that reason.

There was, however, one problem. Marion rejected him. Her thoroughbred upbringing, although abandoned for the most part, showed through when it came to matrimony. For agonizing months, Emil tried to persuade her of his sincerity and his love and his devotion, but his failed marriages and his haste to tie the marital knot made him suspect in her eyes. When she finally agreed to marry him, she insisted on a long engagement: two years!

For the first time in his life, Emil was able to laugh at himself. For years, he had postponed having a relationship with a woman because of the time-consuming courting that might be expected of him. Now he was faced, not only with lengthy courting, but long-distance courting at that. Still, he couldn't bring himself to give her up.

It was worth the wait. Unlike Marcy and Clarle, who had had their own agendas, Marion had no goals to strive for, no recognition to seek. She was satisfied with who she was and where she was. She heard the crickets sing, and she shared the sounds with Emil.

After his retirement from Sudduth, they settled on the bayou that had captured his emotions the first time he saw it. With the fierceness of a lifetime, he painted the town and its people, and he taught many of them to paint as well.

He didn't forget about George. When the young man completed his pre-medical education at a Negro college in the South, he was eventually accepted in medical school. Emil and Marion saw him through, financially. He became a medical doctor and practiced in his home state. He spent his leisure hours painting and teaching others of his race to paint, always without compensation.

With the nation's largest Air Force base situated just a few miles away from Niceville, the area grew, bringing in a community college. Together, the college and Holzhauer introduced culture to the art-starved area. Eventually, he donated his life's work to Okaloosa-Walton Community College, which is situated in the center of cricket-singing territory, part of a five hundred thousand acre government preserve.

Holzhauer died in 1986 at the age of ninety-nine. After his death, Okaloosa-Walton Community College was the recipient of a twenty-one million dollar grant for the construction of a fine and performing arts center on the Niceville campus. People in the fast-growing resort area donated another five million. The ultra modern center houses a two thousand square foot Holzhauer gallery for permanently displaying his work.

About the Author

Like Holzhauer, Audrey Edwards was born into poverty, a dilemma she made every effort to rectify through education. She earned a Ph.D. from Florida State University where she studied gerontology, speech pathology, and higher education. Like Holzhauer, she discovered late in life, the rewards of teaching. Since 1993, she has trained teachers in China and Vietnam for teaching English and American culture. As Holzhauer's friend and neighbor for over twenty years, she became as passionate for writing his story as he had been for artistic expression.

Dr. Edwards still resides in Niceville, Florida, a remote village Holzhauer dubbed "cricket singing territory". She is married to Edward Nowogroski, Colonel, USAF (Ret).

Bibliography

Art Digest. "Prizes at Chicago Water Color International Go to Modernists," 1 April, 1930.

Art Institute of Chicago. "The Cribbage Champion, Emil Holzhauer," *American Painting and Sculpture Magazine*, 1930.

Bulliet, C.J. "Water Colors Fail To Reveal American Genius," *Chicago Evening Post Magazine*, 25 March, 1930.

Bolz, Diane M. "The Ashcan Artists take on New York," *Smithsonian* 26 (February, 1996): 28.

Buhner, Karl Hans Dr. "Das Spatwerk Fehrles," *Einhorn 106* (Schwabisch Gmund, Germany) August, 1971, 200-208.

D'Souza, Dinesh. *Liberal Education: The Politics of Race and Sex on Campus*. New York: The Free Press, 1991.

Hackney, Fiona and Isla Hackney. *The Art of the World's Greatest Watercolourists*. Secaucus, New Jersey: Chartwell Books, 1990.

Henri, Robert. *The Art Spirit*. New York: Harper & Row, 1958.

Holzhauer, Emil. "Ein Gmunder Zog in Die Weit." *Einhorn-Jahrbuch*, (Schwabisch Gmund, Germany) 1976, 200-207.

Homer, Innes, assisted by Violet Organ. *Robert Henri: and his Circle*. Ithaca & London: Cornell University Press, 1969.

Hughes, Robert. "The Epic of the City," *Time 147* (19 February, 1996) 62-63.

Isenberg, Gerhard. “Der Kreis Schwabisch Gmund aus der Sicht der Regionalplanug,” *Einhorn 87* (Schwabisch-Gmund, Germany) June, 1968, 148-149.

Kahn, David. *Seizing the Enigma: The Race to Break the German U-Boat Codes*. Boston: Houghton Mifflin, 1991.

Literary Digest Magazine. “Satirists: Angry and Furious,” 29 February, 1936.

Munson-Williams-Proctor Institute. *1913 Armory Show: 50th Anniversary Exhibition*. Utica: Henry Street Settlement, 1963.

Perlman, Bennard B. *Painters of the Ashcan School: The Immortal Eight*. New York: Dover Publications, 1979.

_________. *Robert Henri, His Life and his Art*. New York: Dover Publications,1991.

Schenk, Friedrich. “Wurttemberg-Ost im Verkehrsschatten,” *Einhorn 87* (Schwabisch-Gmund, Germany), June, 1968.

University of Georgia Press. Lamar Dodd, *A Retrospective Exhibition*. Athens: University of Georgia Press, 1970.

Newspapers and Exhibitions

Atlanta Journal. "Art Department Presents Exhibit in Atlanta Gallery," 23 October, 1949.

Atlanta Constitution. "Holzhauer wins Southern States top Art Award," 7 April, 1946.

________. "Art Notes," 25 April, 1943.

Baer, Donald. "Holzhauer's Water Colors, New York of Paul Julian," *Santa Barbara News-Press*, 2 April, 1944.

Baltimore Sun. "Moderns Taking to Medium," 28 October, 1934.

Blanton, Scarlet. "Emil Holzhauer, Artist Spends Holidays Here Painting." *The Brunswick (Georgia) News*, 27 December, 1947.

Bosch, Gulnar. "Holzhauer Paintings rival Brilliant Colors of Fall," *Macon (Georgia) Telegraph and News*, 24 October, 1948.

Coburn, F. W. "In the World of Art," *Boston Herald*, 14 January, 1923.

Croughton, Amy H. "Much Beauty in Paintings by Holzhauer," *Rochester Democrat*, 16 December, 1928.

DeMarko, Sharon. "'I've Had a Rich Life. Ah, Such a Rich Life,'" *Pensacola Journal*, 10 September, 1971.

_________. "Emil Holzhauer. Artist emeritus at 96: he reminisces, but his ageless works are still on tour," *Ft. Walton Beach, Florida Daily News*, 19 August, 1983.

Detroit Free Press. "'Mildred,' oil by Emil Holzhauer, courtesy of Morton galleries, New York," 5 April, 1931.

Devree, Howard. "Recent Metropolitan Purchases Raise Anew Problems of Public Support," *New York Times*, 14 July, 1940.

Ft. Walton Beach (Florida) Daily News. "Artist Emil Holzhauer to be honored Saturday," 11 November, 1982.

Ft. Walton Beach (Florida) Playground Daily News. "Emil Holzhauer Featured in Retrospective Show," 16 April, 1980.

Greenville (South Carolina) Piedmont. "Holzhauer Exhibit," 22 June, 1942.

Greenville (South Carolina) News. "In The Gallery," 14 June, 1942.

Guarisco Gallery, Ltd. *Emil Holzhauer: A retrospect*, Washington, D.C., Undated exhibition brochure.

Jewell, Edward Allen. "Beal At His Best in Water-Colors," *New York Times*, 8 December, 1933.

________. "Exhibition by Holzhauer," *New York Times*, 25 March, 1931.

Kansas City Journal-Post. "To Be Seen at the Art Institute," 6 September, 1931.

McBride, Henry. "Cribbage Players," *New York Evening Sun*, 26 April 1930.

M'Cormick, William B. "Beauty and Grandeur of Palisades Told on Canvas by a Young Artist," *New York Times*, 4 August, 1916.

Miami Herald. "Art Show, Music Hours Mark Week," 7 February, 1943.

Moore, Gertrude Herdle. "Affords View of Contrast In Painting," *Rochester Democrat*, 15 October, 1933.

Newark Evening News. "Four Jersey men as Water Colorists," 13 December, 1933.

New York Evening Mail. "The Glories of the Palisades," 3 August, 1916.

New York Evening Post. "Emil Holzhauer," 28 March, 1931.

___________, "The G.R.D. Gallery," 25 October, 1930.

New York Times. "Brooklyn Bridge. Emil Holzhauer, at the G.R.D. Studios," 26 October, 1930.

Palm Beach Post-Times. "Norton Exhibits 'American' By Artist Emil Holzhauer," 27 December, 1942.

Pittsburgh Post Gazette. "Guide Through New York Art Land," 4 April 1931.

__________. "A Holzhauer Canvas," 17 October, 1931.

Simonton, Thomas. "Water Color Show At Whitney Museum: Other Exhibitions," *New York American*, 22 February, 1936.

Vaughan, Malcolm. "Subjective Art Dominates Salons of America Display," *New York American*, 27 April 1930.

Wolfe, Karl. "Outstanding American Painters to Be Featured at "Water-Color Exhibition," *Jackson (Mississippi) Daily News*, 24 March 1946.

Holzhauer's Legacy

Listed in:

Who's Who in Art in the South and Southeast

Who's Who in American Art

Mallets' Index of Artists, International Edition, 1948.

Benezit's Pictionnaire des Peintres, 1966.

Allgemeiner Lexicon Directory, Bildenen Kuntsler, 1953.

AWARDS

Painting, *Village Street, January*, exhibited at New York World's Fair and selected by National Art Society for its portfolio of sixteen colored reproductions of the most representative pictures in the exhibition.

Painting, *Village Street, January* selected for descriptive broadcast over the NBC Radio Network, 1940.

Carnegie grant for study in Mexico, 1947; 1949.

Logan Medal and Purchase Prize at International Watercolor Exhibition, Chicago, 1930.

First Place Prizes:

North Carolina Artists' Exhibition, Asheville, North Carolina, 1942.
Art League Exhibition in Atlanta, 1946.
First Southeastern Annual Exhibition, Atlanta, 1946
Alabama Artists's Medal, watercolor, Auburn, 1948.
Southeastern Annual, Atlanta, 1954.

PERMANENT COLLECTIONS

Museum fur Natur & Stadtkicultur, Schwabisch-Gmund, Germany
Whitney Museum of American Art, New York
Institute of Art, Chicago
Museum of Fine Art, Denver
Art Association, Los Angeles
Memorial Art Gallery, Rochester
Institute of History and Art, Albany
Museum of Fine Arts, Syracuse
Dudley Peter Allen Memorial Museum, Oberlin, Ohio
Monhegan Island Museum, Monhegan Island, Maine
Newark Museum, Newark
University of Georgia, Athens
The High Museum, Atlanta
Pensacola Art Center, Pensacola, Florida
Municipal Art Gallery, Mobile
Museum of Arts and Science, Macon, Georgia
Panama City Art Association, Panama City, Florida
Okaloosa-Walton Community College, Niceville, Florida
Roberson Center for the Arts, Binghamton, New York